ADVANCE PRAISE FOR

First-Generation College Student Experiences of Intersecting Marginalities

"This book is an important contribution to more than one field of inquiry: working-class studies, student affairs, and campus diversity. The essays complicate and enrich our understanding of who the first-gen student actually is, just as first-gen students also complicate and enrich our nation's campuses. The book promises to help colleges and universities better understand first-gen students and support them in meaningful, effective ways, moving beyond discussion of 'access' alone and toward retention and graduation. The book is a valuable addition to the literature driving change to make higher education both more welcoming and more responsive to the needs and aspirations of all students."
—Carolyn Leste Law, Thesis/Dissertation Advisor at Northern Illinois University and coeditor of *This Fine Place So Far from Home: Voices of Academics from the Working Class*

"Contributors to this volume reveal how demographics such as race, ethnicity, gender, and sexual orientation intersect with first-generation college students, the book's unifying theme, to hinder marginalized groups before, during, and after graduation. These authors' writings demonstrate why every institution of higher education should sponsor an organization that addresses the disparate needs of its first-generation students."
—Ken Oldfield, Emeritus Professor of Public Administration at the University of Illinois at Springfield

"The essays in this collection offer vivid and at times deeply moving insights into the class dynamics and intersectional politics of U.S. universities. In a corporatized culture that likes to talk a lot about the 'student experience,' the book should be read by any faculty, administrators and support workers who want to meaningfully understand the different life stories and dispositions that students bring to campus."
—Sean Phelan, Associate Professor at Massey University (New Zealand)

First-Generation College Student Experiences of Intersecting Marginalities

Virginia Stead, H.B.A., B.Ed., M.Ed., Ed.D.
GENERAL EDITOR

VOL. 10

The Equity in Higher Education Theory, Policy, & Praxis series
is part of the Peter Lang Education list.
Every volume is peer reviewed and meets
the highest quality standards for content and production.

PETER LANG
New York • Bern • Berlin
Brussels • Vienna • Oxford • Warsaw

First-Generation College Student Experiences of Intersecting Marginalities

Edited by Teresa Heinz Housel

PETER LANG
New York • Bern • Berlin
Brussels • Vienna • Oxford • Warsaw

Library of Congress Cataloging-in-Publication Data

Names: Housel, Teresa Heinz, editor.
Title: First-Generation College Student Experiences of
Intersecting Marginalities / Edited by Teresa Heinz Housel.
Description: New York: Peter Lang, 2019.
Series: Equity in higher education theory, policy, & praxis; vol. 10
ISSN 2330-4502 (print) | ISSN 2330-4510 (online)
Includes bibliographical references and index.
Identifiers: LCCN 2018028674 | ISBN 978-1-4331-5702-8 (hardback: alk. paper)
ISBN 978-1-4331-5703-5 (paperback: alk. paper)
ISBN 978-1-4331-5521-5 (ebook pdf) | ISBN 978-1-4331-5522-2 (epub)
ISBN 978-1-4331-5523-9 (mobi)
Subjects: LCSH: First-generation college students—United States.
Minorities—Education (Higher)—United States.
People with social disabilities—Education (Higher)—United States.
Classification: LCC LC4069.6 .F57 2019 | DDC 378.1/9820973—dc23
LC record available at https://lccn.loc.gov/2018028674
DOI 10.3726/b14422

Bibliographic information published by **Die Deutsche Nationalbibliothek**.
Die Deutsche Nationalbibliothek lists this publication in the "Deutsche
Nationalbibliografie"; detailed bibliographic data are available
on the Internet at http://dnb.d-nb.de/.

The paper in this book meets the guidelines for permanence and durability
of the Committee on Production Guidelines for Book Longevity
of the Council of Library Resources.

*Dedicated, with gratitude, to two treasured mentors
who encouraged me to dream, fearlessly:
Melody Snure and Donna Rehm*

Contents

Preface

Carolyn Calloway-Thomas

In *The Faraway Nearby*, Rebecca Solnit (2013) writes, "What's your story? It is all in the telling. Stories are compasses and architecture; we navigate by them, we build our sanctuaries and our prisons out of them, and to be without a story is to be lost in the vastness of a world that spreads in all directions like arctic tundra or sea ice" (p. 3). *First-Generation College Student Experiences of Intersecting Marginalities* contains moving stories of first-generation students' search for identity and belonging. The book also provides compelling insights into identity variables such as ethnicity, race, class, gender, sexual orientation, mental illness, spirituality, and family, which testify to the centrality of social position and accessibility in a complex and various world. This preface opened with Solnit's (2013) "'story about story,'" which "'signifies that storytelling or the human narrative is as old as humankind. The New Testament Book of John records that 'In the beginning was the word'" (John 1:1) (Calloway-Thomas, 2017, p. 57). As Burke asserts, "'story came into the world' when our primal ancestors became able to go from sensation to words when they could duplicate the experience of tasting an orange'" (Fisher, 1987, pp. 65–66, cited in Calloway-Thomas, 2017, p. 57). Using a metaphor, Fisher (1987) conceptualizes his "narrative paradigm" with claims that we are *homo narrans*, or human storytellers.

Harari (2015), in discussing the relationship between the subjective ("something that exists depending on the consciousness and beliefs of a single individual") and the inter-subjective, argues crucially, "The inter-subjective is something that exists within the communication network linking the subjective consciousness of many individuals. If a single individual changes his or her beliefs, or even dies, it is of little importance. However, if most individuals in the network die or change their beliefs, the inter-subjective phenomenon will mutate or disappear" (p. 117). This telling perspective is a vivid reminder of how much we rely on the views of others for how to go about our daily lives and interact with others. Harari's (2015) perspective also suggests that human identity-making is embodied through storytelling, with profound consequences for individuals, from our quotidian existence, to our efforts to find meaning in classrooms and college settings. Furthermore, inter-subjectivity is a sharp lens through which we view our social position with its sometimes subtle signs and huge magnifications of identify and belonging, status, and class. In other words, how humans behave toward each other has social meaning, from reactions to food stamp recipients, to whether one eats kale as opposed to spinach, or whether the president of a company has fresh flowers delivered to his office daily.

Regardless of points of origins or philosophical perspective, human beings are keenly shaped by social mobility, or lack thereof. Therefore, one of the best ways to look at *First-Generation College Student Experiences of Intersecting Marginalities* is to focus on how identity, with its social meaning, intrudes upon the lived experiences of so many, with consequences for how people order their lives. Within the past few years, powerful books have examined how social background forms an intricate part of humans' scramble for status and equality, including Piketty's (2014) *Capital in the Twenty-First Century*; Vance's (2016) *Hillbilly Elegy: A Memoir of a Family and Culture in Crisis;* Isenberg's (2016) *White Trash: The 400-Year Untold History of Class in America*; Reeves' (2017) *Dream Hoarders: How the American Upper Middle Class is Leaving Everyone Else in the Dust, Why That is a Problem, and What to Do About It;* and most recently, Currid-Halkett's (2017) *The Sum of Small Things: A Theory of the Aspirational Class.*

First-Generation College Student Experiences of Intersecting Marginalities by implication draws on some of the central themes outlined in the aforementioned sobering books about class and identity, including the impact of words, social encounters, marginalization, and markers of status, wealth and inequality, on human behavior. Such impactful variables greatly influence how who gets what, when, and with what effect, can scathingly call into question the very essence of who we are. Gilroy (2000) captures the distinctive social DNA of identity and belonging this way: "Identity helps us to comprehend the formation of that perilous pronoun 'we' and to reckon with the patterns of inclusion and exclusion that it cannot help creating" (p. 99). The essays in this book grapple keenly with what happens when first-generation college students (FGCS) confront huge contrasts between identity and difference and sameness and otherness. How did they grapple? How did they move from challenges to their identity to positions of leadership in outstanding colleges and universities? The essays provide insights into the authors' search for identity, which is so powerfully intertwined with social distinctions.

Overview of This Book's Chapter Themes

Although the specific histories of the authors in this volume are different, they coalesce around the central idea that FGCS struggle to attain the key elements of a good life in America. Although the purpose of this book is not to offer readers a primer for a way out of confining spaces and places, it manages to do so compellingly, because the stories of how some authors overcame the deep encroachments upon their identity, are pregnant with ideas about how to cope meaningfully, like a Tibetan Sherpa leading determined climbers skillfully to the top of Mt. Everest.

In Chapter 1, Teresa Heinz Housel opens the book's first section, "The Weight of Intersectioning Marginalized Identities," to offer theoretical background materials and a framework for how to contextualize the narratives of FGCS, with emphasis on invisibility syndrome, intersectionality theory, and other concepts for understanding the signifiers of class and identity. Of course, the connectivity between identity and class is not a new social construct, but this chapter offers revealing insights into understanding the trajectories toward intergenerational upward mobility. Although earlier research offers sharp glimpses into and an understanding of the cultural DNA and challenges to social mobility, Housel analyzes the intersections of identity for an entirely different purpose. She examines how FGCS navigate their histories from their first encounters in college into the world of academia, a sometimes-daunting place to confront identity and selfhood.

Chapter 2 looks at what is crucial to understanding the specific stories of first-generation students, with emphasis on how stories of identity can provide an intersectional approach to the multifaceted nature of social capital and oppression. Ethnicity and race, care-giving, and income levels are all intertwined with the choices FGCS make and how less privileged people cope with the intricate dimensions of oppression, sharply grounded less in material things and more in marginalization. Audra K. Nuru, Tiffany R. Wang, Jenna Abetz, and Paris Nelson also shed light on the importance of understanding how objectified systems of cultural capital work across individuals, groups, and institutions.

Trott Nely Montina and Jonathan Mathias Lassiter (Chapter 3) focus on how FGCS and first-generation college professors (FGCP) navigate the academy, while grappling strenuously with hierarchies and differences in order to affirm their humanity. The authors complicate matters by adding potent variables such as cisgender, spirituality, and lower-middle-class status to the essay. Furthermore, Montina and Lassiter use invisibility syndrome and optimal theories to better our understanding of the intersectional dialogues between FGCS and FGCPs.

Looking at the world of identity through the lens of Hispanic and nontraditional college students, how does context inform intersectional marginalization? Chapter 4 wrestles with the temporal aspects of intersectional marginalization, raising serious issues about the chronological stages of experiencing marginalization. Micaela Rodriguez, Sascha Hein, and Leslie A. Frankel also raise the following questions: What's different about adolescent identity, and how does one stage inform subsequent stages of identity formation, along with three factors: context, continuity, and interactions?

Chapter 5 morphs into the area of self-efficacy and cultural values gaps. Paulette D. Garcia Peraza and Angela-MinhTu D. Nguyen examine the career choices of first-generation female college students. This emphasis is different from research literature, which typically focuses on academic performance and achievement of first-generation students. By moving into the realm of career choices that first-generation students make, the authors found that the degree of cultural identity and social support predicted "career decision self-efficacy," making a strong case for college administrators, advisors, and professors to be more attentive to the impact of human capital upon the allocation of economic resources.

Looking at the world from the prospective of double marginalization, Rebecca Mercado Jones (Chapter 6) wrestles with some first-generation students' profound feelings of isolation, tapping into how both familial and classroom "encounter modalities" can be problematic. In such instances, how does one interrupt what Gilroy (2000) calls "the ontologization of place"? (p. 122). By extension, Jones makes the case that stories are indeed geography, and that sometimes they "are the quicksand in which we thrash," get stuck, and then free ourselves, to use Solnit's (2013, p. 3) language. Jones explains how the fusion of identity as "marginal" and "intersectional" informed a great deal of her dreams and shaped her odyssey.

Chapter 7 introduces the reader to the book's second section, "Considering Invisible Marginalities," vivifying the idea that marginalization is sometimes double-sided, demonstrating how identities are fused with geopolitical events, including intrusions into labor, living costs, and the workforce in general, with disturbing consequences for Housel's family. Housel shows, among other things, how an interlinking of tertiary institutions and class identity can impact a single-parent family, although the impetus of the forces may be multiple and intersectional.

Chapter 8 looks at a topic that is rarely discussed in the literature on health and well-being: How do FGCS cope with mental health issues while being surrounded by individuals who might be tempted to heap shame upon them because of the stigmatizing resonance of such predicaments. In a complicated and signifying way, Andrea L. Meluch makes the case that to be a first-generation student with mental health challenges can be a double-whammy.

In Chapter 9, readers see how the encompassing nature of identity is complicated by layering first-generation transgender foster care students' positionality on self-shaping. Using the case study approach, Jacob O. Okumu and Kay-Anne P. Darlington discuss how Nuru, a first-generation transgender college student, copes with a legacy of foster care. The case provides fresh news about the incremental aspects of identities and their jarring consequences. For example, what happens when a foster care student enters a pristine university campus for the first time and witnesses two-parent families pitted against the backdrop of his/her history—with the absence of visible parents?

"I Belong Here, Too" is a fitting title for Chapter 10, which undertakes to account for what Danica A. Harris calls "the struggle to find place in the academy" by showing the financial and cultural burdens that confront FGCS in university settings. The importance of situational embeddedness and the interplay between sometimes mismatched cultural settings are also discussed. Reeves (2017) provides compelling information about how the "top fifth of the income distribution… are separating from the rest" (p. 3). Crucially, Reeves (2017) notes that such separation impacts a great deal of our lived experiences, including "education, family structure, health and longevity, even in civic and community life" (p. 3). In this regard, Harris's search for a more inclusive environment has huge implications for how institutions of higher learning conduct their cultural business.

Chapter 11 opens the book's third section, "The Role of Intersecting Marginalized Identities in Institutional Socialization." In keeping with this section's general theme, Chapter 11 acknowledges that although journals, newspapers, blogs, and other media sites deal with systems of thought about first-generation students, too much of the literature looks at such students through a deficit lens. Further, Xamual Bañales argues that scholars must also open a window on what happens to FGCS, from the application process to concordance, or lack thereof, between non-first-generation students. Currid-Halkett (2017) and Reeves (2017) both probe how family structure, intellectual and social capital, attitudes and lifestyle, what Bourdieu (1984) calls the "habitus" of everyday life, shape how we view the world, with urgent consequences for upward or downward mobility. Bañales reminds readers of the intricate enmeshment that obtains between things that happen on campus and things that happen off campus, long before first-generation students enter the university.

Gloria Aquino Sosa, Pietro A. Sasso, and Tracy Pascua Dea (Chapter 12) also examine facets of the college environment for students, using the Dynamic Student Development Metaeodel (DSDM) as a model for examining student success on university campuses. Their research stresses the crucial significance of a more holistic look at the multifaceted nature of college students' search for identity, belonging, and academic success. The authors also provide implications for their work and how institutions of higher learning may gain invaluable insights into more useful ways of shaping how FGCS think and what they do.

The final chapter discusses how faculty and others might employ pedagogy and other tools to address one of the most concerning aspects of the twenty-first century, and the role that the university may play in understanding the consequences of inaction. Significantly, by implication Housel invites readers to participate in an online collection of resources to help faculty, staff, administrators, and any others who work with FGCS. Strategic university policies and pedagogy can help university personnel think harder about the connectivity between first-generation student success and "hoarding the dream." *First-Generation College Student Experiences of Intersecting Marginalities* is an engaging and thought-provoking examination of how first-generation students organize meanings—story making—in their search for identity and belonging.

Reference

Bourdieu, P. (1984). *Distinction: A social critique of the judgement of taste*. Cambridge, MA: Harvard University Press.

Calloway-Thomas, C. (2018). Empathetic literacy and intercultural storytelling: Compasses and architecture. In A. Atay & D. Trebing (Eds.), *The discourse of special populations: Critical intercultural communication pedagogy and practice* (pp. 55–66). New York: Routledge.

Currid-Halkett, E. (2017). *The sum of small things: A theory of the aspirational class*. Princeton, NJ: Princeton University Press.

Fisher, W. (1987). *Human communication as narration: Towards a philosophy of reason, value, and action*. Columbia, SC: University of South Carolina.

Freedman, L. (2013). *Strategy: A history*. New York, NY: Oxford University Press.

Gilroy, P. (2000). *Against race: Imagining political culture beyond the color line*. Cambridge, MA: The Belknap Press of Harvard University Press.

Harari, Y. N. (2015). *Sapiens: A brief history of humankind*. New York, NY: HarperCollins Publishers.

Isenberg, N. (2016). *White trash: The 400-year untold history of class in America*. New York, NY: Viking Press.

Piketty, T. (2014). *Capital in the twenty-first century (A. Goldhammer, Trans.)*. Cambridge, MA: Belknap Press of Harvard University Press.

Reeves, R. V. (2017). *Dream hoarders: How the American upper middle class is leaving everyone else in the dust, why that is a problem, and what to do about it*. Washington, DC: Brookings Institution Press.

Solnit, R. (2013). *The faraway nearby*. New York, NY: Penguin Group.

Vance, J. D. (2016). *Hillbilly elegy: A memoir of a family and culture in crisis*. New York, NY: HarperCollins.

Acknowledgments

TERESA HEINZ HOUSEL

As I reviewed the contributing authors' chapters while completing this book, I repeatedly noticed a common thread among their essays. Their theoretical perspectives and topics may differ, but almost all mention at least one mentor who helped them along the path toward higher education.

The specific form of mentorship differs among the contributors. For some, an attentive teacher noticed that they had unused talents. Other contributors received insightful support from a research lab supervisor or academic advisor. Still others benefited from a helpful classmate, supportive parent, or even a historical figure whose understanding of marginalization inspired the contributor to become an advocate for other first-generation college students (FGCS).

Similar to many of our contributors, I definitely attribute hard work, intelligence, luck, and just plain grit for helping me become the first in my family to complete undergraduate and postgraduate degrees. Duckworth, Peterson, Matthews, and Kelly (2007) quantitatively examined grit's influence on a person's ability to succeed, with their findings suggesting that talent, "but also the sustained and focused application of talent over time," helps someone achieve difficult goals (p. 1087). As a young person, I sometimes referred to the hardest days as "faith days," or days when I needed to work diligently toward my dreams without imminently seeing certain end results. However, similar to the experiences of many of this book's contributors, I had many helping hands, too, as loving mentors poured out wisdom, kindness, and even financial resources as I reached many of my career and life goals.

My mentors have ranged from a famous Oberlin College graduate in the journalism world to an elderly neighbor, Molly, in East Fremantle, Australia. Molly dedicated her life to helping others after enduring the loss, trauma, and pain in being removed from her Aboriginal family as a child to work as a domestic in White households as part of the country's Stolen Generations. "I can't speak my tribal name," Molly once told me, alluding that her unchosen personal history was too painful to vocalize. Like Molly, many of my mentors did not have university educations, but it doesn't matter: They believed in me and had wisdom and compassion that in many cases were borne out of their own struggles.

I've contemplated the role of mentors while completing this book. On a recent trip to the United States, I visited my family and longtime friends in northeastern Ohio. One of my first expeditions was to drive down wintry rural roads so that I could quietly visit my childhood church, Chippewa Church of the Brethren, in the flat countryside near Wooster, Ohio. I had actually not visited the church since my undergraduate years at Oberlin College. At that time, I was trying to distance myself from my working-class background as I managed the difficult cultural divides between campus and home. I had not yet gained the life experience to realize that my becoming was *because of,* not in spite of, my class background.

Because I arrived on a Sunday evening, the church was locked and silent in the graying winter sunset. I parked the rental car and walked across the street from the church to the small country graveyard. As I walked amongst the graves, I noticed names of many now-deceased women who emotionally supported me during my upbringing as the daughter of a single father in this rural community: Marie McFadden, Betty Young, Donna Rehm. I was humbled to realize how many had passed on as the years seemingly evaporated.

In this book's preface, Carolyn Calloway-Thomas describes how we tell stories to both affirm and make sense of our identity. Indeed, this graveyard visit reminded me how we do not write our stories alone. I had actually dreaded taking the long flight from Wellington, New Zealand because I wanted to enjoy a leisurely Southern Christmas and a barbeque along the beach, perhaps at a cozy rented bach (holiday house) somewhere near Glenorchy on the South Island, the one place in the world where I can truly relax. However, as I paused before many of the graves in the fading gray light, sometimes taking photos to help remember their inscriptions, I was powerfully overcome by the realization that on this frozen ground was exactly where I needed to be. No matter how far away I travel, or how many new life experiences that I may have outside of this tiny dot of a community in Ohio farm country, I needed to be right here at this very moment, in a place that held others who will always be part of my story.

I particularly remember Donna Rehm. Donna operated a small beauty salon in her home on a large farm on Apple Creek Road. She was the first person I met who had traveled overseas. When she hosted our youth church school class at her home, I watched and listened raptly as she shared slides of their missionary trips to Africa, Israel, and Britain. The images from overseas piqued my longstanding fascination with other countries. My family home had many world maps and *National Geographic* magazines because my father shared my international interests. I poured over them and made mental lists of places I someday hoped to experience. Donna's colorful slides helped make these places real. She always assured me that I would achieve one of my life goals of someday teaching around the world. Donna passed away in late 2013, but her influence lives on as I speak of her encouragement often to my family and students.

During this same recent trip to Ohio, I visited another childhood mentor, Melody Snure. As a high school freshman, I boldly wrote to Melody, who was then managing editor of the Wooster daily newspaper, *The Daily Record*, asking if she might consider hiring me as a reporter or columnist. My hutzpah no doubt reflected my father's influence. For better or for worse, my father would dream big and then let the practicalities fall into place as he went along. Melody kindly wrote back and encouraged me to pursue journalism as a future career. In the meantime, she suggested, I should get as much experience as possible through my school newspaper, yearbook, and other logical avenues available at my school.

I no longer remember what prompted my decision to write Melody back a year later, but my father's reading of three newspapers a day, plus my love for writing fiction books that I illustrated and stitched together with thread, must have inspired me to offer my services again. Much to my surprise, she offered me a job writing a monthly teen column and occasional articles on youth-related topics. I leapt at the opportunity.

Other than my teachers at school and some professionals in our community, Melody was one of the first people I knew who had completed a university education. Hearing her stories about taking courses and developing her journalism career inspired me to believe that I could follow a similar path. I loved writing the monthly editorials and articles at *The Daily Record*. The experience taught me how to cultivate knowledge across a broad range of topics, develop story ideas, conduct research, encourage sometimes shy or reticent people to open up to me, and synthesize information from different sources into a narrative, all skills that I would later use in my first career as a journalist and now as an academic and freelance writer.

Although I had heard inklings of Melody's childhood experiences when I was in high school, I learned during my recent trip that she was also a first-generation student. I was surprised to discover that when she encountered some resistance to her desire to attend college, key mentors such as her mother assisted to make her dream possible. Her recollections again reminded me that we do not arrive to any destination alone.

Both Donna and Melody's examples affirm my goal to mentor other first-generation students. As many of this book's contributors point out, researchers have long-documented the many emotional, academic, financial, and social struggles that FGCS encounter as they complete their education. In my own case, most people encouraged me, but a few (particularly in my doctoral studies) sometimes tried to make me feel as if I didn't belong in higher education, or that my voice and story were not as important as theirs. I particularly remember one classmate who made a point of interrupting me when I spoke in graduate seminar discussions, or another person from financial privilege who sometimes laughed at my expense. Though their actions were intended to silence me, they in fact inspired me even more to help others as a future educator. Their actions also remind me that for every person who tries to inhibit our journey, there are many more whose support we carry along our path toward higher education.

I am privileged to curate this book's chapters that examine the intersections of marginalized identities in FGCS. Echoing the sentiment of Micaela Rodriguez in "The (Im)possible Dream" (Chapter 4), to the reader from a FGCS background who may be reading this: Your voice is just as important as everyone else's. You have a right to be on that campus or in that classroom, whether you are a student, administrator, faculty, or staff. You *are* good enough. You are part of the story. In fact, higher education desperately needs your perspectives.

To readers who are faculty, administrators, and staff, I hope that this book will assist you in effectively supporting the FGCS in your care. Together we can lift our students toward learning and reaching their goals. Together we can build truly inclusive communities that value many perspectives. Thank you for your interest in first-generation students and in this book.

References

Duckworth, A. L., Peterson, C., Matthews, M. D., & Kelly, D. R. (2007). Grit: Perseverance and passion for long-term goals. *Journal of Personality and Social Psychology, 92*(6), 1087–1101. doi: https://doi.org/10.1037/0022-3514.92.6.1087

Abbreviations

Academic Achievement Test (ACT)
American Identity Measure (AIM)
Association of Jotería Arts, Activism, and Scholarship (AJAAS)
Career Decision Self-Efficacy (CDSE)
continuing generation college student (CGCS)
Deferred Action for Childhood Arrivals (DACA)
Dynamic Student Development Metatheodel (DSDM)
English Language Learner (ELL)
first-generation college (FGC)
first-generation college professors (FGCP)
first-generation college student (FGCS)
first-generation faculty (FGF)
grade point average (GPA)
Graduate Record Exam (GRE)
growth, learning, and development (GLD)
Hispanic Serving Institution (HSI)
lesbian, gay, bisexual, transgender, or queer (LGBTQ)
Movimiento Estudiantil Chican@ de Aztlán (MEChA)
National Alliance on Mental Health (NAMI)
Post-Traumatic Stress Disorder (PTSD)
Predominantly White Institution (PWI)
Revised Multigroup Ethnic Identity Measure (MEIM)
Scholarship Aptitude Test (SAT)
services, supports, interventions, and programs (SSIPs)
Shame Resilience Theory (SRT)
Significant other (SO)
socioeconomic status (SES)

science, technology, engineering and mathematics (STEM)
Summer Academic Institute for Leaders and Scholars (SAILS)
The Communication Theory of Identity (CTI)
Third World Liberation Front (TWLF)
University Learning Outcomes Assessment (UniLOA)
Young Queers United for Empowerment (YQUE)

Section One: The Weight of Intersecting Marginalized Identities

1. The Importance of Intersecting Marginalized Identities in Considering: What Is Known and Not Known About First-Generation College Students

Teresa Heinz Housel

Introduction

When I first considered my objective to expand and deepen the academic research on first-generation college students (FGCS), my background as a first-generation student and faculty member heavily influenced this motivation. This book draws upon existing research to define a FGCS as the first person in their immediate family to attend college (Balemian & Feng, 2013). My previous two books (co-edited with Vickie L. Harvey) examined the academic, emotional, cultural, and financial challenges that FGCS experience as they complete their undergraduate and graduate studies, and subsequently enter academia and other professional careers (Harvey & Housel, 2011; Housel & Harvey, 2009). Our books built on previous FGCS-related research, which collectively examined this student population's complex academic, social, and mental health needs; cultural transition to higher education; and career journeys after graduation (Lohfink & Paulsen, 2005; Nunez & Cuccaro-Alamin, 1998; Reid & Moore, 2008; Strayhorn, 2006; Watt, Johnston, Huerta, Mediola, & Alkan, 2008; Zwerling & London, 1992).

Since the publication of my previous two books (Harvey & Housel, 2011; Housel & Harvey, 2009), the burgeoning field of FGCS research has broadened scholars' understanding of this student population's educational journeys before, during, and after college. Indeed, scholars now know a great deal about first-generation students. Primarily, many administrators realize that they cannot ignore this population whose numbers are rapidly increasing on American college and university campuses. More students than ever attend college in a growing knowledge economy in which many jobs require critical information literacy and technical skills. Many employers now require a college degree, regardless if the job is a professional or blue-collar one (Conway, 2009, pp. 322–323; Provasnik et al., 2007; Snyder, de Brey, & Dillow, 2016). Statistics on FGCS at American colleges and universities tend to lag a few years behind, but Banks-Santilli's (2014) recent study points out that one in six first-year students at American four-year colleges and universities today are first generation (see also Saenz, Hurtado, Barrera, Wolf, & Yeung, 2007). Other researchers calculate slightly different student numbers. Of the undergraduates enrolled in American tertiary institutions, nearly a third are FGCS (Chen, 2005; Eagan et al., 2014, p. 7). Though the statistics on FGCS in American higher education differ among researchers, the studies collectively indicate that FGCS are now enrolled in dramatically higher numbers compared to two generations ago, when a college education mostly served to groom affluent White men for their family businesses and other white-collar careers (Harris, in press; Ryan & Sackrey, 1996).

As more FGCS attend college today, we know that rising education costs mean that many of them take on heavy student loan debt, whether or not they graduate (Lee & Mueller, 2014; Tompor, 2015). When I attended Oberlin College in the early 1990s, the cost of a year's education with tuition and board (meals and housing) had not yet reached $30,000. My single father made less than $30,000 annually at Goodyear Tire & Rubber Company in Akron, Ohio. He struggled to pay my monthly school fees even though I received government grants and heavy financial assistance from Oberlin's endowment. The cost of American higher education continues to skyrocket far beyond average wages and living costs. In 1980, the average annual cost for undergraduate tuition, room, and board at four-year public institutions was $6,381 and $13,995 at private institutions; by 2010, estimated annual costs were $15,605 and $31,975, respectively (U.S. Department of Education, National Center for Education Statistics, 2012). Meanwhile, funding from Federal Pell Grant and Work Study programs to cover education costs at public, four-year institutions fell from 77 percent in 1980 to 41 percent in 2007 (Engle, 2007). I now live in New Zealand, where students usually have to take out interest-free government loans to pay for their school fees (though this is a recent development with the introduction of university fees from

1989 onwards) (Kenny, 2012; Robson, 2009). However, the first year of university or training program is now free under a new Labour government initiative (Labour, 2018).

Researchers have widely documented that despite financial aid programs designed to help level out unequal access for American college students, FGCS typically encounter various barriers to success once they arrive on campus. As I previously pointed out (Harvey & Housel, 2011), the difficulties that FGCS face differ depending on their campus environments, which vary between community colleges, private liberal arts colleges, and large universities in urban and rural locations. However, their academic challenges are well-documented: FGCS frequently struggle academically, participate in fewer extra-curricular activities, receive lower grades, and work more hours to finance their education than their non-first-generation peers (Bui, 2002; Glenn, 2004; McCarron & Inkelas, 2006; Moschetti & Hudley, 2008; Reid & Moore, 2008; Ryan & Glenn, 2002/2003; Stephens, Fryberg, Rose Markus, Johnson, & Covarrubias, 2012).

In addition to academic challenges, many first-generation students experience social, cultural, and emotional marginalization on campus (Bui, 2002; Francis & Miller, 2008; Lundberg, Schreiner, Hovaguimian, & Miller, 2007). Housel and Harvey (2009) discuss how faculty, administrators, and staff may find it difficult to identify these challenges because they stem from unspoken social mores and cultural expectations in higher education. "[FGCS] often lack social capital, such as overseas travel and exposure to cultural arts that wealthier students might take for granted" (Housel & Harvey, 2009, p. 15). Other researchers document first-generation students' cultural transition to their institutions' middle- and upper-class cultures. Similar to many other academics from first-generation and/or working-class backgrounds, Lubrano (2004) discusses how first-generation students must learn to navigate the unwritten social rules of their peers, professors, and academic administrators, many of whom come from middle- and upper-class backgrounds. When first-generation students have to straddle their home and campus cultures, this cultural and identity tension often leads to mental stress and fewer visits home. I previously wrote about my study abroad experience as an Oberlin College undergraduate for the *Chronicle of Higher Education*: "I sometimes spent school breaks on the campus to avoid the anxiety of negotiating two different cultures. It was easier to read magazines in the near-empty campus dormitory than to go home" (Housel, 2012). By my junior year, I had learned to successfully navigate my college's middle- and upper-class culture, and even held leadership roles in several campus media organizations. However, even as I learned how to culturally maneuver through one situation, new experiences such as completing a national magazine internship in New York City or going to my academic advisor's home for lunch required whole new sets of unknown cultural knowledge and performances.

Institutions have much work ahead in helping FGCS access higher education and successfully complete their studies. However, more colleges and universities now recognise that increasing diversity through student enrolment will benefit their institutions (Garrison & Gardner, 2012). I am encouraged that many institutions now include socio-economic diversity in their efforts and target first-generation students (Greenwald, 2012). Many also recognize the barriers that FGCS face and have created initiatives to financially and academically assist them. In 2007, my undergraduate alma mater launched a financial assistance program (Oberlin Access Initiative) that gives Pell Grant-eligible students loan-free financial aid packages (Bader, 2007). In December 2007, Harvard University began replacing student loans with grants for families earning less than $180,000 a year (Kinzie, 2007, p. A08). These initiatives are necessary because students, faculty, and staff all benefit from having a diverse student body. As this volume points out, diversity spans all identities—and not just visible ones.

Intersections of Marginalized Identities: Addressing What Is Not Yet Known About FGCS

Despite the general expansion of research on FGCS, the field needs research that takes a multi-dimensional approach to their identities that are often marginalized in higher educational contexts. While completing my last book (Harvey & Housel, 2011), the contributing authors often informally shared anecdotes with us about how they had to simultaneously negotiate their different identities such as class, ethnicity, sexuality, and mental health issues with their first-generation status. Identities not only have a complex relationship with each other, but are also differently marginalized and salient across various contexts and times in a student's life. Grier-Reed and Ganuza (2012) discuss how "in attempting to negotiate their multiple identities across multiple contexts," students can experience marginality as they bridge disconnections between their home and college life (p. 464; see also Orbe, 2004).

This identity saliency is certainly true in my case, when my first-generation student identity felt more salient as I completed assignments early on in my undergraduate education. I initially struggled in my history and English literature classes because I had not learned to actively read an academic text, integrate connections across a course's themes, or write an analytical essay, unlike my peers who had attended wealthy public and private schools. Much later on, in my academic positions at a private liberal arts college, and now at a public research university in New Zealand, my rural working-class background is sometimes more salient when I interact with faculty and administrators from economically privileged backgrounds. I am well qualified for my positions, but I've still somewhat internalized my father's top-down view of his workplace, where the "big shots" (his words) occupied the offices that he cleaned as a custodian.

Orbe (2004) argues that it is "incumbent on studies focusing on identity negotiation among FGC [first-generation college] students to acknowledge that the salience of FGC student status will vary among participants" (p. 133). This book responds to this challenge. With its focus on intersecting marginalized identities, this book seeks to move beyond the well-documented findings on FGCS' experiences in higher education and examine what is not yet known about this student population. My initial call for chapters solicited a broad range of theoretical-based narratives as well as quantitative and qualitative studies. The enthusiastic response to the chapter call affirmed that others sense the same strong need for research on intersecting marginalized identities.

This book's contributors are predominantly first-generation undergraduates, graduate students, faculty, administrators, and staff who have experienced intersections of marginalized identities. As the chapters examine identity saliency across different contexts, they expand our knowledge about students' complex, everyday performances of identities that involve much more than being the first in their families to attend college. My objective for this book's essays is that their knowledge will help institutions, faculty, administrators, and staff where students most need it: on the ground. In other words, in the classroom, residence halls and informal social spaces, institutional policy, campus programs that assist FGCS, and outreach activities for families of FGCS.

To this book's readers: I am creating a digital knowledge base that will be a resource for first-generation students, faculty, administrators, staff, and those who work with them in any capacity. I invite you to contact me with your strategies for reaching FGCS at the classroom and institutional level so that we can add your knowledge to an online resource library of community-based knowledge: http://teresaheinzhousel.com/intersectionsofmarginality/. These resources will help caring and concerned faculty, staff, and administrators create learning environments where all students can feel valued, safe, and can learn.

References

Bader, R. (2007). A question of access. *Oberlin Alumni Magazine, 103*(2). Retrieved from http://www2.oberlin.edu/alummag/summer2008/features/access.html

Balemian, K., & Feng, J. (2013). *First generation students: College aspirations, preparedness and challenges.* Slides presented at the Advanced Placement Annual Conference, Las Vegas, NV. Abstract retrieved from https://eric.ed.gov/?id=ED563393

Banks-Santilli, L. (2014). First-generation college students and their pursuit of the American dream. *Journal of Case Studies in Education, 5* (February). Retrieved from http://www.aabri.com/manuscripts/131657.pdf

Bui, K. V. (2002). First-generation college students at a four-year university: Background characteristics, reasons for pursuing higher education and first year experiences. *College Student Journal, 36*(1), 3–11.

Chen, X. (2005, July). First-generation students in postsecondary education: A look at their college transcripts. Retrieved from U.S. Department of Education, National Center for Education Statistics. Retrieved from http://nces.ed.gov/pubs2005/2005171.pdf

Conway, K. M. (2009). Exploring persistence of immigrant and native students in an urban community college. *The Review of Higher Education, 32*(3), 321–352.

DeMott, B. (1990). *The imperial middle: Why Americans can't think straight about class.* New York, NY: William Morrow.

Eagan, K., Stolzenberg, E. B., Ramirez, J. J., Aragon, M. C., Suchard, M. R., & Hurtado, S. (2014). *The American freshman: National norms fall 2014.* Los Angeles, CA: Higher Education Research Institute, UCLA.

Engle, J. (2007). Postsecondary access and success for first-generation college students. *American Academic, 3*(1), 25–48.

Francis, T. A., & Miller, M. T. (2008). Communication apprehension: Levels of first-generation college students at 2-year institutions. *Community College Journal of Research and Practice, 32*(1), 38–55. doi: https://doi.org/10.1080/10668920701746688

Garrison, N. J., & Gardner, D. S. (2012). Assets first generation college students bring to the higher education setting. Paper presented at the Association for the Study of Higher Education (ASHE) Annual Conference (Las Vegas, NV, Nov 15, 2012). Abstract retrieved from https://eric.ed.gov/?id=ED539775

Glenn, D. (2004, September 3). For needy students, college success depends on more than access, study finds. *The Chronicle of Higher Education, 51*(2), p. A41.

Greenwald, R., (2012, November 11). Think of first-generation students as pioneers, not problems. *The Chronicle of Higher Education.* Retrieved from https://www.chronicle.com/article/Think-of-First-Generation/135710

Grier-Reed, T., & Ganuza, Z. (2012). Using constructivist career development to improve career decision self-efficacy in TRIO students. *Journal of College Student Development, 53*(3), 464–471. doi: 10.1353/csd.2012.0045

Harris, D. A. (in press). I belong here, too. In T. H. Housel (Ed.), *Intersections of marginality for first-generation college students*. New York, NY: Peter Lang.

Harvey, V. L., & Housel, T. H. (Eds.). (2011). *Faculty and first-generation college students: Bridging the classroom gap together*. San Francisco, CA: Jossey-Bass.

Housel, T. H. (2012, October 29). First-generation students need help in straddling their 2 cultures. *The Chronicle of Higher Education*. Retrieved from https://www.chronicle.com/article/Helping-First-Generation/135312

Housel, T. H., & Harvey, V. L. (Eds.). (2009). *The invisibility factor: Administrators and faculty reach out to first-generation college students*. Boca Raton, FL: BrownWalker Press.

Kenny, K. (2012, May 7). The birth of student loans. *Critic—Te Arohi*. Retrieved from https://www.critic.co.nz/features/article/1925/the-birth-of-student-loans

Kinzie, S. (2007, December 12). Other colleges eye Harvard's plan to increase affordability. *The Washington Post*, p. A08.

Labour. (2018). *Making tertiary education and training affordable for all*. Retrieved from http://www.labour.org.nz/tertiaryeducation

Lee, J., & Mueller, J. A. (2014). Student loan debt literacy: A comparison of first-generation and continuing-generation college students. *Journal of College Student Development, 55*(7), 714–719. doi: 10.1353/csd.2014.0074

Lohfink, M. M., & Paulsen, M. B. (2005). Comparing the determinants of persistence for first-generation and continuing-generation students. *Journal of College Student Development, 46*(4), 409–428.

Lubrano, A. (2004). *Limbo: Blue-collar roots, white-collar dreams*. Hoboken, NJ: John Wiley & Sons.

Lundberg, C. A., Schreiner, L. A., Hovaguimian, K., & Miller, S. S. (2007). First-generation status and student race/ethnicity as distinct predictors of student involvement and learning. *NASPA Journal (Online), 44*(1), 57–83.

McCarron, G. P., & Inkelas, K. K. (2006). The gap between educational aspirations and attainment for first-generation college students and the role of parental involvement. *Journal of College Student Development, 47*(5), 534–549. doi: https://doi.org/10.1353/csd.2006.0059

Moschetti, R., & Hudley, C. (2008). Measuring social capital among first-generation and non-first-generation, working-class, white males. *Journal of College Admission, 198*(Winter 2008), 25–30.

Nunez, A., & Cuccaro-Alamin, S. (1998). First-generation students: Undergraduates whose parents never enrolled in postsecondary education (NCES Report No. 98–082). Washington, DC: National Center for Educational Statistics.

Orbe, M. P. (2004). Negotiating multiple identities within multiple frames: An analysis of first-generation college students. *Communication Education, 53*(2), 131–149. doi: https://doi.org/10.1080/03634520410001682401

Provasnik, S., KewalRamani, A., Coleman, M. M., Gilbertson, L., Herring, W., & Xie, Q. (2007). Status of Education in Rural America (NCES 2007–040). National Center for Education Statistics, Institute of Education Sciences, U.S. Department of Education. Washington, DC.

Reid, M. J., & Moore, J. L. (2008). College readiness and academic preparation for post-secondary education: Oral histories of first-generation urban college students. *Urban Education, 43*(2), 240–261. doi: https://doi.org/10.1177/0042085907312346

Robson, S. (2009, April 27). A short history of tertiary education funding in New Zealand. *Salient.* Retrieved from http://salient.org.nz/2009/04/a-short-history-of-tertiary-education-funding-in-new-zealand/

Ryan, M. P., & Glenn, P. A. (2002/2003). Increasing one-year retention rates by focusing on academic competence: An empirical odyssey. *Journal of College Student Retention, 4*(3), 297–324. doi: https://doi.org/10.2190/KUNN-A2WW-RFQT-PY3H

Ryan, J., & Sackrey, C. (1996). *Strangers in paradise: Academics from the working class.* Lanham, MD: University Press of America.

Saenz, V. B., Hurtado, S., Barrera, D., Wolf, D., & Yeung, F. (2007). *First in my family: A profile of first-generation college students at four-year institutions since 1971.* Los Angeles, CA: Higher Education Research Institute. Retrieved from http://www.heri.ucla.edu/publications

Snyder, T. D., de Brey, C., & Dillow, S.A. (2016). Digest of Education Statistics, 2015 (NCES 2016–014). U.S. Department of Education. Washington, DC: National Center for Education Statistics. Retrieved from https://nces.ed.gov/pubsearch/pubsinfo.asp?pubid=2016014

Stephens, N. M., Fryberg, S. A., Rose Markus, H., Johnson, C.S., & Covarrubias, R. (2012). Unseen disadvantage: How American universities' focus on independence undermines the academic performance of first-generation college students. *Journal of Personality and Social Psychology, 102*(6), 1178–1197. doi: https://doi.org/10.1037/a0027143

Strayhorn, T. L. (2006). Factors influencing the academic achievement of first-generation college students. *NASPA Journal Online, 43*(4), 82–111.

Tompor, S. (2015, June 8). College student's nightmare: Loan debt and no degree. *USA Today.* Retrieved from https://www.usatoday.com/story/money/columnist/tompor/tompor/2015/06/07/student-loans-repay-delinquency-federal-reserve/28562447/

U.S. Department of Education, National Center for Education Statistics. (2012). Digest of Education Statistics, 2011 (NCES 2012–001). Tuition costs of colleges and universities. Retrieved from http://nces.ed.gov

Watt, K. M., Johnston, D., Huerta, J., Mediola, I. D., & Alkan, E. (2008). Retention of first-generation college-going seniors in the college preparatory program AVID. *American Secondary Education, 37*(1), 17–40.

Zwerling, L. S., & London, H. B. (Eds.). (1992). *First-generation students: Confronting the cultural issues.* San Francisco, CA: Jossey-Bass.

2. "I Felt the Invisible Hand of Inequity Fall Firmly on My Shoulders, Holding Me Back": Exploring the Intersectional Identities of First-Generation College Student Women

AUDRA K. NURU, TIFFANY R. WANG, JENNA ABETZ, AND PARIS NELSON

[*Authors' Notes:* The authors would like to thank the first-generation college student women who participated in this study and shared their stories to offer an invaluable glimpse into their unique life experiences. The authors would also like to thank the editor, Dr. Teresa Heinz Housel, as well as the anonymous reviewers for their helpful input. Correspondence to: Audra K. Nuru, University of St. Thomas, Department of Communication and Journalism, 2115 Summit Avenue, St. Paul, MN 55105, USA. E-mail: anuru@stthomas.edu.

To maintain confidentiality, pseudonyms were assigned rather than using the real names of the narrators.]

Each life is a collection of complex events that can be organized into a coherent and meaningful life story (McAdams, 2001). Although there is a strong body of research in adult life stories, less is known about adolescent life stories. This development stage is interesting to study because adolescence is a time of exploration, experimentation, consolidation, and commitment. First-generation college students (FGCS) are one group of adolescents who reflect this development stage. These students must work to negotiate home and campus identities while maintaining strong ties to their family and home community.

Benmayor (2002) asserts that storytelling is one way that FGCS can fulfill their commitment to their home communities. These students are devoted to improving the lives of their families and communities by creating a legacy of college completion, serving as role models for future generations of potential college students, and realizing a "personal and collective dream of achieving a college education" (Benmayor, 2002, p. 97). This commitment complements their "concern for and commitment to promoting the development and well-being of future generations" (McAdams, 2006, p. 81). The current chapter, therefore, adopts a narrative perspective in examining the intersections of FGCS' identities. Examining the ways in which FGCS construct the different facets of their lived experience may inform us about the ways adolescents understand and interpret marginality.

First-Generation College Student Legacies

Legacies can emerge over time as individuals promote the development and well-being of future generations by sharing their life stories. Past researchers have explored legacies in the context of the family. These stories preserve identity across generations (Langellier & Peterson, 1993) and communicate simple themes that are easily recalled (Stone, 1988). Thompson et al. (2009) define legacies as "strands of meaning that run through the family in ways that give it identity or sense, are constituted in communication through family storytelling, and are continually reshaped over time" (p. 108). Like life stories, legacies are malleable, fluid and often told, re-told, and re-shaped from generation to generation as "family members embrace, reject, and/or extend family legacies" (Thompson et al., 2009, p. 107). This malleability and fluidity is especially apparent during adolescence, when college students leave home, enter college, and begin to develop and explore their identities and life stories (Arnett, 2005). Although past studies have explored how college students preserve identity through intergenerational storytelling, recent research has focused on how FGCS create and promote a legacy of college completion (Arzuaga, 2016; Jehangir, Stebleton, & Deenanath, 2015; Wang, 2012, 2014a, 2014b; Wang & Nuru, 2017). Because FGCS come from families where neither parent completed college, they lack a legacy or tradition of college completion. This population is of particular interest because these students often negotiate multiple identities and maintain strong ties to their families and communities.

Quantitative research has focused on comparing FGCS with continuing-generation college students, who are defined as students who come from families with a tradition of college completion (Hossler, Schmit, & Vesper,

1999), describing the path of transition from high school to college (Terenzini, Springer, Yaeger, Pascarella, & Nora, 1996), and examining the persistence of FGCS in college (Choy, 2001). Recently, qualitative research has begun exploring how FGCS negotiate their identities (Orbe, 2006; Orbe & Groscurth, 2004; Putman & Thompson, 2006; Wang, 2012, 2014a, 2014b; Wang & Nuru, 2017). Orbe (2008) suggests that FGCS experience a time of significant identity negotiation during college. This process often leads to dialectical tensions when FGCS return home to share their experiences with younger family members and community members.

Orbe (2008) identifies individual-social identity and stability-change dialectics as particularly relevant to identity negotiation. Balancing the individual-social identity tension involves negotiating personal identities within larger social groups (Tajfel, 1981; Turner, 1991). This tension highlights the struggle between the individual or personal and social or collective self-concept. At home, this tension requires FGCS to find a balance between independence and interdependence. FGCS desire to create distance from their family while retaining some level of closeness. This creates a struggle between the old and new selves and the established and emerging identities.

Benmayor (2002) suggests that FGCS can use storytelling to successfully negotiate their identities at home and fulfill their commitment to the home community. This desire to provide support to family members and community members is shaped by a generative commitment to improving the lives of their families and communities (Benmayor, 2002). FGCS fulfill this commitment when they take on the role of mentor or role model for younger family members and community members who are considering college. Because these individuals often lack a tradition of college completion within their own families, the presence of current FGCS role models often predicts future FGCS' college success (Tyre, 2006).

Rationale

Although life stories are rooted in the past, they are more than a chronological account of biological facts. They are embedded in a cultural context and differ with respect to theme (McAdams & Bowman, 2001), structural complexity (Woike, Gersekovich, Piorkowski, & Polo, 1999), and coherence and intelligibility (Baerger & McAdams, 1999). Although there is a strong body of research on adult life stories, there is an established need for research on adolescent life stories (Bruner, 1987). Recent research has focused on college students' identity stories (Thompson et al., 2009), but little is known about FGCS' identity stories.

FGCS lack a tradition of college completion. Because there is no family college completion legacy, many FGCS believe it is important to support and improve the lives of their families and communities (Benmayor, 2002). FGCS fulfill this commitment by taking on the role of mentor or role model for future generations considering college (Tyre, 2006). Mentoring and modeling college completion often involves sharing their college identity life stories. Over time, these life stories can become legacies or "strands of meaning that run through the family in ways that give it identity or sense, are constituted in communication through family storytelling, and are continually reshaped over time" (Thompson et al., 2009, p. 108). Although researchers know that storytelling helps FGCS successfully negotiate their identities at home and fulfill their commitment to their families and communities (Benmayor, 2002), little is known about what types of college identity stories FGCS use to create a legacy of college completion.

Intersectionality and Higher Education

Coined by Crenshaw (1989), intersectionality is a metaphor for understanding how privilege and marginalization intersect in overlapping, multiplicative, and fragmented ways. Intersectionality address myriad interlocking oppressive effects of marginalization (Collins, 1990; Crenshaw, 1989; DeFrancisco, Palczewski, & McGeough, 2014; King, 1988) and is therefore central not only to understanding individual identities, but also the systems, such as higher education, where inequalities are reproduced (Collins & Bilge, 2016).

Scholars have articulated numerous metaphors to help visualize intersectionality. Frye (1983) suggested a birdcage where each wire in the cage represents a different aspect of marginalization. King (1988) coined the term "multiple jeopardy" to argue against the idea of Frye's (1983) additive notion that aspects of inequality could be separate. King instead argued that racism, sexism, and classism operate as three interdependent operations of power. Collins (1990) suggested the metaphor of the "matrix of domination" to describe a broad structure of domination in which multiple interlocking-isms (racism, classism, sexism, etc.) operate.

Intersectional approaches are particularly important for understanding how marginalization shapes experiences in higher education (Ostrove, Stewart, & Curtin, 2011). Stewart and Dottolo (2005) assert that "women students, students of color, and students who did not identify as heterosexual had experiences in the academy that were markedly different from those with dominant social identities" (p. 750). In addition, other researchers have argued that women (Tokarczyk & Fay, 1983) as well as students from the working class (Provitera McGlynn, 2011; Ryan & Sackrey, 1996; Welsch, 2004) felt a lack of belonging, making academia a balancing act of straddling different worlds.

Intersectionality inherently rejects the notion that one aspect of identity (such as race, class, sex, and sexuality) is more salient than others (Jehangir et al., 2015; Orbe, 2004), and allows one to see how identity shifts over time and context. For example, Orbe (2004) notes how FGCS status surfaced as more central when it was interwoven with race/ethnicity, age, class, and gender. Thus, for some FGCS, the privilege linked with being male, European American, middle/upper class, and/or within the traditional age for college students allowed the FGCS identity to exist on the periphery of students' daily lives. Understanding how intersectionality shapes marginalized FGCS' experiences can be a first crucial step in producing a more inclusive and supportive environment to increase the belonging, well-being, and academic success of these students.

Method

Intersectionality refers to a holistic approach of observing how different identity categories interact in individuals' lives. Thus, by its very nature, intersectional analysis is challenging because it requires simultaneous attention to several axes of identity. In an effort to paint a more complete portrait of FGCS' experiences, our methodological choices centered on providing rich context, depth, and multivocality. As such, we collected three personal narratives from currently-enrolled undergraduate FGCS. By interweaving the personal narratives of Bre, Maril, and Morgan, we are able to illuminate three voices that lend unique insights into the processes of negotiating multiple intersecting identities as FGCS.

Narrative Data Collection

As part of a larger study on experiences of adversities during their collegiate journeys, we engaged in purposeful selection (Baxter & Babbie, 2004) to locate narrators who met the U.S. Department of Education's (1998) definition of FGCS: neither parent completed a bachelor's degree. Narrators ranged in age from 18 to 20 and self-identified as belonging to low-income and racially underrepresented groups. Through semi-structured interviews, narrators were asked to tell their college scholarship story, to describe a story about hardships experienced in high school, as well as a story about adversities experienced during college. Each interview averaged 70 minutes in length.

Data Analysis

To analyze the data, each interview was transcribed verbatim. Next, we explored categories of meaning by grouping the emerging themes on a master list (Smith, 1995). This step involved looking for consistent patterns among the narratives by using an iterative process of open, axial, and selective coding. Using Owen's (1984) criteria, we identified themes based on recurrence (multiple instances within each narrative), repetition (multiple uses of the same wording), and forcefulness (emphasis on particular words or phrasing). To make certain our themes were reflections of the meanings conveyed by the narrators, we engaged in critical discussion to vet and refine final categories (Lindloff & Taylor, 2002).

Results

The purpose of this chapter was to better understand the storied experiences of FGCS as they navigate the complex, fragmented, and overlapping intersectionalities of multiple identities. For purposes of clarity, we first delineate each identity category in detail, discussing each theme in order of most to least represented in the FGCS narratives. Then, we draw attention to the ways in which these identities overlap. Although we organize these experiences around four broad categories, we do so with the understanding that they do not exist in isolation of one another. In what follows, we discuss the intersectionality of marginality for FGCS by attending to four broad themes: intersectionalities of FGCS and social capital; intersectionalities of FGCS and income; intersectionalities of FGCS and caregiving; and intersectionalities of FGCS and ethnicity-race. We then call attention to the ways in which these identities intersect and how the narrators describe navigating multiple disenfranchised social positions. Further, by presenting the stories of three FGCS women in conversation with one another, we illuminate the ways in which these overlapping identity categories impact the college experience. We begin by discussing the intersectionalities of FGCS and social capital.

First Theme: Intersectionalities of FGCS and Social Capital

When referring to "social capital," we adopt the definition advanced by Bourdieu (1986), who describes it as "the aggregate of actual or potential resources which are linked to possession of a durable network of more or less institutional relationships" (p. 248). This theme was most prominently portrayed in the FGCS narratives through assertions that their continuing generation college student (CGCS) peers had access to systems of knowing that were unbeknownst to them. For instance, the narrators explain that the parents of CGCS were seemingly more involved in the process of applying to school, securing scholarships, and providing social support because they were able to draw on their personal experiences and social networks to help their children understand college expectations. As such, parents of CGCS passed down social and cultural capital to their children that helped them succeed. Bre, Maril, and Morgan explain that because going to college was a new and unfamiliar experience for their families, they did not inherit the social and cultural capital needed to navigate the college experience (Arzuaga, 2016). Bre shares:

> I had worked so hard during high school, taken honors classes, worked two jobs, completed over 250 hours of community service, had a bout of homelessness and was able to maintain a 4.3 GPA and was so sure that my hard work would pay off. Yet, as I failed to land scholarships, I became acutely aware that my hard work just wasn't good enough. My ACT score didn't reflect the double wait-ressing shift I did the night before a big exam I made an "A" on; it didn't reflect my drive, my passion, and most importantly it did not reflect my potential. I was sick with aggravation and anxiety and for the first time I felt the invisible hand of inequity fall firmly on my shoulders, holding me back. Career counselors at my high school encouraged me to keep an open-mind toward changing my goal of going to a four-year school, bidding me to be "realistic." That was the first time that I realized that no matter how hard I had worked, for every seven steps I took forward, I was still three steps behind my CGCS friends.

Bre explains that although she earned a high GPA while facing unimaginable circumstances, she felt as though she could not get ahead. Unlike her CGCS peers, she lacked the cultural capital of knowing *who* and *how* to ask for funding. Like Bre, Maril illustrates that she, too, lacked an understanding of the process for applying for scholarships. She explains that she initially thought that college was not a possibility for her because none of her family members had attended. She states:

> One day my AP Biology teacher asked me about college. I hadn't submitted any applications or anything. [...] I was telling her nobody ever went to college. I didn't know how to apply or where to start. I found out I had missed all the deadlines for scholarships. I couldn't afford college so I wasn't looking into it. [....] She took me under her wing and showed me how to apply for schools. [...] I'm really grateful for teachers like her because without her I would probably not be in school. [...] With her help, I ended up getting one of the highest scholarship amounts in my graduating class. I wasn't even going to school. I figured I would be at home taking care of my parents for the rest of my life. [My scholarship foundation] took a child who wasn't going to college because the rest of her siblings didn't go to college, her parents didn't go to college, and they made it possible.

Here, Maril explains that because she did not understand the application process, she missed deadlines for scholarships. She continues by elucidating the influential role her AP Biology teacher played in sharing necessary cultural capital, whom she credits as the sole reason she was able to apply for college and secure scholarships.

Yet, FGCS students like Morgan highlight that applying for college is just the beginning. Morgan points to the fact that while she, too, needed help with her college application, what was perhaps most frustrating for her was that her CGCS peers had support systems in place to protect them if they made mistakes. She explains that because her parents did not have the social capital to help her, she was "on her own." Morgan reflects:

> I noticed that a majority of the kids had parents that were extremely invested in their future. They had these parents who had been to college. [...] These kids came from drastically different backgrounds than I did. [...] I couldn't convey why I was so frustrated with them. If I screwed up, then I was screwed three ways. If they screwed up they could bounce back. [...] I don't have a support system like they do. If I mess up I'm on my own. If my friends mess up they have parents that can catch them.

Overall, Maril, Morgan and Bre show that the educational experience is impacted by the intersectionalities of FGCS and social capital in that unlike their CGCS peers, FGCS do not inherit social capital from their parents. Instead, FGCS often enter college life without social support systems in place and are therefore charged with the additional strain of establishing them along the way.

Second Theme: Intersectionalities of FGCS and Income

Within conversations about the intersections of FGCS identity and social capital, Maril, Bre, and Morgan gave voice to a second theme: intersectionalities of FGCS and income. Often discussed abreast conversations of social capital, the narrators underscored how living in low-income households presented unique struggles related to social class. Reflecting on her own circumstances, Morgan explains that academic success "has a lot to do with income too. If you're rich enough you can fix your problems, but if you're poor, you can't." Like Morgan, both Maril and Bre describe how being financially disenfranchised created obstacles in that they perpetually struggled to secure basic resources including food, shelter, and running water. Maril recalls:

> [My mom] was our primary source of income, so her losing her job led to utilities being cut off and us not having food in the house, me not having the things I essentially needed. We had no heat so she would be boiling water on the stove

so we could take hot baths. Luckily my grandmother left us the house and it was paid for, so we didn't lose our house. There were a lot of times we didn't have stuff we needed. It just kept going downhill from there. [...] We would go to the church and they would give us boxes of food, so we could have food in the house. That was a very painful time because my mom used to give—we never had a lot but we had enough to give to others, [...] but I could tell stuff really hurt her pride and it hurt me because she would rather go hungry than to have to go pick up that box.

According to Allen (2004), inferior living conditions, such as those in which Maril describes, can constrain students' potential to learn. Allen (2004) argues that restricted access to basic resources may negatively impact potential for longevity and success as well as self-esteem. Further, national statistics demonstrate that low-income students are disproportionately labeled as low-status and may receive less help in class (Allen, 2004; Jehangir et al., 2015). Consistent with these trends, Maril, Bre, and Morgan describe how they forged through these limitations. Bre shares that she knew education was her only hope for social mobility:

I was used to having less than others around me and learned at a young age the value of hard work. I remember my single dad coming home from work tired to the bone helping me with homework, his calloused hands struggling to turn a page in my textbooks. I learned then that we had it hard and knew from an early age that I did not want to live in poverty forever. My father's greatest gift to me was instilling in me a deep appreciation for education and always encouraging me to achieve in my studies. I found education as an escape from poverty with the knowledge that if I studied really hard, worked as hard as my dad did, then I would be able to escape the quick-sand pit of poverty. Growing up poor taught me to be resourceful, thankful, and to work very hard. I still carry those lessons with me today and am thankful for the work ethic my father taught me which helped me to land a free ride to college. My father's encouragement in education led me to achieve highly in school, in college, and find my passion in advocating for education in the U.S. I would not be where I am today without him.

Collectively, Bre, Maril, and Morgan's storied experiences demonstrate that being educational pioneers and being financially disenfranchised forces FGCS to have to work much harder to experience the things that those with social capital and financial means take for granted (if they ever experience them at all).

Third Theme: Intersectionalities of FGCS and Caregiving

A third theme that emerged from the FGCS narratives involved caregiving for family members who were dealing with addiction, mental illness, or (dis)ability. Although they were just high school students at the time, Bre,

Morgan, and Maril explained that they were often called to take on adult caregiving roles. For example, Maril recalls attending to her parents' medical needs:

> I was the primary caregiver—anything they needed. I've seen the gross side of medicine. I've changed [...] and cleaned feeding tubes [...]. I was the one who went to doctors' appointments, scheduled doctors' appointments, going to the hospitals, and doing all the medical stuff, taking care of the house. [...] It's hard, especially when you have to go from being a child to being a caretaker. You're not ready for that. [...] When I was little I had to go from being a kid to being mature and responsible—stuff that children don't do. My mom can't see to fill out paperwork; she can't see to file her taxes. That's stuff I'm having to do. That's stressful.

As Maril explains, oscillating between being a child and a caregiver was a struggle. On top of completing her schoolwork, she served as the primary caregiver for both of her parents, routinely driving them to and from doctors' appointments even before she was legally permitted to drive.

Similarly, Morgan notes that because her single mother was typically at work, she took on the role of caregiver for her younger siblings. Along with completing her homework and researching scholarships, Morgan explains that she also served as a tutor and guardian for her younger sisters. She shares:

> I didn't do my sisters' homework [for them], but I made sure they did it and helped them out with it. [...] I would cook dinner, make sure they had their stuff ready for the next day. Just taking care of them.

Like Morgan, Bre also lived in a single-parent household, which demanded that she take on adult roles and responsibilities. In addition to working a job to help pay for household bills, Bre also served as a caregiver for her grieving father. Throughout her narrative Bre discusses the impact that her mother's schizophrenia diagnosis had on her family structure. Because her mother resides at a mental health facility and is largely absent from her life, Bre and her father had to work as a team to survive. For these reasons, it was incredibly difficult for her to move away to college as it meant leaving her father behind. She shares:

> I remember feeling as if I abandoned my father back home. I remember feeling really torn about leaving my dad knowing that if I were there he wouldn't be alone and would have someone to help with money. [...] Delaying the gratification of getting a job out of high school was difficult for me because all I could think about was how money would help our situation immediately. But, I keep telling myself that after I earn my degree I will have greater earning potential which will help to pull my family out of poverty.

Overall, the narrators illustrate that being FGCS and primary caregivers is taxing in that they occupy simultaneous roles of inexperience and authority. Further, as they move away from home to pursue educational goals, they must navigate ongoing struggles of feeling guilty for leaving their family behind and pride for creating new educational legacies.

Fourth Theme: Intersectionalities of FGCS and Ethnicity-Race

The final theme to emerge within the FGCS narratives focused on the intersectionalities of FGCS and ethnicity-race. Although nearly every university across the U.S. celebrates some commitment to diversity, faculty of color continue to represent less than 25% of all full-time professors (Gutiérrez y Muhs, Niemann, González, & Harris, 2012; Myers, 2016). Further, faculty of color are largely concentrated at the lowest-ranks of academe (Gutiérrez y Muhs et al., 2012). As such, many students of color routinely earn college degrees without ever taking a course with a professor who shares their ethnic-racial background. For Maril, this was just the case. She recalls noticing racial divides in her classrooms and among the faculty and staff at her school:

> I started noticing little things like how if we were in a classroom, all the White kids were on one side and all the Black kids were on the other side. [...] Or like, most of the janitors are Black, but most of the instructors are White.

As a student of color, Maril describes in this excerpt that she came to realize the marginality of ethnicity-race on her university campus. In concert with Maril, Morgan illustrates the challenges of being a student of color among an overwhelming majority of White students and faculty members. She recalls:

> I was constantly having to not be a stereotype. [...] If you were visibly upset, you're an angry Black woman. It was constantly having to deal with that. I was shocked. I had never been around people that acted this way. People having low expectations for you, and then getting upset when you surpass their expectations.

In Morgan's experience, both professors and students alike underestimated her potential to succeed. In fact, during one point of her narrative, Morgan recalls a professor doubting her ability to complete her exam quickly without engaging in some form of academic misconduct. For Morgan, racial stereotypes presented insurmountable obstacles that impacted her willingness to engage in class.

Further, Bre also struggled to navigate ethnic-racial stereotypes. Bre recalls being called to enact a "model minority" role within her classes (Allen, 2004). She shares:

> I am the daughter of a Korean immigrant, something I feel has been an enriching experience but not without some adversity. [...] There are people who still believe that mixing races is a "bad" thing or "product of sin" so there was no shortage of stares from strangers growing up. [...] I never really saw teachers, mentors, or celebrity icons that looked like me [...] In school I was never very talented in STEM subjects and yet I was the "Asian" of the class and looked to excel in those subjects. To this day, I struggle with imposter syndrome and I struggle to believe that I'm good enough to get through my courses or that I'm good enough for my major.

By pointing to challenges of navigating a multiethnic-racial identity in a rural and mono-racial cultural environment, Bre illustrates how ethnic-racial marginality impacts sense of self. In addition to dealing with ethnic-racial stereotypes and a lack of ethnic-racial representation in her community, Bre notes these types of interactions lead her to question her ability to succeed. In sum, each of the narrators describe that being students of color on university campuses without faculty of color in leadership roles makes navigating the college experience increasingly more difficult.

The Intersectional Experience of FGCS Women

Crenshaw (1989, p. 140) describes the "intersectional experience" as one in which discretely marginalized component identities are intrinsically linked, creating a whole self that is multiply-burdened. She explains that the interaction of these marginalized identities compounds experiences of disadvantage in ways that are greater than the sum of singular acts of discrimination (racism, sexism). In consonance with Crenshaw, Bre, Maril, and Morgan illuminate the ways in which FGCS women simultaneously experience the intersections of multiple disenfranchised identities. Bre shares:

> For a long time, I saw my identities and experiences—poor, mixed heritage, first generation, and troubled family history—as roadblocks or potholes in my life. I feel that because of my identities, when one person takes three steps forward, I must take seven just to catch up to where they had been. [...] I feel like I am carrying my family name and our chance for a better life on my shoulders [...]. I feel that because of my identities, I play a perpetual game of catchup socially, academically, and emotionally.

Here, Bre explains that coming from multiple disenfranchised social groups created obstacles that those with more privileged social positions (those in more powerful social groups, or those navigating single-axis oppression) do not encounter. She notes that the pressure of establishing a new educational legacy for her family and bettering her family's social position weighs heavily on her. To this end, she illustrates that because she must manage several over-lapping disadvantages from multiple identity groups, she was overwhelmed in that she has to constantly work harder to counterbalance these hardships. Maril echoes these sentiments:

> As a lower-class, African American, female I have faced many obstacles in college. I can't get things as easily as my White [CGS] peers can which is hard when you are working towards a degree that seems like every semester they have some new big fee or stipulation for you to continue. [...] Especially being in the nursing school, I now have added finances from the program that are not completely covered by my scholarship. This added additional stress to the program—the biggest being insurance. I can't really afford to pay for it but I need it for my program. Stuff like that kind of makes you sad because I had to struggle to get where I am and now that I'm here I have to struggle to stay here when my classmates don't have to think twice about something as simple as health insurance. [...] I've enjoyed my time in college but I have had to struggle for basic things they I am aware that others don't have to think twice about.

In this excerpt, Maril articulates the ways in which her experience on-campus differs from her peers. Given that one of her parents receives Medicare and the other is uninsured, Maril has to purchase individual health insurance in order to maintain enrollment in her courses. Unlike her peers who are able to stay on their parents' insurance throughout college, her family is unable to afford the cost of family coverage. Maril also highlights that she has encountered challenges as an African-American female at a predominantly White institution.

Like Maril, Morgan underscores that the intersections of ethnicity-race, income, and gender have presented challenges for her during her college career. Morgan shares:

> I would say my income has made it harder to be carefree in life. I'm also aware that my race will probably cause me difficulty in some social interactions. I'm constantly aware that certain behaviors will lead people to think of me as a certain way, and in a very negative light. [...] Black women are often at the bottom of "Power Tower," but I've always been a firm believer that knowledge is power and I want power, so it made me want my education more. It's made me more serious about college than some of my peers. [...] My classes often [...] leave out Black women [...] and the constant negative statistics that are constantly brought up are very demoralizing. I'm a public health major and the only time we talk about Black women is when it comes to the HIV/AIDS infection rate or the teen parent status. Not all Black women or even a majority live this way or experience this.

Along with the challenges of coming from a low-income household, Morgan highlights how race and sex discrimination create disadvantages within the classroom. Although Morgan understands the power of education in elevating her social position, she notes that her class readings fail to represent the lived experiences of most African-American women in the U.S. In doing so, Morgan highlights that her lived experience is underrepresented or mischaracterized within the educational system. Overall, Bre, Maril, and Morgan call attention to an "intersectional experience" (Crenshaw, 1989, p. 140) through which they are navigating multiply-burdened identity categories as FGCS.

Discussion

In this chapter, three FGCS women give voice to the intersectionality of marginality across four broad themes: intersectionalities of FGCS and social capital; intersectionalities of FGCS and income; intersectionalities of FGCS and caregiving; and intersectionalities of FGCS and ethnicity-race. Understanding how the intersections between these axes of identity emerge in the lived experiences of FGCS enables unique insight into the complex construction of marginality for FGCS. Although presented as four discrete themes, these facets of identity are neither additive nor separable; rather, each facet is always salient and interwoven. A qualitatively different situation is created when aspects of identity are seen as interwoven. The barriers these FGCS experienced created an absence of viable choices in *different* ways and at *different* times, but functioned *similarly* to impact access to resources afforded to students with family legacies of college completion. In addition, while different identities emerged as salient at different times, the presence of multiple interlocking identities are always present as wires in the metaphorical birdcage (Frye, 1983) that constrain the lives of FGCS. For example, lacking social capital emerged as salient when these women navigated the college application process. Ethnicity-race emerged as salient when they encountered stereotypes from faculty on campus based on the color of their skin. When we step back and look macroscopically, however, we see that FGCS cannot simply fly around individual wires in the birdcage because the intersection of the wires functions to cage and constrain their movement.

Fundamentally, what these women illustrate is that there is no monolithic FGCS identity, but instead the multiple threads of their identity complicate and inform their lived experiences. This is consistent with previous research (Langhout, Rosselli, & Feinstein, 2007) indicating that FGCS experience systematic discrimination based on multiple aspects of their identity, such as their economic capital and ethnicity. This chapter's findings demonstrate the interlocking oppressive effects of less privileged social positions (DeFrancisco et al., 2014). Importantly, they give insight not only into individual identities, but also the systems where challenges are perpetuated across individuals, groups, and institutions (Collins & Bilge, 2016).

The narratives of FGCS in the present chapter illuminate several important points regarding the intersectionality of marginality. First, without a legacy of college completion in their families, the uncertainty faced in preparing for college, particularly regarding expenses, funding, and degree expectations is especially isolating. Although college-educated parents can guide their children through understanding the culture of higher education and its place in their future success (Pascarella, Pierson, Wolniak, & Terenzini, 2004), these FGCS show how lacking the networks, resources, and support systems present for students with college-educated parents means lacking a cushion to break their fall or to soften the blow of even a minor setback.

Second, the ways in which this lack of resources posed particular difficulties for their financial needs lends insight into the ways in which social capital intersects with social class. Working-class students often experience economic burdens necessitating that they work and spend less time accessing institutional agents (Morschetti & Hudley, 2008) or individuals who can transmit or help communicate opportunities and resources available on campus. This is especially powerful because communication with these individuals is linked to the beliefs of FGCS, but not students with college-educated parents (Moschetti & Hudley, 2008). In other words, the students who need this contact the most may not have been encouraged to seek it (because they lack social capital) or they may not have the time to access it (because of their class-based needs). Subsequently, their confidence and sense of connection and belonging suffers.

Third, stereotypes and tokenization based on these women's visibility as a person of color trapped them in "simultaneous and intersecting systems of relationships and meaning" (Andersen & Collins, 1992, p. xiii). In some cases, this meant that positive actions (such as doing well on a test or finishing an exam quickly) violated others' expectations of them while in other cases, it created the pressure to uphold stereotypes (such as the model minority). These myriads of overlapping and conflicting forces illuminate the ways in which these students may feel like "outsiders within" (Collins, 1990), or those who are on the fringes, for whom navigating the college experience is challenging. This pattern continues throughout higher education and into the academy as faculty women of color describe how their competence is questioned (Gutiérrez y Muhs et al., 2012). As members of two minority groups, women faculty of color experience identity taxation that is unique from either female faculty or faculty of color (Hirshfield & Joseph, 2012).

Although this chapter explored the stories of three women FGCS at one point in time, it would be useful for researchers to explore how these narratives may shift or change throughout their college years. One avenue that would be rich for a textual analysis of FGCS narrative would be the use of diary studies. Journaling about their goals, their communication with institutional agents, family, and peers over time would allow scholars to explore the ebb and flow of the college years as they unfold naturally. In addition, exploring the intersectional influences of FGCS men and women would enable deeper insight into the college experience. Exploring the intersections of identity for FGCS allows for a more holistic and nuanced portrait of marginality as it is lived.

References

Allen, B. J. (2004). *Difference matters: Communicating social identity*. Prospect Heights, IL: Waveland Press.

Andersen, M. L., & Collins, P. H. (1992). *Race, class, and gender: An anthology*. Belmont, CA: Wadsworth.

Arnett, J. J. (2005). The developmental context of substance use in emerging adulthood. *Journal of Drug Issues, 35*(2), 235–253. Retrieved from http://journals.sagepub.com/loi/jod

Arzuaga, A. (2016). Family engagement for first-generation families and families of color. In V. Pendakur (Ed.), *Closing the opportunity gap: Identity-conscious strategies for retention and student success* (pp. 10–24). Sterling, VA: Stylus Publishing.

Baerger, D., & McAdams, D. P. (1999). Life story coherence and its relation to psychological well-being. *Narrative Inquiry, 9*(1), 69–96. Retrieved from http://www.ingentaconnect.com/content/jbp/nari

Baxter, L. A., & Babbie, E. (2004). *The basics of communication research*. Belmont, CA: Wadsworth.

Benmayor, R. (2002). Narrating cultural citizenship: Oral histories of first-generation college students of Mexican origin. *Social Justice, 29*(4), 96–121. Retrieved from http://www.socialjusticejournal.org/Backiss.html

Bourdieu, P. (1986). The forms of capital. In J. G. Richardson (Ed.), *Handbook of theory and research for the sociology of education* (pp. 241–258). New York, NY: Greenwood Press.

Bruner, J. S. (1987). Life as narrative. *Social Research, 54*(1), 11–32. Retrieved from http://newschool.edu/centers/socres/backissues.html

Choy, S. P. (2001). *Findings from the condition of education 2001: Students whose parents did not go to college: Postsecondary access, persistence, and attainment* (NCES 2001–126). U.S. Department of Education, National Center for Education Statistics. Washington, DC: U.S. Government Printing Office.

Collins, P. H. (1990). *Black feminist thought: Knowledge, consciousness, and the politics of empowerment*. Boston, MA: Unwin Hyman.

Collins, P. H., & Bilge, S. (2016). *Intersectionality.* Malden, MA: Polity Press.

Crenshaw, K. (1989). Demarginalizing the intersection of race and sex: A Black feminist critique of antidiscrimination doctrine, feminist theory and antiracist politics. *The University of Chicago Legal Forum, 1989,* 139–167. Retrieved from https://philpapers.org/archive/CREDTI.pdf?ncid=txtlnkusaolp00000603

DeFrancisco, V. P., Palczewski, C. H., & McGeough, D. D. (2014). *Gender in communication: A critical introduction* (2nd ed.). Thousand Oaks, CA: Sage.

Frye, M. (1983). *The politics of reality: Essays in feminist theory.* Freedom, CA: Crossing Press.

Gutiérrez y Muhs, G., Niemann, Y. F., González, C. G., & Harris, A. P. (Eds.). (2012). *Presumed incompetent: The intersections of race and class for women in academia.* Ogden, UT: Utah State University Press.

Hirshfield, L. E., & Joseph, T. D. (2012). "We need a woman, we need a Black woman": Gender, race, and identity taxation in the academy. *Gender & Education, 24*(2), 213–227. doi: 10.1080/09540253.2011.606208

Hossler, D., Schmit, J., & Vesper, N. (1999). *Going to college: How social, economic, and educational factors influence the decisions students make.* Baltimore, MD: Johns Hopkins University Press.

Jehangir, R., Stebleton, M., & Deenanath, V. (2015). *An exploration of intersecting identities of first-generation, low-income students.* Columbia, SC: National Resource Center for the First Year Experience.

King, D. K. (1988). Multiple jeopardy, multiple consciousness: The context of Black feminist ideology. *Signs, 14*(1), 42–72. Retrieved from http://www.jstor.org/stable/3174661

Langellier, K. M., & Peterson, E. E. (1993). Family storytelling as a strategy of social control. In D. K. Mumby (Ed.), *Narrative and social control: Critical perspectives* (pp. 49–76). Newbury Park, CA: Sage.

Langhout, R. D., Rosselli, F., & Feinstein, J. (2007). Assessing classism in academic settings. *The Review of Higher Education, 30*(2), 145–184. doi:10.1353/rhe.2006.0073

Lindlof, T. R., & Taylor, B. C. (2002). *Qualitative research methods* (2nd ed.). Thousand Oaks, CA: Sage.

McAdams, D. P. (2001). *The person: An integrated introduction to personality psychology* (3rd ed.). Fort Worth, TX: Harcourt.

McAdams, D. P. (2006). *The redemptive self: Stories Americans live by.* New York, NY: Oxford University Press.

McAdams, D. P., & Bowman, P. T. (2001). Narrating life's turning points: Redemption and contamination. In D. P. McAdams, R. Josselson, & A. Lieblich (Eds.), *Turns in the road: Narrative studies of lives in transition* (pp. 3–34). Washington, DC: American Psychological Association.

Moschetti, R., & Hudley, C. (2008). Measuring social capital among first-generation and non-first-generation, working-class, White males. *Journal of College Admis-*

sion, 198(Winter 2008), 25–30. Retrieved from https://files.eric.ed.gov/fulltext/EJ829418.pdf

Myers, B. (2016, February 14). Where are the minority professors? *The Chronicle of Higher Education.* Retrieved from https://www.chronicle.com/interactives/where-are-the-minority-professors

Orbe, M. P. (2004). Negotiating multiple identities within multiple frames: An analysis of first-generation college students. *Communication Education, 53*(2), 131–149. doi: 10.1080/03634520410001682401

Orbe, M. P. (2006, December). *Latino/a first-generation college students: Similarities and differences across predominantly Latino and predominantly White campuses.* Paper presented at the annual meeting of the Speech Communication Association of Puerto Rico, San Juan, P.R.

Orbe, M. P. (2008). Theorizing multidimensional identity negotiation: Reflections on the lived experiences of first-generation college students. *New Directions for Child and Adolescent Development, 120,* 81–95. doi: 10.1002/cd.217

Orbe, M. P., & Groscurth, C. R. (2004). A co-cultural theoretical analysis of communicating on campus and at home: Exploring the negotiation strategies of first generation college (FGC) students. *Qualitative Research Reports in Communication, 5,* 41–47.

Ostrove, J. M., Stewart, A. J., & Curtin, N. L. (2011). Social class and belonging: Implications for graduate students' career aspirations. *Journal of Higher Education, 82*(6), 748–774. doi: 10.1353/jhe.2011.0039

Owen, W. F. (1984). Interpretive themes in relational communication. *Quarterly Journal of Speech, 70,* 274–287. doi: 10.1080/00335638409383697

Pascarella, E. T., Pierson, C. T., Wolniak, G. C., & Terenzini, P. T. (2004). First-generation college student: Additional evidence on college experiences and outcomes. *Journal of Higher Education, 75*(3), 249–284. doi: 10.1353/jhe.2004.0016

Provitera McGlynn, A. (2011). *Envisioning equity: Educating and graduating low-income, first-generation, and minority college students.* Madison, WI: Atwood Publishing.

Putman, A., & Thompson, S. (2006). Paving the way: First-generation Mexican American community college students in a border community speak out. In M. Orbe, B. Allen, & L. Flores (Eds.), *The same and different: Acknowledging the diversity with and between cultural groups* (pp. 121–142). Washington, DC: NCA Press.

Ryan, J., & Sackrey, C. (1996). *Strangers in paradise: Academics from the working class.* Lanham, MD: University Press of America.

Smith, J. A. (1995). Semi-structured interviewing and qualitative analysis. In J. A. Smith, R. Harré, & L. V. Langenhove (Eds.), *Rethinking methods in psychology* (pp. 9–26). Thousand Oaks, CA: Sage.

Stewart, A. J., & Dottolo, A. L. (2005). Socialization to the academy: Coping with competing social identities. In G. Downey, J. S. Eccles, & C. M. Chatman (Eds.), *Navigating the future: Social identity, coping, and life tasks* (pp. 167–187). New York, NY: Russell Sage Foundation.

Stone, E. (1988). *Black sheep and kissing cousins: How our family stories shape us.* New York, NY: Times Books.

Tajfel, H. (1981). *Human groups and social categories: Studies in social psychology.* Cambridge, England: Cambridge University Press.

Terenzini, P. T., Springer, L., Yaeger, P. M., Pascarella, E. T., & Nora, A. (1996). First generation college students: Characteristics, experiences, and cognitive development. *Research in Higher Education, 37*(1), 1–22. doi: 10.1007/BF01680039

Thompson, B., Koenig Kellas, J., Soliz, J., Thompson, J., Epp, A., & Schrodt, P. (2009). Family legacies: Constructing individual and family identity through intergenerational storytelling. *Narrative Inquiry, 19*(1), 106–134. doi: 10.1075/ni.19.1.07tho

Tokarczyk, M., & Fay, E. (Eds.) (1993). *Working-class women in the academy: Laborers in the knowledge factory.* Amherst, MA: University of Massachusetts Press.

Turner, J. C. (1991). *Social influence.* Milton Keynes, England: Open University Press.

Tyre, P. (2006). The trouble with boys. *Newsweek, 44,* 46–52. Retrieved from http://www.newsweek.com/id/47522

U.S. Department of Education. (1998). *Higher Education Act of 1965, 1998 Higher Education Act Amendments* (P.L. 105–244). Retrieved from http://www2.ed.gov/about/offices/list/ope/trio/triohea.pdf

Wang, T. R. (2012). Understanding the memorable messages first-generation college students receive from on-campus mentors. *Communication Education, 61*(4), 335–357. doi: 10.1080/03634523.2012.691978

Wang, T. R. (2014a). Formational turning points in the transition to college: Understanding how communication events shape first-generation students' pedagogical and interpersonal relationships with their college teachers. *Communication Education, 63*(1), 63–82. doi: 10.1080/03634523.2013.841970

Wang, T. R. (2014b). "I'm the only person from where I'm from to go to college": Understanding the memorable messages first-generation college students receive from parents. *Journal of Family Communication, 14*(3), 270–290. doi: 10.1080/15267431.2014.908195

Wang, T. R., & Nuru, A. K. (2017). "He wanted me to achieve that for our family and I did, too": Exploring first-generation students' experiences of turning points during the transition to college. *Journal of Family Communication, 17*(2), 153–168. doi: 10.1080/15267431.2016.1264401

Welsch, K. A. (Ed.). (2004). *Those winter Sundays: Female academics and their working-class parents.* Lanham, MD: University Press of America.

Woike, B. A., Gersekovich, I., Piorkowski, R., & Polo, M. (1999). The role of motives in the content and structure of autobiographical memory. *Journal of Personality and Social Psychology, 76*(4), 600–612. doi: 10.1037/0022–3514.76.4.600

3. From Invisible Trailblazers to Insurgent Leaders: An Intergenerational Narrative of Transcendence at the Intersection of Race, Class, Sexual Orientation, and Spirituality

Trott Nely Montina and Jonathan Mathias Lassiter

Introduction

It is rewarding, challenging, and sometimes lonely—all at once—being the first person in one's family to achieve something for the first time in the family's history. First-generation college students (FGCS) are trailblazers who must navigate several barriers in their process of achieving higher education. These obstacles include lack of social and cultural capital as well as financial strain (Housel & Harvey, 2009; Owens, Lacey, Rawls, & Holbert-Quince, 2010). For FGCS who have interlocking marginalized social identities, these challenges are compounded (Orbe, 2004, 2008). For example, a FGCS who is also Black and from a lower middle-class economic background may not only have to cope with economic difficulties, but also with White supremacy. This student may find that their experiences are pushed to the margins due to having social identities that are considered subordinate in class and racial paradigms (Purdie-Vaughns & Eibach, 2008). The matrices of oppression that FGCS—and similarly first-generation college professors (FGCP) who were once FGCS themselves—with intersecting marginalized identities must endure may contribute to them feeling invisible and dehumanized in their attempts to succeed in academia.

FGCS and FGCP at the intersection of race, class, sexual orientation, and spirituality often have the experience of being invisible. Franklin and Boyd-Franklin (2000) described Black males as often having a "feeling of not being seen as a person of worth" (p. 33). Often these men must grapple with cultivating a sense of self in a world that does not affirm their humanity (Parham, 1999). This crucial process can sometimes cause people to undergo psychic dissonance in which they feel part of two worlds and are not fully comfortable in either. Black FGCS and FCGP often find themselves in liminal spaces that require them to either prefer one part of their identity to gain favor in a particular context, or dare to embrace all of themselves at the risk of being misinterpreted and mistreated. Previous researchers have found that this sort of liminal existence often contributes to FGCS and FGCP feeling unaccepted in a Predominantly White Institution (PWI) and distant from family members and peers in their often under-educated communities and families-of-origin (Longwell-Grice, Adsitt, Mullins, & Serrata, 2016; Perez, 2008). These first-generation academics often are subjected to microaggressions (Sue, Capodilupo, & Holder, 2008; Sue et al., 2008; Sue et al., 2007). Microaggressions are "brief and commonplace daily verbal, behavioral, and environmental indignities, whether intentional or unintentional, that communicate hostile, derogatory, or negative racial slights and insults to the target person or group" (Sue et al., 2007, p. 273). Intersectionality is a conceptual framework that may explain the complexity of this group's experience as first-generation academics.

Intersectionality theory draws attention to the ways in which multiple identities at the individual level (race, socioeconomic status, spiritual/religious affiliation) interlock with matrices of privilege and oppression at the structural level (White supremacy, capitalism, religio-cultural hegemony) (Bowleg, 2012; Cho, Crenshaw, & McCall, 2013; Crenshaw, 1989). From an intersectional perspective, all people have both marginalized and privileged identities that are environmentally dependent (Bowleg, 2012). For example, being a Black heterosexual cisgender male may provide privilege for a FGCS in the company of heterosexual Black peers, but subject that same student to implicit gendered racism (for example, White female college students moving from a sidewalk after noticing a Black male student walking in the distance). Furthermore, identities that used to be important may dwindle in their influence on one's lived experience across his lifespan (Bowleg, 2012). For example, a Black, same-gender-loving (SGL) man who once believed that he had to speak on behalf of all Blacks in all-White contexts and represent all SGL people in all-heterosexual contexts, may develop a sense of self that is secure and no longer feels compelled to respond to every act of prejudice and discrimination to humanize himself. Intersectionality theory provides a framework for understanding how people with interlocking marginalized and privileged identities understand themselves and their experiences in the world, and how these things change over time.

Optimal theory, an Afrocentric framework, provides a paradigm for understanding and achieving a holistic identity that is greater than the sum of one's parts—a transcendent existence. Optimal theory highlights the existence of a person as simultaneously a spiritual and physical manifestation. This diunital existence allows the person to inhabit the present moment and at the same time project one's self into a future moment where one is connected with those who came before and those who will come after (Myers, Montgomery, Fine, & Reese, 1996). This connection imbues a person with a power that is essential for survival and achievement. This diunital existence can help one maintain a sense of purpose and hope for a future, although the present moment may be difficult. For FGCS and FGCP, attending and graduating college is a shared goal to fulfil both their and families' dreams. Attaining a college education emphasizes success for both FGCS and FGCP and their families.

The experiences of FGCS and FGCP who occupy spaces at the intersections of race, class, sexual orientation, and spirituality are seldom highlighted (Mitchell & Means, 2014; Strayhorn, 2010). These narratives could be useful in providing insight about how such people in academia navigate and transcend deleterious systems to affirm their humanity (LaSala, Jenkins, Wheeler, & Fredriksen-Goldsen, 2008; Turner, Gonzalez, & Wood, 2008). Towards this aim, this chapter describes our experiences as a first-generation Black heterosexual, Christian, lower-middle class, cisgender male student and a first-generation Black SGL, spiritual-identified, cisgender male professor from a working-class background at a PWI. The psychological theories and concepts discussed above (i.e., invisibility syndrome, microaggressions, intersectionality theory, and optimal theory) are referenced throughout the narratives to provide a frame for understanding first-generation academics' experiences.

A First-Generation College Student's Perspective: Invisibility and Microaggressions

When my father brought me to America, it was so that I could benefit from the myriad advantages of United States citizenry. My parents taught the importance of education through their words and example. They made sure that I kept appropriate educational priorities either by explicitly lecturing me or by using their current position in life to serve as examples of the daily stresses and restlessness that comes with working minimum-wage jobs.

My father once looked me straight in the eyes stating, "Si objektif ou nan lavi se pa sèvi ak lide ou lè sa a ou ap toujou gen yon travayè"— If your purpose in life is not to use your mind, then you will always be a laborer. My parents wanted a future for me that did not simply require the physical labor of using my hands to find work. Rather, my parents wanted me to use not just my hands, but also my intellect to succeed in life. This lesson was one of the most influential lessons in my life and contributed to me applying to and attending an elite liberal arts college in the U.S. However, the elite academic exposure was coupled with exposure to the harsh realities of White supremacy and class-based barriers that I was not expecting to encounter as a FGCS. Because [my parents] had not attended college, they could not have prepared me for the complexity and subtleness of the oppressive forces I would face on campus.

Encountering Unexpected Microaggressions

In my first week of college, my campus acclimation group and I were in the basement of my dorm getting to know one another when a White male student revealed to us, without any provocation, that he was paying full tuition. He then proceeded to pose questions to me about my status on campus, such as: "What sport do you play here?" and "Are you on scholarship?"

His questions flustered me. In his mind, I couldn't simply be a student who got accepted to the same college as he because of my academic credentials and potential. Nor did it occur to him that I could be anything other than economically disadvantaged. No, to him, my Black skin signaled poverty, and I had to be attending college due to receiving a sports scholarship. With his microaggression, he communicated that I did not belong on a college campus, except as someone whose body the school could "buy" to bring it athletic accolades in exchange for a place on campus. The wholeness of my humanity was rendered invisible. My intellectual possibilities cast aside. Unfortunately, this dehumanizing experience was a precursor to the types of questions [I would get] about how I got to college and my place there.

Although I am from a family with limited economic resources and did eventually play sports at my college, these factors are just a part of my story and do not define me. However, I continued to experience microaggressions that not only communicated that I did not belong, but also that I was a second-class citizen. A second-class citizen is one who is a person belonging to a social or political group whose rights and opportunities are inferior to those of the dominant group in a society (Sue et al., 2008). Such microaggressions denied me the right to define my own image and destiny, and threatened to crush me into the confines of race and class-based negative stereotypes.

As a FGCS with intersecting traditionally marginalized identities, I have often experienced microassaults (such as racial and gendered epithets) (Sue et al., 2008) that are more blatant and unapologetic in their harshness. This was the case when some of my teammates continuously said the N-word around me. The following text is part of an email that I sent to a couple teammates after having enough of some microassaults:

> When you guys were uttering the N-word around like it's nothing, it really didn't put me at ease. I have literally dealt with people using the N-word and making racial comments on this team before. The first time it happened was when [Teammate One] blurted out the N-Word when we were all in New Science Building. Ya'll knew what he said was out of line. I was calm about it and talked with him so that he could understand the implications of his using the racialized N-Word. He said sorry to me, but like was he really sorry, or was he sorry because he got caught saying the N-Word when I was there? Another case of when I had to deal with racial comments on this team is when ya'll saw [Teammate Two] making the comment about me sitting at the back of the bus. Ya'll reacted to his comment and knew what he said was wrong. I addressed [Teammate Two's] racial comment with him and we reconciled things out. After [Teammate One] and [Teammate Two's] comments, I immediately started to refrain myself from the team because I really didn't feel comfortable being around the team. However, I still continued to talk with you guys because I thought ya'll were different. I thought that I wouldn't have this conversation with ya'll because I thought I knew that you guys understood my feelings on racial comments and racialized usage of the N-Word. The thing is, you guys, as my teammates, I thought could be my bros. And I do call you guys bros, but why are my bros shaking my hand, embracing me, but then when they walk away from me use such a racially oppressive term. I know you guys understand the implications of N-Word.... So each time that I hear you guys casually use the N-Word it irritates me. Again, this issue didn't start with you guys, but it is with you guys that I am saying enough is enough.... It just sucks that I can't feel at ease with this team because you guys (and others) fail to realize the implications of using the N-Word and other racial comments when you all are fully aware of the connotations of the racialized term. Honestly, I am still good with you guys and I know that you are all good people, but just that I am not obligated to keep quiet about this issue.

When my teammates, whether in my presence or behind closed doors, committed acts of microaggressions it serves as "status reminders by their implicit suggestion of unworthiness" (Burt, 2009, p. 28).

I resented having to deal with microaggressions at my PWI, which communicated to me that I was a second-class citizen. I developed a double-consciousness with my real self in the background, while presenting a performative self in PWI spaces to make others comfortable. However, I was always uncomfortable. I allowed myself to feel uncomfortable for the hope that I will not be read as one of many Black stereotypes. In situations of race and class-based microaggressions encountered at college, I pretended to ignore them and act as though I was not aware that I was being microaggressed.

A Black Faculty Member's Perspective: Guidance From Experience

Black students and faculty are a statistical minority on my campus. African-American students make up 3.2%, and African-American faculty make up 2.3% of the ethnic diversity at Muhlenberg College.[1] Being one of the few Black students, I sometimes feel intimidated in class and in social settings. During my freshman year, this intimidation contributed to me being mute during classes because I did not want attention directed at myself. My encounter with the White, male student during my first week of classes proved and reminds me that I am a Black person who will be observed through a lens that is clouded by preconceived notions about who I am. I was conflicted by being simultaneously hypervisible (as a racial and classed being) and invisible (in regard to the wholeness and intricacies of who I am a person) on campus to the point where I started to internalize a sense of hopelessness and powerlessness in my purpose for attending college.

However, before I drowned in my internalized feelings, I met professors of color who motivated and reminded why I chose to go to college. This is especially helpful because as a FGCS, I do not have a lot of models of people of color I know personally who went to college. In terms of academic and social performance, not having parents who have already navigated college can make many FGCS unsure about how to manage the college experience. I have begun to seek the help of my professors, especially those of color, to help me navigate my experience as a FGCS. For example, I shared my experiences and emotions in the classroom with my academic advisor (a faculty member of color). She encouraged me to speak up. She listened to my struggles of being a Black student in a pool of Whiteness, and gave me advice as to how to navigate through those struggles. She and the other few Black faculty serve as a reference group of what is possible for me in the future as a Black person—that I am not just limited by negative stereotypes. Seeing them gives me hope as a FGCS navigating white supremacy and financial stressors.

First-Generation College Professor's Perspective: Coming Full Circle

I was excited to go to college! I knew that education would be my way out of the working-class lifestyle into which I had been born. I had excelled in my studies in grade school and during my secondary education, so I had no doubts about my academic abilities. However, being a FGCS, I had no idea about how much I didn't know. Looking back now, I did not understand the importance of social capital. I was unaware that social capital (e.g., support and mentorship from faculty and administrators) could be the difference between an A- and an A in a difficult class or whether I received a position in the student leaders' program. My naiveté regarding social capital is common among FGCS who often do not interact with faculty as much as non-FGCS (Arum & Roksa, 2011; Soria & Stebleton, 2012; Terenzini, Springer, Yaeger, Pascarella, & Nora, 1996).

My parents, who had never been to college, had instilled in me working-class values of self-reliance and diligence. They taught me that I could only depend on my own efforts to get me the things I wanted. So my first year of college, I worked tirelessly, studied late hours, joined several student organizations (pre-medicine club and Black Students Alliance), and volunteered at the local Boys & Girls Club. Furthermore, when I ran into an obstacle (such as not understanding academic material in class), I did not ask for help, but tried to overcome it on my own. My values of self-reliance and independence convinced me that my professors were not interested in my struggles and that they would respect me more if I did not "bother" them with my concerns. I also believed that if I was unable to achieve something, then it was a problem with me that I had to figure out, and not the concern of faculty and administrators. My working-class background and FGCS status intersected in a way that in my attempt to succeed, I did not use resources such as professors' help, which could have made my experience easier. Again, my experience is unfortunately a common one. Researchers have found that FGCS often have difficulties making meaningful, helpful connections with faculty, and thus often struggle academically (Próspero & Vohra-Gupta, 2007; Saunders & Serna, 2004). This is unfortunate, given that FGCS are the ones who often need their professors' help the most.

My working-class upbringing heightened the importance of being a FGCS and eventually first-generation college graduate. Being the first person in my immediate family to attend college was a significant responsibility. I felt both honor and pressure. I was honored to be the realization of a dream for my parents who had sacrificed their time, energy, and money for me to make it to college. However, my parents' pride and my own ambition weighed heavily on me. I often felt as if I only had one opportunity to graduate from college and to "do it right" (make all A's, graduate with honors, and get a "good job"), and that if I did not capitalize on the opportunity, I would be doomed to a working-class life forever. This feeling manifested outwardly as discipline and perseverance, but on the inside it manifested as anxiety and cognitive rigidity. I always felt like I had to *be* "a right way" and *do* the "right thing." I did not believe I had any room for error.

It was not until late in my second semester as a freshman that I realized that my classmates whose parents were college graduates and middle class did not hold such notions of independence. These classmates of mine seemed to be more carefree and experimental in their course selection and approach to classwork. On the contrary, I had come to college knowing I would major in psychology and pre-medicine. I stuck to that plan all the way through to graduation. Sometimes, I heard my middle-class and non-FGCS classmates lament that they were only in college because their parents wanted them to be there. I remember one classmate stated, "I'm just here because my dad wants me to get a degree so I can take over the [family] business."

My classmates who were not FGCS also seemed to expect more out of the professors and administration. They seemed more entitled. They would complain that professors were "unrealistic" in expecting them to read 50 pages in one night because they had other classes for which to do homework. My classmates also asked their professors for extensions on assignments and to raise their grades. I remember being shocked by these requests, and never imagined being able to do so for fear that my professors would think of me as dumb and lazy. But my classmates' parents told them that the professors had a responsibility to them as students, and that students did not have a responsibility to the professors. The intersection of my working-class and FGCS statuses contributed to me working hard (sometimes to the point of exhaustion), but also to me not taking advantage of the opportunities for support.

First-Generation Tenure-Track Professor: Spirituality at the Intersection

I am now a first-generation tenure-track professor of psychology. The intersections of my racial, sexual orientation, and class identities meld with my spirituality to inform my current work as teacher, mentor, and scholar. My spirituality—which is not related to any specific religious doctrine—is the animating force that seamlessly ties all my identities together into something greater and helps me not only remain resilient, but also to resist the systems of oppression that I have had to face my entire life and continue to handle. My spirituality is four-dimensional and helps me live a holistic life. It connects me to a unifying spirit-being greater than myself, the natural world, those who have come before me (my ancestors—biological and cultural), and those who will come after me (my nephews and nieces, mentees) (Myers, 1993). This four-dimensional connection helps me devise strategies to not only personally navigate systems of oppression, but to also be a leader for other marginalized students, faculty members, and citizens in the larger communities around me. While my spirituality is not connected to a formal religious tradition, professors of several religious backgrounds have reported that their spirituality often is a personal resource for them in navigating academia and in their pedagogical praxis (Shahjahan, 2010). Spirituality, both connected to and disconnected from organized religion, can have a positive impact on FGCP personal and professional practices.

As I view the world through an intersectional perspective that acknowledges ways in which our identities interlock to bestow both oppression and privilege, I am aware that my FGCP status offers a positionality that comes with autonomy and prestige (at least in some venues) that allows me access to traditionally restricted venues (i.e., nonprofit organizations' boards; speaking engagements in communities and universities), where I can further my work toward social justice. I enjoy the autonomy that I have to teach the classes I want, research what I choose, and have the schedule I prefer. I cherish being a mentor for FGCS who have intersecting marginalized identities. I work to provide opportunities for students' academic and personal growth. This work is consistent with my spirituality that connects me with the world around me and those who come after me (my mentees).

The values I have discussed in this section have helped me become a FGCS and eventually a FGCP. I now use the lessons I learned along the way to advocate for the FGCS who are in my classes. I am particularly attuned to facilitating the success of FGCS with intersecting marginalized identities. The challenges that they must handle are multifaceted and interlocking. I intimately understand the obstacles that many of them must face, and work to pass along the knowledge and create welcoming environments where they can achieve holistic well-being. This sharing of knowledge is aligned with an optimal psychology and spirituality that connects me with my students holistically.

My unique positionality as a FGCP with traditionally marginalized identities (Black, SGL, from a working-class background) fuels my on-campus advocacy. For example, I use my personal experience and professional expertise to argue for scholarly and financial resources in faculty meetings. As an institutional review board member, I also encourage faculty and student researchers on campus to be more thoughtful in their study recruitment to more purposively include ethnic and racial minority students or scientifically rationalize their exclusion from their studies. Additionally, I am often engaged in the work of community building. I deliberately work to create safe spaces by having dinners, emotional processing meetings, and informal conversations related to self-care with my colleagues and students. Through these activities, I try to cultivate better academic productivity, holistic well-being, and authenticity.

A Dialogue Between a FGCS and FGCP

FGCS often pursue an education for the hope of a successful future. However, the process of education is most often rife with marginalization that one must navigate in addition to academic challenges. Below are excerpts from a dialogue with this chapter's first author (Trott Nely Montina, FGCS) and the second author (Jonathan Mathias Lassiter, FGCP). This dialogue highlights several themes: (a) FGCP and FGCS are burdened by the task of being the representative for Black communities; (b) FGCS' use of spirituality to maintain their mental health and relationships with those who are ignorant towards them; (c) Black college professors and students have parallel processes of in-class White supremacist hostility; and (d) both FGCS and FGCP use college as a tool to reject the social conditions in which they were raised.

Burden of Representation

MONTINA: So how did you feel being the "only one"[2] in class?

LASSITER: I guess at first, like freshman year it was—I was—because I went to a fairly integrated high school. And so it was weird to me to be in class with all these White people. And I knew that White people were like racist, but like how ingrained it was shocking. And so I think for me I found myself feeling like I had to be like the voice of Black people a lot.... And so they—because they would just say such ignorant things. And so I was like, "Okay, I have to speak up." So that was—that happened a lot. And that became tiring after a while.

MONTINA: So when I'm in class and like similar to you, like if someone says something like that I found particularly...was just ignorant or that was just like not as correct thinking, once I see someone do that, then...automatically I say something, regardless of whatever's happening I have to say something because for me, I just can't sit there.

LASSITER: But it takes you out of the space. It takes you out of your educational process. Here you are trying to absorb the information like everyone else and it takes you away from that where it's almost kind of like you're thrown into this Bizarro world,[3] right, like you were saying, where it affects your cognitive thinking.

MONTINA: Once it happens and I see one of my classmates has [expressed] some negative sentiments or whatever, then I basically like I am [physically] in the classroom, but my mind is not in the classroom because I am so consumed by my thoughts and like getting enraged.

Discussion of Theme. The first theme, "Burden," highlights the strain that FGCS and FGCP with intersecting marginalized racial and class identities face when combating ignorance on campus. Being the "only one" as a racial and class minority FGCS and FGCP is sometimes overwhelming and frustrating. Black male FGCS and FGCP have disclosed wanting to be viewed as an individual and not as stereotypical aggressive or physically-overdeveloped Black men (Fries-Britt & Turner, 2001; McCabe, 2009; Sawyer & Palmer, 2014). Unfortunately, many FGCS and FGCP with intersecting marginalized identities are not afforded this recognition of their uniqueness.

Spirituality

LASSITER: There's this sense that if there's no one else to turn to, you can always turn to God. And God is always there to listen and to comfort. And I hear you talk about this, that spirituality gives you this intrinsic sense of self-worth that it's not based on having as much as your classmates have or doing everything they're doing or talking the way they're talking or even what society tells you that you should be, as a first-generation Black male student. But it's about, no, I have a connection with the higher power, I'm here, and I'm valuable. I'm valuable, period. And that definitely does help you maintain your mental health, helps you maintain perseverance, helps you maintain love for yourself, and not engage in some of those negative health behaviors that a lot of college students get into.

MONTINA: Also that allows me to still want to form a relationship with those who have wronged me. When I deal with ignorant people on campus, I do not automatically close off myself to them. Because of my spirituality, I'm able to accept those even if they don't accept me. For example, I didn't utter to my teammates, who were very ignorant towards me, "Hey, you guys are not my friend anymore. I hate you." You know what I'm saying?...[al]though they [teammates] did like a microaggression towards me, I was able to like talk to them in a personal way. Using my religious values of acceptance and love, I was able to articulate to them, "You guys were my brothers." I found that forming a connection with those with clouded perceptions about others to be helpful. A connection with them allows me to say, "Hey, guys, here's what happened. This is how I feel, and whether it was intentional or unintentional, let's fix this. Let's connect."

LASSITER: It is that axiological stance that Myers talks about in Optimal Theory about the value of the relationships, and what I'm hearing you saying is that the spirituality allows you to cultivate relationships and not give out the nastiness or the hate that others may project towards you, whether intentionally or just out of ignorance.

Discussion of Theme. The second theme, "Spirituality," discusses spirituality's role in helping FGCS and FGCP connect with others and forgive them for prejudiced behavior. Spirituality is often a resource for helping people navigate and cope with systemic oppression. Spirituality, whether in the context of organized religious settings or in nontraditional practices, has been found to help college students challenge oppressive behaviors and messages from peers and professors on campus (Means, 2017). It has also been linked to faculty members of color being resilient in PWIs—which can often be subtly racially oppressive and classist—and cultivating joy and purpose in their profession in order to meet scholarly and tenure requirements (Fong, 2009; Hendrix, 2009). However, to the authors' knowledge, there is no scholarly literature that explores the influence of Afrocentric spirituality on Black FGCS and FGCP's academic and professional experiences. Afrocentric spirituality centers on the interconnectedness of human beings as spiritual projections in physical form (Myers et al., 1996). The experiences of the authors illuminates the ways in which spirituality is both a resource that allows one to connect deeper with one's self and also build deeper, more purposive connections with others.

Parallel Processes

LASSITER: I think this happened in my class last semester. So let's break that down because I couldn't unpack that the way I would have liked to in that moment. But tell me what was going on for you because that was a situation—here you are, first-generation, Black male student in the class with a Black male professor and we're talking about ways to diffuse prejudice and things like that. And then I forget…the comment [of your White female classmate]. Do you remember what? I remember it was like….

MONTINA: …that we live in a post-racial society now, and that things were progressing…and then for me that was—the fact that her point of view and her worldview [made her come to the conclusion] that we live in a post-racial society [alerted me that her comment was problematic]. So then I had to speak up and I said, "Whoa, whoa, whoa, you can't just [say] that because we don't live in a post-racial society...." There was another thing I said when another student was talking about immigration and how "they're not supposed to be here" and that "they're supposed to be deported." And then I was talking to her and then like, "Wait, what are you talking about? Like no. And like, first of all, we're all immigrants here."

LASSITER: Right. And even she was challenging me, right? Because she kept [talking]—and I literally had to like raise my voice and take a dominant stance in order for her to stop talking.

MONTINA: And then she was going back and forth [inaudible]. And you were like, "Come on, let's go. Let's move on." "But what's everybody looking at me for?" So then once I see that I see that tensions is going up.... So I [get] reserved. I'm like literally like I'm in the classroom, but I don't focus anymore, like my mind is gone. I just want to leave that situation because I'm so uncomfortable.

LASSITER: Right and I notice that you shut down in that class. And I was like, "Damn, he shut down." Because I was really, you know, like as a person who's been in your shoes as first-generation Black male college student like—and who's now on this end I was like ready to be like, okay no, like no, basically. But you can't read students for filth right?[4] You have to have a certain professionalism in this end, right?

Discussion of Theme. The third theme, "Parallel Processes," describes the ways in which White supremacy is encountered in the classroom and disrupts the educational process for both students and professors. This is especially complicated for Black college professors. They not only are responsible for addressing the academic objectives of their courses, but they are also expected to be responsible for handling issues that concern prejudice directed at other students. Black professors are burdened by this, as some are placed in situations where they have the "only one" student in their classrooms; therefore, how they address race relations must be unbiased, but to a PWI point-of-view, the Black professor might be taking sides in favor of the "only one." Many Black college professors are not equipped to handle every racial issue that occurs in the classroom and on campus, but because of their race they are not only professors, but are also expected to be unofficial mediators and peacemakers for the school. These situations often result in faculty with intersecting marginalized identities experiencing a consciousness-powerlessness paradox. This amounts to faculty witnessing FGCS with interlocking marginalized social statuses being subjected to a matrix of oppression, but are unable to intervene due to their own lack of agency within that matrix (Harper & Hurtado, 2007). Due to these experiences, FGCP are directly and vicariously burdened by oppression in PWIs.

Rejection

MONTINA: Sometimes your family [and friends], they want you to go to college and they push you to do your best while at college. However, the process of being educated gives you access to different knowledge that they haven't had. And that opens your world to a whole different worldview that they aren't exposed to—that they can't tap [in]to. So then is that desire for education and for upward mobility, is that a rejection of your family's values or friends that were not fortunate to attend college?

LASSITER: I was thinking about this, about the rejection of your Blackness and rejection of the family values. It's interesting because I was like, well you know, I wasn't rejecting anything. But now that I think about it, if I look at that closer, in a way I was rejecting. I don't know if I was rejecting family values, but I was definitely rejecting the circumstances, the social situation of my family.

MONTINA: I saw rejection as a positive thing, a positive factor because like I was able to see the [socioeconomic] circumstances [of] my family. For example, I recognize the ways in which my family, we struggle. I see my dad working long hours in two minimum wage jobs, but never complains. My dad was always working, so I barely [saw] him. When he came home late at night from his second job, he goes down in the basement, turns on the TV, and within five minutes goes to sleep. This happens over and over again, every single day.... So then it's like I see and reject that lifestyle that he has.... And then from that I want to do better. I don't want to work two jobs. I want to use my brains to get a career that I want to do. So then I see that and I reject that. Rejection of my family circumstances turns to motivation, determination, and aspiration to do better to escape my social standing.

Discussion of Theme. The fourth theme, "Rejection," discusses the rejection of one's disadvantaged socioeconomic background. FGCS and FGCP reject not their families-of-origin, but the marginalized and disenfranchised circumstances and social positioning of their families. It is a pushback against the socioeconomic and other resource-poor, non-affirming environments in which they were raised. They reject such circumstances so they may further provide for not only their own future families, but also their parents and siblings (Phinney, Dennis, & Osorio, 2006; Stieha, 2010; Tseng, 2004). FGCS and FGCP are often required to imagine beyond the limiations of their communities-of-origins so that they may persist in PWIs, and eventually contribute to more financially stable lives for themselves and their families.

Conclusion

Black FGCS have reported having a range of unique experiences both in and outside of the classroom at PWIs. In this context, they must simultaneously render their humanity invisible while making their race and its social connotations hypervisible. Black first-generation students are often a statistical minority in their classrooms (Smith, Allen, & Danley, 2007). Some students have reported that they believe that their professors do not take their concerns and opinions seriously and do not expect them to achieve or work at the same level as White American students (Smith et al., 2007). Black FGCS who also identify as SGL have reported feeling isolated in both Black heterosexual settings and White SGL spaces as well as being the targets of verbal and physical aggression due to their racial and SGL identities (Strayhorn & Tillman-Kelly, 2013). Taken together, FGCS at the intersection of race, class, and sexual orientation are subjected to several challenges that can have a negative impact on their academic achievement and personal well-being.

Unfortunately, the challenges associated with being a FGCS do not always terminate with graduation. The experiences of marginalization can shape that student throughout life. This is often true for FGCS who become first-generation graduate students and college professors. FGCP who are also people of color report incidences of individual and structural White supremacy, scholarly delegitimization, and representational taxation (i.e., being asked to mentor students of color who are not their formal advisees and be the "diversity" representative on campus committees) (Laden & Hagedorn, 2000). Again, this is complicated when these professors also possess additional marginalized identities such as being SGL. Black first-generation, SGL professors may feel uneasy due to concerns about disclosing their SGL identity, being viewed primarily through a racial lens, or being tokenized (LaSala, Jenkins, Wheeler, & Fredriksen-Goldsen, 2008).

Although both FGCS and FGCP must navigate several obstacles, some have cited their spirituality as a source of strength to help them cope on frequently inhospitable or disingenuous campuses. FGCS have shared that spirituality helps them be persistent in earning their education; maintaining resilience in the face of oppression on campus; developing and maintaining a sense of purpose; and forming social networks within religious organizations (Harley, 2008). Spirituality has also helped first-generation faculty of color give meaning to their work and affirm their own self-worth (Harley, 2008). One such meaning that faculty of color make about their work is that of being leaders and advocates for students of color on campus (Laden & Hagedorn, 2000). Spirituality is a fruitful resource that has helped many Black first-generation students and professors persist against daunting odds.

This chapter has highlighted the experiences of two first-generation academics. It has described the ways in which first-generation academics with intersecting marginalized identities both struggle and transcend the negative impact of oppression on college campuses. These first-generation scholars must contend with demeaning microaggressions, having their humanity erased, and being only seen as their Black skin or socioeconomic background. However, they have found ways to push back against oppressive environments through rejection of marginalization and use of a spirituality that centers them as whole, complex human beings. These first-generation academics' stories provide an example of moving from invisibility to visible leadership.

Notes

1. Muhlenberg College Faculty Ethnic Diversity Breakdown taken from the College Factual website (College Faculty, 2018).
2. The "only one" refers to situations in which people of color (primarily Black people) are the sole representation of their race in a PWI environment.
3. Bizarro World refers to a world in DC Comic books in which everything is backwards or inverted (DC Database, 2018).
4. "Reading for filth" is a colloquial term that means to criticize one to the fullest extent. It a term derived from Black SBL culture (Urban Dictionary, 2018).

References

Arum, R., & Roksa, J. (2011). *Academically adrift: Limited learning on college campuses.* Chicago: University of Chicago Press.

Bowleg, L. (2012). The problem with the phrase women and minorities: Intersectionality—an important theoretical framework for public health. *American Journal of Public Health, 102*(7), 1267–1273. doi: 10.2105/AJPH.2012.300750

Burt, C. (2009). Discrimination and deviance: Racial socialization matters. Retrieved from https://getd.libs.uga.edu/pdfs/burt_callie_h_200908_phd.pdf

Cho, S., Crenshaw, K. W., & McCall, L. (2013). Toward a field of intersectionality studies: Theory, applications, and praxis. *Signs: Journal of Women in Culture and Society, 38*(4), 785–810. doi: 10.1086/669608

College Factual. (2018). *Muhlenberg College diversity: How good is it?* Retrieved from https://www.collegefactual.com/colleges/muhlenberg-college/student-life/diversity/

Crenshaw, K. (1989). Demarginalizing the intersection of race and sex: A black feminist critique of antidiscrimination doctrine, feminist theory and antiracist politics. *University of Chicago Legal Forum, 1989*(1), 57–80. Retrieved from http://heinonline.org/ HOL/LandingPage?handle=hein.journals/uchclf1989&div=10&id=&page=

DC Database. (2018). *Htrae*. Retrieved from http://dc.wikia.com/wiki/Htrae

Franklin, A. J., & Boyd-Franklin, N. (2000). Invisibility syndrome: A clinical model of the effects of racism on African-American males. *American Journal of Orthopsychiatry, 70*(1), 33–41.

Fong, M. (2009). The spirit moves where there is a need in higher education. *New Directions for Teaching and Learning, 2009*(120), 87–95. doi: 10.1002/tl.380

Fries-Britt, S., & Turner, B. (2001). Facing stereotypes: A case study of Black students on a White campus. *Journal of College Student Development, 42*(5), 420–429.

Harley, D. (2008). Maids of academe: African American women faculty at predominately White institutions. *Journal of African American Studies, 12*, 19–36. doi: 10.1007/ s12111-007-9030-5

Harper, S., & Hurtado, S. (2007). Nine themes in campus racial climates and implications for institutional transformation. *New Directions for Student Services, 2007*(120), 7–24. doi: 10.1002/ss.254

Hendrix, K. G. (2009). The spirit that strengthens me: Merging the "life of the mind" with "life in the spirit." *New Directions for Teaching and Learning, 2009*(120), 67–75. doi: 10.1002/tl.378

Housel, T. H., & Harvey, V. L. (2009). *The invisibility factor: Administrators and faculty reach out to first-generation college students.* Boca Raton, FL: Brown Walker Press.

Laden, B., & Hagedorn, L. (2000). Job satisfaction among faculty of color in academe: Individual survivors or institutional transformers? *New Directions for Institutional Research, 2000*(105), 57–66. doi: 10.1002/ir.10505

LaSala, M., Jenkins, D., Wheeler, D., & Fredriksen-Goldsen, K. (2008). LGBT faculty, research, researchers: Risks and rewards. *Journal of Gay & Lesbian Social Services, 20*(3), 253–267. doi: 10.1080/10538720802235351

Longwell-Grice, R., Adsitt, N. Z., Mullins, K., & Serrata, W. (2016). The first ones: Three studies on first-generation college students. *NACADA Journal, 36*(2), 34–46. doi: 10.12930/NACADA-13-028

Longwell-Grice, R., & Longwell-Grice, H. (2008). Testing Tinto: How do retention theories work for first-generation, working-class students? *Journal of College Student Retention: Research, Theory & Practice, 9*(4), 407–420. doi: 10.2190/CS.9.4.a

McCabe, J. (2009). Racial and gender microaggressions on a predominantly-White campus: Experiences of Black, Latina/o and White undergraduates. *Race, Gender & Class, 16*(1/2), 133–151. Retrieved from http://www.jstor.org/stable/41658864

Means, D. (2017). "Quaring" spirituality: The spiritual counterstories and spaces of Black Gay and Bisexual male college students. *Journal of College Student Development, 58*(2), 229–246. doi: 10.1353/csd.2017.0017

Mitchell, D., & Means, D. (2014). "Quadruple consciousness": A literature review and new theoretical consideration for understanding the experiences of Black gay and bisexual college men at predominately White institutions. *Journal of Black Males in Education, 5*(1), 23–35.

Myers, L. (1993). *Understanding an Afrocentric world view: Introduction to an optimal psychology* (2nd ed.). Dubuque, IA: Kendall/Hunt Publishing Company.

Myers, L., Montgomery, D., Fine, M., & Reese, R. (1996). Belief system analysis scale and belief and behavior awareness scale development: Measuring an optimal, Afrocentric world-view. In R. L. Jones (Ed.), *Handbook of tests and measurements for Black populations* (pp. 19–35). Hampton, VA: Cobb & Henry.

Orbe, M. (2004). Negotiating multiple identities within multiple frames: An analysis of first-generation college students. *Communication Education, 53*(2), 131–149. doi: 10.1080/0363452041000168240 1

Orbe, M. (2008). Theorizing multidimensional identity negotiation: Reflections on the lived experiences of first-generation college students. *New Directions for Child and Adolescent Development, 2008*(120), 81–95. doi: 10.1002/cd.217

Owens, D., Lacey, K., Rawls, G., & Holbert-Quince, J. (2010). First-generation African American male college students: Implications for career counselors. *The Career Development Quarterly, 58*(4), 291–300. doi: 10.1002/j.2161–0045.2010.tb00179.x

Parham, T. (1999). Invisibility syndrome in African descent people: Understanding the cultural manifestations of the struggle for self-affirmation. *The Counseling Psychologist, 27*(6), 794–801. doi: 10.1177/0011000099276003

Perez, A. (2008). Struggling between two worlds: How college affects identity construction. *Journal of College Admission, 198*, 10–13. Retrieved from https://eric.ed.gov/?id=EJ829411

Phinney, J., Dennis, J., & Osorio, S. (2006). Reasons to attend college among ethnically diverse college students. *Cultural Diversity and Ethnic Minority Psychology, 12*(2), 347–366. doi: 10.1037/1099–9809.12.2.347

Próspero, M., & Vohra-Gupta, S. (2007). First generation college students: Motivation, integration, and academic achievement. *Community College Journal of Research and Practice, 31*(12), 963–975. doi: 10.1080/10668920600902051

Purdie-Vaughns, V., & Eibach, R. (2008). Intersectional invisibility: The distinctive advantages and disadvantages of multiple subordinate-group identities. *Sex Roles, 59*(5–6), 377–391. doi: 10.1007/s11199-008-9424-4

Saunders, M., & Serna, I. (2004). Making college happen: The college experiences of first-generation Latino students. *Journal of Hispanic Higher Education, 3*(2), 146–163. doi: 10.1177/1538192703262515

Sawyer III, D., & Palmer, R. (2014). A different kind of Black, but the same issues: Black males and counterstories at a predominantly White institution. *Journal of Progressive Policy and Practice, 2*(3), 255–272. Retrieved from https://works.bepress.com/robert_palmer/74/

Shahjahan, R. (2010). Toward a spiritual praxis: The role of spirituality among faculty of color teaching for social justice. *The Review of Higher Education, 33*(4), 473–512. doi: 10.1353/rhe.0.0166

Smith, W., Allen, W., & Danley, L. (2007). "Assume the position... you fit the description." Psychosocial experiences and racial battle fatigue among African American male college students. *American Behavioral Scientist, 51*(4), 551–578. doi: 10.1177/0002764207307742

Soria, K. M., & Stebleton, M. J. (2012). First-generation students' academic engagement and retention. *Teaching in Higher Education, 17*(6), 673–685. doi: 10.1080/13562517.2012.666735

Stieha, V. (2010). Expectations and experiences: The voice of a first-generation first-year college student and the question of student persistence. *International Journal of Qualitative Studies in Education, 23*(2), 237–249. doi: 10.1080/09518390903362342

Strayhorn, T. (2010). When race and gender collide: Social and cultural capital's influence on the academic achievement of African American and Latino males. *The Review of Higher Education, 33*(3), 307–332. doi: 10.1353/rhe.0.0147

Strayhorn, T., & Tillman-Kelly, D. (2013). Queering masculinity: Manhood and Black gay men in college. *Spectrum: A Journal on Black Men, 1*(2), 83–110. doi: 10.2979/spectrum.1.2.83

Sue, D. W., Capodilupo, C. M., & Holder, A. (2008). Racial microaggressions in the life experience of Black Americans. *Professional Psychology: Research and Practice, 39*(3), 329–336. doi: 10.1037/0735-7028.39.3.329

Sue, D. W., Capodilupo, C. M., Torino, G. C., Bucceri, J. M., Holder, A. M. B., Nadal, K. L., & Esquilin, M. (2007). Racial microaggressions in everyday life: Implications for clinical practice. *American Psychologist, 62*(4), 271–286. doi: 10.1037/0003-066X.62.4.271

Sue, D. W., Nadal, K. L., Capodilupo, C. M., Lin, A. I., Torino, G. C., & Rivera, D. P. (2008). Racial microaggressions against Black Americans: Implications for counseling. *Journal of Counseling & Development, 86*(3), 330–338. doi: 10.1002/j.1556-6678.2008.tb00517.x

Terenzini, P. T., Springer, L., Yaeger, P. M., Pascarella, E. T., & Nora, A. (1996). First generation college students: Characteristics, experiences, and cognitive development. *Research in Higher Education, 37*(1), 1–22.

Tseng, V. (2004). Family interdependence and academic adjustment in college: Youth from immigrant and US-born families. *Child Development, 75*(3), 966–983. doi: 10.1111/j.1467-8624.2004.00717.x

Turner, C., Gonzalez, J., & Wood, J. (2008). Faculty of color in academe: What 20 years of literature tells us. *Journal of Diversity in Higher Education, 1*(3), 139–168. doi: 10.1037/a0012837

Urban Dictionary. (2018). Read for filth. Retrieved from https://www.urbandictionary.com/define.php?term=read%20for%20filth

4. The (Im)Possible Dream

MICAELA RODRIGUEZ, SASCHA HEIN, AND LESLIE A. FRANKEL

[*Authors' Note*: Correspondence concerning this chapter should be addressed to Micaela Rodriguez, Undergraduate Student, Department of Psychological, Health, and Learning Sciences, University of Houston, 3657 Cullen Blvd, Room 491, Houston, TX 77204–5029. E-mail: micki.rh@gmail.com and phone: (832) 474–5130.]

Before I started working on this narrative, I had never applied the words "intersectional marginality" to my college experiences. Nevertheless, there were times that I felt like I did not belong and felt myself on the outside looking in: not being able to attend college immediately after high school graduation, even though I desperately wanted to; dropping out of my first three attempted semesters at a community college because I would become overwhelmed with anxiety about my ability to complete major assignments; and when I dropped out of my first semester at a major university because I became pregnant. Each of these situations reflected how I perceived marginality. The situations' recurring theme was a feeling that I was not *good enough* to *make it* as a college student. Given these situations, this personal narrative's goal is to elucidate how different experiences of marginality at different points in my life intersected to generate these feelings.

In facing my past during this narrative inquiry, and reflecting on various critical turning points in my life, I began to realize that I have spent my entire adult life (the past 16 years) working towards the goal of earning a bachelor's degree from a four-year university. During this time, I encountered many struggles and setbacks, but my accomplishments point to the fact that I can and have *made it* as a college student. I am about to complete a 16-year journey through the American higher education system as a 35-year-old undergraduate senior and low-income Hispanic mother of two young girls (ages 3 and 5). I will graduate with honors in my major for having completed a senior honors thesis, and my overall grade point average (GPA) is a 3.979 at a Carnegie Tier One research university. I also happened to be the only member of my family to graduate high school.

Despite these accomplishments, I still have a hard time believing I am worthy of these honors. In fact, believing in myself as "good enough" is something I have struggled with for as long as I can remember. Although I knew that this feeling was a big part of what made my college experiences so challenging, this narrative inquiry's purpose is to identify additional factors that may have contributed to my adversity of feeling marginalized in my college experiences. However, I could not explain why I felt this way, why the feeling seemed more salient at some times than others, and why this feeling still perturbs me to this date. In my search for answers, I was drawn to Brown's (2006) research on women and shame, which informs this essay's analysis. Brown (2015) describes shame as "the fear of disconnection" (p. 68), which was that unnamed *something* that had been perplexing me all this time. This sudden realization put everything I had been working on over the last several months into perspective. Shame is the feeling I carried with me all those times I dropped out of college.

Study Design: A Narrative Inquiry View of My Experience

Rather than focusing only on the thoughts and emotions I associated with marginality (I can't do this. I am not good enough. I am a failure.), my mentors encouraged me to step outside the first-person to consider the circumstances that made me feel this way. These feelings of anxiety, lack of confidence in my own ability, my perceived inadequacy, and my frustration with my inability to meet self-defined standards have been described as the "imposter phenomenon" (Clance, 1985), particularly among high-achieving individuals. Little research examines the imposter phenomenon in minority students, or in students experiencing intersectional marginality in particular. However, the available literature points to environmental mastery (the ability to control complex environments) and low affirmation/belonging (a sense of group membership and attitudes toward an individual's ethnic group) as potential correlates of the imposter phenomenon among minority college students (Peteet, Montgomery, & Weekes, 2015). As described in further detail below, for me these feelings of intellectual incompetence were paired with feelings of shame, and oscillated between two poles: my family background and societal expectations.

The following subsection briefly describes the methodology of my narrative inquiry, which is situated in the tradition of studying human experiences and has been applied to narrative inquiries in educational settings (Clandinin, 2006; Connelly & Clandinin, 1990). The form of narrative inquiry used here, that is, autobiographical narrative, can be characterized as narrative inquiry to the self (Freeman, 2007). It therefore encompasses my personal educational experiences and the way they were shaped by intersectional marginality. To further create a conceptual framework for this personal narrative, I employed semi-structured interviews (Gubrium, Holstein, Marvasti, & McKinney, 2012) with my family members. This method of data collection is ideal for contextualizing, substantiating, and situating my personal college experiences through the eyes of my close relatives, and to identify indicators that may point in different directions while allowing enough flexibility and room for my family members' spontaneous descriptions and narratives.

An in-depth description of the results is organized in three subsections, each accentuating varying degrees of intersectional marginality along the dimensions of context, continuity, and interactions (to be defined in the following section). I then discuss the findings through a lens of the Shame Resilience Theory (SRT) (Brown, 2006), and conclude with practical recommendations for higher education institutions that aim to provide equal opportunities for all students.

Autobiographical Narrative Inquiry Methodology

Clandinin (2006) defines narrative inquiry as considering the "social, cultural and institutional narratives within which individual's experiences are constituted, shaped, expressed and enacted" (p. 46). This current study is conducted through an ongoing and revolving process of storytelling, data collection, and data analysis. The stories of experiences are the source for data, called field texts (for example, field notes, photographs, and transcripts of conversations) (Clandinin, 2006). Field texts for my study included: my academic transcripts, which provide a detailed record of my college enrollment; scholarly literature and educational statistics, which inform of the landscape of public higher education in America; and interviews with family members to understand their experiences within the American education system.

Data analysis occurs when the stories and field texts are examined and reorganized in a "metaphoric narrative inquiry space" along three dimensions: context (situation/place), continuity (past, present and future), and interaction (personal and social) (Clandinin, 2006, p. 47). I use these three dimensions to conceptualize an alternate perspective of intersectional marginality, which positions me as a character in a more comprehensive story. The term 'autobiographical' is fitting to distinguish that the starting point for this narrative inquiry is my own experience of intersectional marginality as a Hispanic, nontraditional, first-generation college student (FGCS), who is also now a low-income mother of two young children.

Results of the Autobiographical Narrative Inquiry

Context: Foundational Layers of Intersectional Marginality

In this section I focus on key distinctions between my family context and the context of higher education as potential factors that contributed to the experience of intersectional marginality at the time of my high school graduation. Because occupational status and educational attainment are generally considered to be closely related (Hollingshead, 1975/2011), I give special attention to my family's educational experiences and my parents' work history.

First-Generation Status and Ethnicity

An accumulating body of research documents key demographic differences between FGCS compared to their traditional peers. For example, Terenzini, Springer, Yaeger, Pascarella, and Nora (1996) found that FGCS are more likely to come from low-income backgrounds, are Hispanic, have lower scores on cognitive tests (reading, math, critical thinking), report lower degree aspirations, are less involved with peers and teachers in high school, have more dependent children, take longer to complete their degree, and receive less encouragement from parents to attend college. FGCS also tend to experience more difficulties transitioning from secondary school to college (Inkelas, Daver, Vogt, & Leonard, 2007), and exhibit lower college retention rates than their traditional peers (Ishitani, 2006).

Furthermore, a growing literature focuses on the experiences of ethnic minority college students. For instance, Saunders and Serna (2004) have documented the influences of creating new networks while managing and sustaining old networks on Hispanic students' college experiences. For instance, Ong, Phinney, and Dennis (2006) point to the impact of factors such as ethnic identity, family interdependence, and parental support on the academic achievement of Hispanic college students. Arana, Castañeda-Sound, Blanchard, and Aguilar (2011) apply an ecological model to emphasize the role of the student context, the university context, and the interaction between the two contexts in a student's decision to persist. Yet, research examines first-generation Hispanic undergraduate college students. For instance,

Dennis, Phinney, and Chuateco (2005) found that higher levels of personal/ career-related motivation to attend college predicted higher levels of GPA, whereas lack of peer support predicted lower GPA. However, as Pascarella, Pierson, Wolniak, and Terenzini (2004) point out, we know little about first-generation Hispanic students' psychosocial development during college. By incorporating my feelings of shame into my personal narrative, I sought to address this gap in the literature. Furthermore, as a first-generation, Hispanic college student, my biggest barrier to attending and completing college was the lack of a role model who could provide what Davis (2010) calls "generational wisdom" about the culture of college such as application and enrollment processes, reading and comprehension of syllabus language, and integration into college social networks. As an 18-year-old high school graduate, my biggest influence at the time was my father.

Dad

My father came to the United States as an undocumented Mexican immigrant in 1977, at age 19. In my father's home village of Lagunillas, Michoacán, México, the highest level of primary education one could attain through a free and public institution was sixth grade, which my father completed at age 11. When my father came to the U.S., he began working as a laborer in the steel wire manufacturing industry in Sealy, Texas. For 22 years, my father gradually climbed the career ladder in this industry. He earned his naturalized citizenship in 1989, and then held the title of general manager for six years at a company in Wallingford, Connecticut, and for three more years at a different company in Louisville, Kentucky. In 1999, my family returned to Texas so that my father and his older brother could go into business together in the pressure vessel manufacturing sector of the oil and gas industry in Houston.

Growing up, I used to give my dad birthday cards and Father's Day cards every year, telling him that he was my idol, which is still true today. My father taught me that if I worked hard, I could earn a decent living to support myself. I started working at age 16, and began paying my own expenses: loan payments for my car and gas for transportation; clothes and accessories for school and work; and sometimes for my own meals. When I graduated from high school, I was apprehensive about asking my parents to help me pay the tuition at a nearby community college where I had enrolled in courses with a school friend. When I did ask, my parents never gave me an answer. The payment deadline passed, so I switched to working full-time from part-time at my then-current job and embarked on my journey to climb the career ladder.

Mom

My mother is of Hispanic heritage and was born in El Campo, Texas in 1961. When she was in ninth grade, my mom got pregnant, dropped out of school, and ran away from home. She was a 15-year-old teen mom when she met my dad in 1977, and by the time my mother was 25, my parents had four girls to look after, myself and my three sisters. My parents were married a year after they met, when my mom was 16. My oldest sister was born in Houston, before my parents met, and my youngest sister was born in Meriden, Connecticut, one town over from Wallingford, where my father worked. My mother started her first job at age 16 as a grocer. Like my father, she climbed the ranks to better wages over the years, and now does sales and customer service for an independent cleaning company.

Siblings

After interviewing my parents about their educational experiences, I interviewed my sisters. Interestingly, I found that each of them shared a similar story about their educational experiences. For different reasons, each of them had low attendance during their freshman year of high school that resulted in not earning enough credits to advance to the next grade level. Each also dropped out of school for good the following year.

I asked my sisters if they thought there were any expectations for them to graduate high school, either from our parents or from the schools they attended. Each of them had the same answer: "Zero expectations from anyone," and "No one cared if I finished school." My oldest sister said that she was encouraged to work, and not go to school. At one point, she was working three jobs and said she had had no time for school. She was 16 when she dropped out of high school. My other older sister said that our mother would let her and our oldest sister stay home from school if they would clean the house. She was 15 when she dropped out.

In 2001, at the age of 18, I became the first member of my family to graduate from high school. I hoped that my youngest sister would follow in my footsteps and complete high school, but in her words, "I was like…if our two oldest sisters didn't have to go to school, then I don't, either. School isn't for me."

Intersectional Marginality of First-Generation Status and Ethnicity in Context

By positioning myself within the context of my family, I discovered the disadvantage of my status as a FGCS. As the first and only member of my family to graduate high school, the culture of college intimidated me, and I felt like I did not belong. A number of previous studies have examined such cultural challenges experienced by FGCS (London, 1992; Miller, 2007). Tinto's (1993) model on student persistence resonated well with my thinking in this domain. Specifically, the presence of distinct cultures in the social communities that I encountered in college and my lack of ability to socially integrate with such cultures became most salient when considering that my culture of origin differed from the college's dominant middle-class culture. Moreover, my lack of connected learning with other students and related social support networks—factors known to impact persistence in college (Skahill, 2002)—made it even harder for me to adapt to the culture of college. In addition to the lack of connectedness with other students, my family's commitment to education (or the lack thereof) created a particular challenge for me in the process of adapting to the culture of college. At that time, attending college was more of an impossible dream than an attainable goal. I very much valued education and wanted to pursue a college degree, but it was not an idea that was heavily promoted in my home. In my family, working was highly encouraged; in fact, as soon as I turned 16, my mom made me get a job.

I was heavily involved in extracurricular activities during my first two years of high school in Kentucky, so my mom wanted me to work so I could help pay for supplies and field trips. I worked at a movie theater for a few months before we moved to Houston. Then in Texas, I started working at a grocery store almost immediately after we arrived. Shortly after that, during my senior year of high school, I took a cooperative education course that allowed me to leave school early to go to work at a part-time job that I acquired as part of the program's coursework. My parents' logical expectation for me after high school graduation was to continue working and climb the career ladder as they had done. However, I wanted to be a teacher, which requires a college degree.

The foundational layers of intersectional marginality are formed when considering my status as a Hispanic FGCS within the larger context of American public higher education. As a Hispanic student, I am part of a marginalized ethnic group that has been referred to as the "least educated group in the United States" (Schneider, Martinez, & Owens, 2006), based on educational statistics that show consistently higher status dropout rates for Hispanic high school students and the lowest completion rates among Hispanic college students. The U.S. Census Bureau (Ryan & Bauman, 2016) reports that two-thirds of Hispanic adults (age 25 and older) have at least a high school diploma (67%), compared to nearly all non-Hispanic White adults of this age group (93%). Compared to Hispanic adults, more non-Hispanic White adults have at least a bachelor's degree (15% versus 36%) (Ryan & Bauman, 2016). Made clear in this context are the ground layers of intersectional marginality I faced in attending college, coming from a family with no shared advice or experience of the culture of college, in a society where I am stigmatized as an underperforming minority.

Continuity: The Unfolding of Intersectional Marginality Over Time

While context revealed the foundations of intersectional marginality at the time of my high school graduation, continuity puts emphasis on how it unfolded over the progression of my college journey. Sixteen years have passed since I graduated high school, and I am about to complete my bachelor's degree. The dimension of continuity (past, present, and future) emphasizes the idea that "experiences grow out of other experiences, and experiences lead to further experiences" (Clandinin, 2006, p. 46). As such, my experience of intersectional marginality was novice at the time of my high school graduation. With the passage of time and a natural sequence of events, my experience of intersectional marginality is much more complex today than it was in 2001, when I graduated from high school. In this section, I will uncover two additional layers of intersectional marginality: nontraditional status and low-income mother.

Nontraditional Status

Approaching college as a Hispanic FGCS was intimidating, but it was not intimidation that kept me on the sidelines during the first three years following high school graduation. No student can attend college without paying college tuition. Traditional college students are expected to be financially dependent on their parents (Radford, Cominole, & Skomsvold, 2015). At that time, however, my parents expected me to be, for the most part, financially independent from them, as previously described. As a byproduct of my status as a Hispanic FGCS, I discovered an impasse that wiped out the traditional college track before I could even step foot on it because I did not have the financial means to pay college tuition.

First Attempts at a Community College. For three years following my high school graduation, I bounced around various jobs, always in search of better wages. In 2004, I had worked my way up to shift supervisor, but I wanted to try my luck again at getting a college degree. This time, with prior knowledge of the enrollment process under my belt, and with my father's reluctant (but generous) financial support, I successfully enrolled at the community college and attended my first classes at age 21. It was not long, though, before things went terribly wrong again. And then, again. And again.

Within the span of the next three years, I enrolled twice more in subsequent semesters. Each time, still with my father's financial generosity, I made it a little farther than the last, but never quite to the end. I would start off on a great foot, engaging in class discussions and getting good feedback on my assignments. However, there was always one—just one—major assignment that would completely overwhelm me to the point that I had so much anxiety that I would stop attending classes altogether. Out of eight attempted courses over three semesters, I only earned credit for one: I got a C in an English class because even though I had skipped out on the last few weeks of the semester, I only missed one essay assignment and the professor gave me a C. Each time I failed was more humiliating than the last, yet I could not seem to give up on my impossible dream.

First Signs of Hope. During the first years of my earliest college attempts, I continued the unstable work pattern of always looking for better opportunities, and sporadically helped out at my father's company whenever work was available. In May 2009, I finally cleared a hurdle on the college track, instead of falling flat on my face, yet again: I completed my first semester of college with a 4.0 GPA. During the next two years, I cleared many more hurdles, but still stumbled on a few.

In the fall of 2009, I suffered my first miscarriage, which caused me to fall behind in two of the five classes I was enrolled in that semester. The following semester, in 2010, I got married and for the first time in my adult life, I had a stable home. I also received a Pell Grant for the first time that year. In the fall of 2010, I experienced my second miscarriage, but because I had taken the summer off and was only enrolled in two classes that semester, I pulled through both classes. In the spring of 2011, I earned an associate's degree from the community college and graduated cum laude (3.69 GPA). I made plans to transfer to a university and that summer, I took classes at the community college that would transfer to the university and count towards my major. However, two weeks before beginning classes at the university, the college track began falling apart beneath my feet, when I found out I was pregnant again.

First Attempt at the University. Ten years after I graduated high school, I had overcome so much to complete the seemingly simple, two-year core component of a bachelor's degree. I was well on my way to earning a bachelor's degree when I transferred to a university in the fall of 2011. That semester, I split my enrollment between the community college and the university by taking two courses at the university and three at the community college. I was elated after earning my associate's degree and graduating with honors, and after an amazing summer of engaging in coursework related to my prospective career field, I was so sure of my ability to juggle five classes between two campuses. However, I did not expect that I would get pregnant again. I had had two previous, unexplained miscarriages, and it got to the point that my husband and I were convinced we were never meant to be parents.

With so much anxiety and uncertainty surrounding my pregnancy, the only way I knew how to deal was to withdraw from all my classes, as I had regrettably done so many times before. Only this time, I did not abruptly stop attending classes: I completed the required paperwork and received W's instead of F's on my transcript that semester. My focus then was safeguarding a high-risk pregnancy to a healthy full-term.

Low-Income Mother. In October 2011, much to my dismay, my first attempted semester at the university ended just before the final drop deadline. In April 2012, I gave birth to my first beloved daughter. Two years later, in August 2014, I gave birth to my second beloved daughter. In the spring of 2016, I reenrolled for my second attempt at the university.

My husband was working at a low-wage job at the time, and I was unemployed. I qualified for financial aid for tuition at the university, and child-care tuition assistance through a program of the Texas Workforce Solutions that my husband had learned about when he was collecting unemployment during the previous year. Without these two vital financial resources, I would have essentially no chance at attending the university. Even with these resources, the fact that I only had childcare within the center's specific operating hours means that I have limited hours to attend the university. Furthermore, considering the travel time it takes me to get to and from campus within these hours (from the opposite side of the city), the actual window of time that I have to be on campus (attending classes and completing assignments) is even smaller.

Continuity of Intersectional Marginality. As I reflect on my current situation, and the challenges I faced throughout this 16-year college journey, I realize that the cards are heavily stacked against me. Despite these struggles, I have accomplished a great deal during the past four semesters that I have been enrolled at the university. Carrying what felt like the weight of the world on my shoulders, I somehow managed to complete close to 40 credit hours over the past 18 months, earning all A's at the university. In the fall, I have to complete nine credit hours to earn my bachelor's degree.

So, here I am, one semester away from reaching my long-travelled destination. This last attempt at the university has brought me closer to accomplishing my impossible dream than I have ever been. Yet as much as I have overcome and accomplished to get to this point, I still find it hard to believe that I am so close, or that I might even make it to graduation and *finally* earn my bachelor's degree. Similarly, as much time and effort that I have put into this personal narrative, as I near the conclusion, there is a nagging voice that is still telling me "I cannot do this; I am just not good enough." Because the weight of intersectional marginality, the aforementioned feeling of shame, always lingers in my college experiences, no matter how honorable my transcript may look, or how good of an essay I can write. As a prelude to understanding why even my best college experiences, including writing this personal narrative, are superimposed with the underlying feelings of outsider and not good enough, the following section discusses intersectional marginality through interactions.

Interactions: Personal and Social Domains of Intersectional Marginality

When considering the dimension of interactions from the narrative inquiry view of experience, Clandinin (2006) presents the idea that "people are individuals and need to be understood as [...] always in relation, always in a social context" (p. 46). Thus, personal interactions describe who people are as individuals; and social interactions describe who people are in relation to others. Throughout this narrative, I have described the feeling of seeing myself as an individual who is not good enough to earn a bachelor's degree. In relation to others within my college experiences, I described myself as an outsider who did not belong. This sense of not belonging within the higher education system has been recognized by previous researchers as a critical factor determining college student retention (O'Keeffe, 2013). As previously stated, these feelings have been present in all of my college experiences, but prior to working on this narrative, I had never been able to identify or understand these feelings: I only knew what they *felt* like.

A Newfound Understanding of Intersectional Marginality

By exploring my college experiences through the three narrative inquiry dimensions of context, continuity, and interactions (Clandinin, 2006), I began to understand the intersecting layers of marginality that I encountered. I learned that my status as a FGCS was the reason I have always felt like an outsider who does not belong, because I was the first member of my family to attend college and I had no immediate role models. I discovered that the feeling of not good enough was the product of a stigmatization of low educational attainment that is tied to people of Hispanic ethnicity, like me (Terenzini et al., 1996). I found that as time went on, I encountered additional struggles due to my status a nontraditional college student struggling to pay college tuition, and later as a low-income mother juggling full-time college and parenting of two young children.

At the time of my high school graduation, the intersections of marginality that I discovered were based on my first-generation status, Hispanic ethnicity, and working-class background. As a first-generation student whose parents never attended college or even graduated from high school, I knew nothing of how to navigate college. The only help to apply and enroll in courses came from a friend of mine from high school whom I had been working with for about a year. She and I attended a campus orientation together, and at the end of the orientation, we were instructed on how to register for classes. When I went home that day, I presented to my parents with the tuition fee statement along with my class schedule. My parents' response of silence to my request for them to help pay the tuition can be attributed to our Hispanic and working-class culture.

Discussion: Answers to My Soul-Searching Questions

At the intersection of context and continuity is who I am (present), where I come from (past), and where I am going (future). At the time of my high school graduation, I am identified as a Hispanic FGCS in the context of my family and American public higher education. I provided a history of my family's educational and occupational experiences to describe where I come from; thus, the central conflict lies in the perceived future of where I am going. SRT explains that this perceived future of where I am going is influenced by cultural expectations of who I am *supposed* to be (see Figure 4.1). These cultural expectations are, in turn, expressed by the people we encounter in an interpersonal context (my family and the public institutions of higher education that I attended), and continuously reinforced by media culture such as television, music, and social media (Brown, 2006). To this point, the following section identifies the cultural expectations central to the comprehensive story of this narrative.

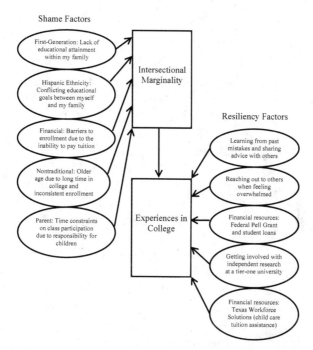

Shame Factors

First-Generation: Lack of educational attainment within my family

Hispanic Ethnicity: Conflicting educational goals between myself and my family

Financial: Barriers to enrollment due to the inability to pay tuition

Nontraditional: Older age due to long time in college and inconsistent enrollment

Parent: Time constraints on class participation due to responsibility for children

Intersectional Marginality

Resiliency Factors

Learning from past mistakes and sharing advice with others

Reaching out to others when feeling overwhelmed

Financial resources: Federal Pell Grant and student loans

Getting involved with independent research at a tier-one university

Financial resources: Texas Workforce Solutions (child care tuition assistance)

Experiences in College

Figure 4.1. Shame factors tied to identities contribute to intersectional marginality. In turn, intersectional marginality contributed to struggles with college experiences such as enrolling, attending, and completing college. Resiliency factors triumph over feelings of shame, leading to better integration and successful matriculation in college.

Dropping Out of College at Various Times

Before I even stepped foot onto a college campus, I already felt like I did not belong. No one in my family had even completed high school, let alone college. Hence, when I did finally enroll in college, this was a feeling I had to constantly battle. At times, I won and things were great, but at the times when I lost that battle, the consequences were disastrous and left me stranded on the outside of where I wanted to be.

This feeling that I was incapable, or not good enough, is supported by Brown's (2006) definition of shame: "the intensely painful feeling or experience of believing we are flawed and therefore unworthy of acceptance and belonging" (p. 45). With this more detailed definition to supplant my own feelings, I understood that the reason I had felt so overwhelmed by these assignments was because I was afraid that anything I had to say would be judged as not good enough. Because I had come from a family who had never been in these situations, I felt like *I* was the one who was flawed; I felt like *I* was just not cut out to be a college student. For a long time, there was no one to prove me wrong. My father did not believe in a formal education, so anytime I expressed some type of concern, he would say something like, "Don't worry about that. You don't need college to have a good job. I will teach you what you need to know and you can make a good living, working here with me." This experience resonates well with research that has found that Hispanic students often receive less encouragement from their parents to go to college (Terenzini et al., 1996). Although my father believed that his advice was in my best interest, he unknowingly reinforced my fear that I did not belong in college. Before learning about SRT, the only explanation I could come up with for the win-loss pattern was that when I was winning, it was because I believed in myself. When I lost, it was because I became overwhelmed by a feeling that I was incapable of completing an assignment. Reading about SRT helped me to understand that when I dropped out of college each of those four times, it was a coping mechanism to escape the shame I was feeling about not fitting in at college.

Eventually, after learning from my previous mistakes, I did figure out how to fit in. Not only did I finally get the hang of college, but I also earned my associate's degree in 2011. Now, six years later, I am working on a senior honors thesis which, if I complete and successfully defend in the fall, will give me a distinguished title of graduating with honors in my major. However, I still experience inescapable feelings of shame, that I am not good enough, or not worthy of these honors. This brings me to my final point of why these feelings still linger, even though I have seemingly already made it to my final destination.

Overcoming the Lingering Feelings of Not Good Enough

Although I believe that my feeling marginalized was inevitable, my feelings of shame should not have happened to me. As an aspiring educator, I truly hope that in the future *something* changes so that students do not feel the way I did. I have come to understand that the only way to overcome these feelings is to *own* who I am and where I come from. Brown (2012) calls this the power to be vulnerable; taking an emotional risk of exposure and uncertainty to honestly let ourselves be seen.

Learning From Past Mistakes and Reaching Out to Others

When I went through my first miscarriage, I remember reaching out to a professor and telling her about what had happened. I told her that I was concerned about a major essay that was coming up. Because I had not yet started the essay, I felt very overwhelmed about getting it done on time. She told me that I could either drop the class, or try to complete the essay and take the best grade. If I dropped the class, she said, I would lose the progress I had already made and have to start completely the next time I attempted the class. On the other hand, if I just stuck it out and completed the class with her, even if I did not earn the A that I wanted, as long as I earned class credit, then I would be done with it and never have to worry about it again.

I ended up turning in a very sloppy, disorganized excuse for an essay that did not earn me much of a grade, but I did pass the course that semester. This professor's advice helped me overcome similar struggles down the road because I always keep in mind that it is better to take a low grade on one assignment than to drop out and lose the progress I already made.

Helping Others Overcome the Struggles of College

At an institutional level, institutions might consider equipping students with skills and resources early on in their college careers to overcome situations in which the student feels overwhelmed and contemplates quitting or dropping a class. For example, institutions could provide students with training during orientation. Institutions can also address the issue in class syllabi with helpful advice and encouragement to approach the instructor for help. Whenever the opportunity presents itself, I always help a classmate overcome the stress of completing an assignment, or the fear of reaching out to the professor for help. When I took online courses last summer, a classmate posted a thread on the message board that is set up for students to reach out for help. The classmate had not yet purchased the class textbook, so she asked if someone could share their textbook so that she could complete the chapter quiz due the first week of class. I went out of my way to scan the textbook pages to send to her so that she could complete her quiz. I put myself in her shoes and imagined that this situation had caused her stress, and since I had already encountered my fair share of debilitating stress about completing assignments, I wanted to save my classmate from making the same horrible mistakes I had in the past. Empathy, or the ability to perceive a situation from another person's perspective, is the acclaimed weapon for combatting shame (Brown, 2006).

Getting Involved on Campus

When I started attending the university last year, I remember feeling so nervous, but excited at the same time. I was glad to be back in college, but afraid that I would fail again, like I had many times in the past. Not to mention that by this time, I felt like most of the other students in my classes were at least 10 years younger than me. However, I found my niche when I participated in a couple different research studies on campus, just a few weeks after beginning my first semester. In one of the studies, I was interviewed about the stresses associated with parenting. I became interested in the researcher's work, and decided to apply as an assistant in her lab. When she offered me the position, I could not believe it. I have worked in her research lab for three semesters, and she is now directing my honors thesis.

Recommendations for Administrators, Faculty, and Students

After 16 years, and countless college experiences, I have overcome a great deal to get to this point. To me, it feels like my past is riddled with more downs than ups, but I have to remember to be proud of where I came from and what I have been through. Even though the future scares me, and I have a hard time believing that I am good enough to accomplish my dreams, I now know that this is where I belong. If there is anything that I have learned from writing this personal narrative, it is that I have *always* been good enough, but I let shame hold me back.

The reason that this mission to earn a bachelor's degree has been so important to me, that I never gave up regardless of how many times I failed, is because education has always been a core value of mine. It has always been my dream to work with families to educate children. Because I came from a family with limited and broken experiences in the American education system, I never believed I was good enough to be an educator. Considering the barriers that I have encountered in my college experiences as a Hispanic, first-generation, nontraditional college student and low-income mother, it is more important to me today than it has even been before to reach a place in my academic career where I can be an advocate for marginalized students.

So, to any college student reading this, I implore you to not be ashamed of who you truly are. I promise you—you *are* good enough. Reach out for help when you feel overwhelmed; I have found that, more often than not, faculty and staff understand the struggles we face as students, and want to help us succeed. Find some way to get involved on campus; if there is nothing available that interests you, try starting your own student organization to make your presence known. Chances are, there are more students like you looking for something to belong to. Use all available resources; applying for financial aid or seeking counseling services may seem intimidating, but those resources are there for a reason. We all need help sometimes, and you deserve support from those resources just as much as anyone else.

It took me almost a decade before I became familiar enough with the culture of college to learn these resiliency tools. Looking back, I regret how much time I wasted suffering in silence with my shame. What makes it worse is that out of those first eight courses that I attempted and failed at the community college, not one single person (classmates, faculty, or staff) ever reached out to *me* to see if I was okay, to ask if there was anything they could do to help me get back on track. Maybe if someone had, my dream may not have seemed so impossible.

To the professors and administrators who are reading this, perhaps these tools for resilience are something colleges and universities need to work harder at teaching students. Who they are, where they come from, and who they aspire to be in the future should not be reasons that FGCS feel shame in college in the way they have been for me in my college experiences. Yes, there will always be students who feel marginalized, but college educators and administrators need to ensure that marginalized students do not suffer through shame as I have. If this issue is addressed in the future, hopefully then, FGCS' dreams will not seem as impossible as mine once did.

References

Arana, R., Castañeda-Sound, C., Blanchard, S., & Aguilar, T. E. (2011). Indicators of persistence for Hispanic undergraduate achievement: Toward an ecological model. *Journal of Hispanic Higher Education, 10*(3), 237–251.

Brown, B. (2006). Shame resilience theory: A grounded theory study on women and shame. Families in Society. *The Journal of Contemporary Social Services, 87*(1), 43–52.

Brown, B. (2012). Listening to shame [Video file]. Retrieved from http://www.ted.com/talks/brene_brown_listening_to_shame

Brown, B. (2015). *Daring greatly: How the courage to be vulnerable transforms the way we live, love, parent, and lead.* New York, NY: Penguin Random House.

Clance, P. R. (1985). *The impostor phenomenon: Overcoming the fear that haunts your success.* Atlanta, GA: Peachtree Publishers.

Clandinin, D. J. (2006). *Handbook of narrative inquiry: Mapping a methodology.* Thousand Oaks, CA: Sage.

Connelly, F. M., & Clandinin, D. J. (1990). Stories of experience and narrative inquiry. *Educational Researcher, 19*(5), 2–14.

Davis, J. (2010). *The first generation student experience: Implications for campus practice, and strategies for improving persistence and success.* Sterling, VA: Stylus Publishing.

Dennis, J. M., Phinney, J. S., & Chuateco, L. I. (2005). The role of motivation, parental support, and peer support in the academic success of ethnic minority first-generation college students. *Journal of College Student Development, 46*(3), 223–236.

Freeman, M. (2007). Autobiographical understanding and narrative inquiry. In D. J. Clandinin (Ed.), *Handbook of narrative inquiry: Mapping a methodology* (pp. 120–145). Thousand Oaks, CA: Sage.

Gubrium, J. F., Holstein, J. A., Marvasti, A. B., & McKinney, K. D. (2012). *The SAGE handbook of interview research: The complexity of the craft.* Thousand Oaks, CA: Sage.

Hollingshead, A. B. (1975/2011). Four factor index of social status. *Yale Journal of Sociology, 8,* 21–52.

Inkelas, K. K., Daver, Z. E., Vogt, K. E., & Leonard, J. B. (2007). Living-learning programs and first-generation college students' academic and social transition to college. *Research in Higher Education, 48*(4), 403–434.

Ishitani, T. T. (2006). Studying attrition and degree completion behavior among first-generation college students in the United States. *The Journal of Higher Education, 77*(5), 861–885.

London, H. B. (1992). Transformations: Cultural challenges faced by first-generation students. *New Directions for Community Colleges, 1992*(80), 5–11.

Miller, R. (2007). The association of family history knowledge and cultural change with persistence among undergraduate low-income, first-generation college students. *Research and Teaching in Developmental Education, 24*(1), 29–45.

O'Keeffe, P. (2013). A sense of belonging: Improving student retention. *College Student Journal, 47*(4), 605–613.

Ong, A. D., Phinney, J. S., & Dennis, J. (2006). Competence under challenge: Exploring the protective influence of parental support and ethnic identity in Latino college students. *Journal of Adolescence, 29*(6), 961–979.

Pascarella, E. T., Pierson, C. T., Wolniak, G. C., & Terenzini, P. T. (2004). First-generation college students: Additional evidence on college experiences and outcomes. *The Journal of Higher Education, 75*(3), 249–284.

Peteet, B. J., Montgomery, L., & Weekes, J. C. (2015). Predictors of imposter phenomenon among talented ethnic minority undergraduate students. *The Journal of Negro Education, 84*(2), 175–186.

Radford, A. W., Cominole, M., & Skomsvold, P. (2015). *Demographic and enrollment characteristics of non-traditional undergraduates: 2011–12.* Washington, DC: National Center for Education Statistics. Retrieved from http://nces.ed.gov/pubs2015/2015025.pdf

Ryan, C. L., & Bauman, K. (2016). *Educational attainment in the United States: 2015.* Washington, DC: National Center for Education Statistics. Retrieved from https://www.census.gov/library/publications/2016/demo/p20-578.html

Saunders, M., & Serna, I. (2004). Making college happen: The college experiences of first-generation Latino students. *Journal of Hispanic Higher Education, 3*(2), 146–163.

Schneider, B., Martinez, S., & Owens, A. (2006). Barriers to educational opportunities for Hispanics in the United States. In M. Tienda & F. Mitchell (Eds.), *Hispanics and the future of America* (pp. 179–227). Washington, DC: The National Academies Press.

Skahill, M. P. (2002). The role of social support network in college persistence among freshman students. *Journal of College Student Retention: Research, Theory & Practice, 4*(1), 39–52.

Terenzini, P. T., Springer, L., Yaeger, P. M., Pascarella, E. T., & Nora, A. (1996). First-generation college students: Characteristics, experiences, and cognitive development. *Research in Higher Education, 37*(1), 1–22.

Tinto, V. (1993). *Leaving college: Rethinking the causes and cures of student attrition* (2nd ed.). Chicago, IL: University of Chicago Press.

5. Latinx First-Generation College Students' Career Decision Self-Efficacy: The Role of Social Support, Cultural Identity, and Cultural Values Gap

PAULETTE D. GARCIA PERAZA AND ANGELA-MINHTU D. NGUYEN

What drives or hinders college students from pursuing their desired career? How do students' family, friends, teachers, and the students themselves influence this desire for a career? Deciding on a career, along with navigating the higher education system, learning to manage time, negotiating workload and parental demands, and networking and making new friends, is a major stressor for university students (Robotham & Julian, 2006). Although these stressors are ubiquitous, first-generation college students (FGCS) (defined as students whose parents did not earn a college degree) encounter unique challenges that pervade academic, career, interpersonal, and psychological domains (Chen, 2005; Pascarella, Pierson, Wolniak, & Terenzini, 2004; Terenzini, Springer, Yaeger, Pascarella, & Nora, 1996). Demographically, most FGCS are Latinxs (Terenzini et al., 1996), one of the largest ethnic minority groups in universities. Academically, Latinx students typically fall behind their European-American counterparts (Fry & Lopez, 2012); feel less prepared and have more doubt about their academic abilities (Smedley, Myers, & Harrell, 1993); and are less likely to explore career options (Leal-Muniz & Constantine, 2005; Lent, Brown, & Hackett, 2000). Moreover, compared to European-American non-FGCS, students with intersecting Latinx and FGCS identities have a lower sense of belonging in college and are more likely to experience race-related stereotypes and discrimination (Gloria & Castellanos, 2012). This chapter examines social support and cultural identity as predictors of career decision self-efficacy (CDSE) for Latinx FGCS, and the role that cultural values gap plays in the model.

Ideally, a bachelor's degree should enable university graduates to have more prestigious and financially lucrative careers than those without bachelor's degrees. However, this depends on whether university students opt to pursue such careers. The belief in one's ability to choose a career, or CDSE (Hackett & Betz, 1981), is especially important for marginalized and oppressed groups, such as racial and ethnic minorities and those from lower socioeconomic backgrounds (Betz, Hammond, & Multon, 2005; Gloria & Hird, 1999). Having high CDSE encourages students to engage in activities that actually allow them to acquire their desired careers (Lent, Brown, & Hackett, 1994). Conversely, low CDSE may impede academic performance and college persistence, preventing students from advancing towards their career goals (Betz, Klein, & Taylor, 1996). Therefore, low CDSE may negate the bachelor's degree potential to lead to upward social mobility (Arbona, 1995; Lent, Brown, & Larkin, 1984).

This study examined two variables that may predict CDSE: social support and cultural identity. Social support refers to the actions that create feelings of love, esteem, and sense of belonging from a network of individuals, including parents, peers, and siblings (Cobb, 1976; Gushue, 2006). For Latinxs, social support from close family acts as a buffer against stressors and promotes better well being (Gomez et al., 2001; Rodriguez, Mira, Myers, Morris, & Cardoza, 2003), as well as higher CDSE (Metheny & McWhirter, 2013; Whiston & Keller, 2004). Sibling support, specifically, is also linked to positive outcomes such as higher academic competence and higher self-esteem (Cicirelli, 1989; Conger & Little, 2010; Connidis, 1992; Volling, 2003). Furthermore, siblings may provide a different type of social support (with regard to career aspirations) compared to other family members (Schultheiss, Palma, Predragovich, & Glasscock, 2002).

For any research on Latinx, it would be remiss to not include cultural identity; therefore, we examine cultural identity as a potential predictor of CDSE. Cultural identity is a type of social identity, which is a person's self-concept stemming from membership in social groups (Tajfel & Turner, 1979). Latinxs in the United States have three cultural identities: ethnic, national, and bicultural identities. First, ethnic identity, which includes feelings of ethnic belonging and pride, and positive attitudes toward one's ethnic group (Phinney, 1990), has been linked to higher CDSE (Arbona, 1995; Gushue, 2006). Second, national identity, which refers to the commitment to, exploration of, and attachment to the norms and traditions of the U.S. (Schwartz et al., 2012; Schwartz, Unger, Zamboanga, & Szapocznik, 2010), is related to higher self-esteem (Kiang, Yip, & Fuligni, 2008), which may relate to higher CDSE. Third, bicultural identity involves simultaneously maintaining ethnic and national identities (Nguyen & Benet-Martínez, 2007), and has been linked to greater CDSE (Mejia-Smith & Gushue, 2017). Despite Latinxs' being multicultural, previous studies (Arbona, 1995; Gushue, 2006) on CDSE tend to focus on only one type of cultural identity, failing to recognize Latinxs' cultural complexity. Furthermore, these previous studies (Mejia-Smith & Gushue, 2017) only examined cultural identity at the neglect of other social identities, failing to recognize Latinx FGCS' multiple identities and the intersection of those identities. Beyond including multiple types of cultural identity (ethnic, national, and bicultural), the current study also focuses on the intersection of cultural identity with another social identity: FGCS.

Because most Latinx students come from immigrant families (Fry, 2002), it is necessary to include cultural values gap as a possible predictor of CDSE. Cultural values gap is a difference in cultural values (American and Latinx cultures) between parents (immigrants) and children (reared in the U.S.), which may create distance in the parent-child relationship (Hwang, 2006). Theoretically, cultural values gap is a component of acculturative family distancing, and acculturative family distancing is a form of acculturation gap, which is the discrepancy between parents and children in their adaptation to American culture and the maintenance of their Latinx cultures (Hwang & Wood, 2009). This cultural values gap may impact vocational tasks, such as deciding on a career (Constantine, Kindaichi, & Miville, 2007; Hwang, 2006). It may also influence the two predictors of interest in this study (social support and cultural identity) and their relationships with CDSE. For example, Latinxs who do not share their parents' values may experience less family cohesion (Dennis, Basañez, & Farahmand, 2010), which in turn, may lead to less family support (Rivera et al., 2008). Furthermore, Latinxs who are in conflict with their parents (or their primary representatives or models of their ethnic culture) (Padilla, 2006) may have low identification to their ethnic group as a whole. Therefore, we proposed that cultural values gap would moderate the relationship between social support and CDSE, and the relationship between cultural identity and CDSE. In other words, whether and how social support and cultural identity predict CDSE depends on the size of Latinx FGCS' cultural values gap with their parents.

For this study, we take an interdisciplinary and intersectionality perspective. Social cognitive career theory (from the field of counseling and career development) proposes that high self-efficacy (e.g., CDSE) predicts positive outcome expectations and career interests or goals (Lent et al., 1994). However, this model fails to include variables such as cultural identity that are related to ethnicity or race. Therefore, we turned to Lewin's (1951) person-environment model (from social psychology) as a supplement. According to Lewin (1951), behavior is a product of the interaction between the person (for example, mental states, traits, and attitudes) and the environment (ecological or social variables). For Latinx FGCS, person factors may include cultural identity, whereas environmental factors may refer to social support. Together, these person and environmental variables may predict students' career decisions and their CDSE.

We conduct the current study from an intersectionality perspective (Crenshaw, 1989), in that we acknowledge the unique experience of being both Latinx and FGCS. Intersectionality theory highlights the distinct experiences of those with multiple social identities (Cole, 2009; Settles & Buchanan, 2014); therefore, predictors of CDSE may be different for Latinxs, FGCS, and Latinx FGCS. In addition, intersectionality theory emphasizes the importance of studying these identities in context (Warner, 2008). For example, the saliency of Latinx FGCS' identities may differ depending on whether s/he is enrolled at a Hispanic Serving Institution (HSI) versus a Predominantly White Institution (PWI). By using an intersectionality perspective, we contribute to the literature by extending psychology research beyond the over-studied groups, such as White and middle-class individuals (Cole, 2009).

Current Study

This chapter examines the role of cultural values gap in a person-environment model of CDSE for Latinx FGCS. We hypothesized that overall, Latinx FGCS with greater social support (both family support and sibling support) would have higher CDSE. Furthermore, we hypothesized that overall, Latinx FGCS with stronger cultural identities (ethnic, national, and bicultural identities) would have higher CDSE. However, we hypothesized that the strength of these relationships would depend on the extent to which Latinx FGCS experience a cultural values gap with their parents. More specifically, the relationship between social support and CDSE would be stronger for those who hold similar cultural values to their parents (small cultural values gap) than for those who subscribe to values that conflict with their parents. Similarly, the relationship between cultural identity and CDSE would be stronger for

Latinx FGCS with smaller cultural values gap than those with larger cultural values gap.

The current study contributes to the field in several ways. First of all, it examines the CDSE of students with intersecting identities: Latinx FGCS. Secondly, it investigates cultural identity and social support in a single study in order to understand both person and environmental correlates of CDSE. Third, this study includes sibling support and bicultural identity, potentially relevant aspects of social support and cultural identity, respectively, for Latinx FGCS that have been thus far neglected in research.

Method

Participants

Participants were 130 Latinx FGCS recruited from the psychology subject pool at a large, public, comprehensive HSI on the West coast. The sample consisted of 84% women with an age range of 17 to 62 years ($M = 19.71$, $SD = 4.27$). Approximately half of the participants (51%) were freshmen, and 25% were psychology majors. A majority (90%) were born in the U.S. Most participants were from lower-middle-class (35%) and middle-class (42%) backgrounds. Participants self-identified as Mexican (68%), Hispanic (unspecified; 17%), Salvadoran (6%), Latinx (unspecified; 3%), Guatemalan (2%), American (2%), and Other (2%). The eligibility criteria for this study were (a) having parents who did not graduate from college, and (b) having ancestors from Mexico, Central America, or South America. Compensation for participation was research credit to partially fulfill requirements for the introduction to psychology course.

Measures

The Career Decision Self-Efficacy Short Form scale (Betz et al., 1996) assesses the level of confidence in completing tasks related to career decisions, such as self-appraisal, planning, problem solving, gathering information, and selecting goals. This 25-item questionnaire used Betz et al.'s (2005) modified 5-point Likert-type scale ranging from 1 (*no confidence at all*) to 5 (*complete confidence*). We computed a mean score with higher scores indicating greater CDSE. The internal-consistency reliability for this sample was excellent: $\alpha = .94$.

We measured social support using the Multidimensional Scale of Perceived Social Support (Zimet, Dahlem, Zimet, & Farley, 1988). We used the family subscale to measure perceived social support from family. For example, questions on the family subscale included items such as, "I get the emotional help and support I need from my family (in general)." The sibling subscale was adapted from the family and peer subscales by replacing "family" or "peers" with "siblings" like in the item "I can talk about my problems with my siblings." Participants rated responses on this 12-item questionnaire (6 items per subscale) using a 7-point Likert-type scale ranging from 1 (*very strongly disagree*) to 7 (*very strongly agree*). We computed the mean, with higher scores indicating greater social support. Both family and sibling subscales demonstrated excellent internal-consistency reliability in this sample, $\alpha = .90$ and $\alpha = .92$, respectively.

We measured cultural identity using two corresponding scales, the Revised Multigroup Ethnic Identity Measure (MEIM) (Roberts et al., 1999) and the American Identity Measure (AIM) (Schwartz et al., 2012). First, the 12-item MEIM assesses ethnic identity, and includes items such as "I have a strong sense of belonging to my own ethnic group." The original MEIM is rated on a 4-point Likert type scale ranging from 1 (*strongly disagree*) to 4 (*strongly agree*). However, to match the rating scale of the AIM (see below), it was modified to a 5-point Likert-type scale ranging from 1 (*strongly disagree*) to 5 (*strongly agree*). We computed the mean, with higher scores indicating stronger ethnic identity. The MEIM scores demonstrated excellent internal-consistency reliability in this sample: $\alpha = .91$. Second, the 12-item AIM assesses national identity, and includes items such as "I feel good about being American." We rated items on a 5-point Likert-type scale ranging from 1 (*strongly disagree*) to 5 (*strongly agree*). We computed a mean score, with higher scores indicating stronger American identity. The AIM scores demonstrated excellent internal-consistency reliability in this sample: $\alpha = .90$. Third, we computed bicultural identity by multiplying the mean MEIM and AIM scores. Low scores on bicultural identity refer to weak ethnic and national identities, while high scores signify strong ethnic and national identities. Scores near the center indicate average values for both identities, or that one cultural identity is strong while the other is weak.

Finally, we used the 22-item Acculturative Family Distancing Youth Report (Hwang, 2006) to assess cultural values gap with items like "My parent(s) and I share the same values" (reverse-coded). Items were rated on a 7-point Likert-type scale ranging from 1 (*strongly disagree*) to 7 (*strongly agree*). We computed the mean, with higher scores indicating larger cultural values gap (or fewer shared cultural values between participants and their parents). There was good internal-consistency reliability for this sample: $\alpha = .84$.

Procedure

Participants completed an online Qualtrics questionnaire through SONA systems. After giving informed consent, participants spent approximately 45 to 60 minutes completing the measures above and responding to demographic questions regarding gender, age, year in school, academic major, number of siblings, generation status, socioeconomic background, ethnic background, and parents' education. For confidentiality of responses, participants were only identified with an identification number in order to compensate them for their participation.

Results

In the initial sample, 21 participants were not FGCS or did not specify FGCS status, 7 participants did not have siblings. Therefore, these participants were removed from the dataset, yielding a final sample size of 130 participants. It is important to note that the sample consisted of mostly women. Table 5.1 contains descriptive statistics for study variables and correlations among those variables. As indicated in Table 5.1, there were significant correlations between social support and cultural identity, specifically between national identity and family support, and between ethnic identity and sibling support.

We conducted a series of hierarchical regression analyses to examine the predictors of CDSE for Latinx FGCS and cultural values gap as a possible moderator of these relationships. For each regression analysis, we centered the predictor variables (social support or cultural identity) and the moderator variable (cultural values gap), such that the mean was subtracted from each variable. We entered the predictor variables in the first step and the moderator variable in the second step. Then, to determine the moderating effect of cultural values gap, we multiplied the centered variables to compute the interaction terms, and entered these terms in the third step.

First, we hypothesized that social support, including family and sibling support, would predict CDSE, but that the magnitude of these relationships would depend on participants' level of cultural values gap. Social support did not predict greater CDSE [$R^2 = .04$, $F(2, 127) = 2.89$, $p = .06$], with neither family nor sibling support predicting greater CDSE [family: $ß = .14$, $t(127) = 1.36$, $p = .18$; sibling: $ß = .09$, $t(127) = 0.87$, $p = .39$]. Further, cultural values gap did not moderate the relationship between family support and CDSE, $ß = -.18$, $t(124) = -1.55$, $p = .12$. However, partially supporting our hypothesis, cultural values gap was a significant moderator of the relationship between sibling support and CDSE, $ß = .33$, $t(124) = 2.88$, $p = .005$.

Table 5.1 Correlations, Means, and Standard Deviations (N = 130)

Variable	1	2	3	4	5	6	7
1. CDSE	—						
2. SS-F	.19*	—					
3. SS-S	.17*	.57***	—				
4. ETHID	.13	.15	.28***	—			
5. NATID	.15	.18*	.15	.23**	—		
6. BICULTID	-.12	.02	.00	-.15	.13	—	
7. CVG	-.26**	-.51***	-.25**	-.13	-.27**	-.03	—
M	3.52	5.40	4.99	3.85	3.73	0.11	3.41
SD	0.63	1.25	1.49	0.69	0.67	0.51	0.79

Note. CDSE = Career Decision Self-Efficacy, SS-F = Social Support Family, SS-S = Social Support Siblings, ETHID = Ethnic Identity, NATID = National Identity, BICULTID = Bicultural Identity, CVG = Cultural Values Gap; *p < .05; **p < .01; ***p < .001.

To better understand the nature of the moderating effect of cultural values gap on the sibling support-CDSE relationship, we conducted a test of simple slopes. When cultural values gap is large, sibling support significantly predicted CDSE, $t(126)$ = 2.64, p = .01. However, at average or small levels of cultural values gap, sibling support did not significantly predict CDSE [average cultural values gap: $t(126)$ = 1.21, p = .23; small cultural values gap: $t(126)$ = -0.80, p = .42]. Therefore, sibling support was predictive of greater CDSE only for participants who had a larger gap in their cultural values (fewer shared cultural values between participants and parents). Note that the nature of this moderating effect is the opposite of what we hypothesized because we focused our rationale on family social support, especially participants' closeness with their parents.

Furthermore, we also predicted that ethnic, national, and bicultural identity would predict CDSE, but the strength of these relationships would depend on the extent to which participants experience a cultural values gap with their parents. Contrary to our hypothesis, cultural identity did not predict greater CDSE, R^2 = .05, $F(3, 126)$ = 2.03, p = .11. Stronger ethnic, national, and bicultural identities did not predict greater CDSE [ethnic: ß = .08, $t(126)$ = 0.88, p = .38; national: ß = .14, $t(126)$ = 1.57, p = .12; bicultural: ß = -.13, $t(126)$ = -1.40, p = .16]. Additionally, cultural values gap did not moderate the relationship between ethnic identity and CDSE [ß = .15, $t(122)$ = 1.57, p = .12], the relationship between national identity and CDSE [ß = -.06, $t(122)$ = -0.71 p = .48], or the relationship between bicultural identity and CDSE, ß = .09, $t(122)$ = 1.00, p = .32.

Discussion

We used survey data to determine whether social support and cultural identity predicted Latinx FGCS' CDSE, and whether the magnitude of the predictive relationships above depends on cultural values gap. Contrary to expectations, neither social support (family, siblings) nor cultural identity (ethnic, national, bicultural) predicted greater CDSE. Although cultural values gap did not moderate the family support-CDSE relationship or any of the cultural identity-CDSE relationships, it did moderate the relationship between sibling support and CDSE. Specifically, sibling support was a significant predictor of CDSE only for Latinx FGCS who had a large cultural values gap.

Our finding that social support did not predict CDSE is inconsistent with previous studies that found that support from family members (in general) was an important part of Latinas' career process and success (Gomez et al., 2001), and college students' CDSE (Metheny & McWhirter, 2013), and that sibling support is important for making a career decision (Gomez et al., 2001; Schultheiss, Kress, Manzi, & Glasscock, 2001; Schultheiss et al., 2002). One possible explanation for this incongruence in findings is that "family (in general)" (as stated in the family support subscale) is too vague, not referring to specific family members. Also, asking about "family (in general)" and "sibling(s)" may be confusing to participants because the two sources of support are not mutually exclusive. Perhaps if "family (in general)" were changed to "parent(s)," then results may be different. Parental support, though potentially influential, may be less available for Latinxs FGCS. Or, other family members, such as grandparents and aunts/uncles, may supplement parental support. In addition, the nature of the sibling relationship (e.g., warmth, conflict) or sibling closeness may influence the perception and availability of sibling support (Conger & Little, 2010; Schultheiss et al., 2001).

Our study was the first to explore the role of cultural values gap in the relationship between social support and CDSE. Related to the discussion above regarding family versus parental support, cultural values gap (our hypothesized moderator variable) may be more relevant to the relationship between *parental* support and CDSE, rather than *family* support and CDSE. For example, participants with a large cultural values gap may be less inclined to turn to their parents (as opposed to consulting with family members in general) when deciding on a career. Interestingly, cultural values gap significantly moderated the degree of the sibling support to CDSE relationship. Specifically, sibling support predicted greater CDSE, but only for those who had a large cultural values gap (fewer shared cultural values with parents). This finding is not surprising because distancing from parents may contribute to a decrease in the perception and acceptance of parental emotional support, and with a lack of parental support, participants may turn to siblings as a compensatory source of support (Milevsky, 2005). That is, Latinx FGCS with a large cultural values gap may rely on sibling support because they may not have parental support. On the other hand, for participants with small or average cultural values gap, sibling support may not be as important to their CDSE because they have parental support. These findings lend insight into the role of sibling support for CDSE in the presence of acculturation gaps.

Our finding that cultural identity did not predict CDSE is incongruent with prior research. Ethnic identity has been found to predict CDSE for Latinxs (Gushue, 2006; Gushue & Whitson, 2006; Mejia-Smith & Gushue, 2017) and for ethnic minorities in general (Gloria & Hird, 1999). Moreover, national identity has been linked to better academic adjustment and higher self-esteem (Kiang et al., 2008; Phinney, Horenczyk, Liebkind, & Vedder, 2001), and biculturalism is positively associated with career self-efficacy (Gomez et al., 2001) and sociocultural adjustment (Nguyen & Benet-Martínez, 2013). One possible explanation for this discrepancy is that our Latinx FGCS attended a HSI; therefore, for these students, social identities other than cultural identity may be more salient and more predictive of CDSE. At a PWI, Latinxs may be more likely to experience isolation, discrimination, or lack of belonging because of their ethnic background. In comparison, Latinxs may be more likely to fit in at a HSI, where they are with students from a similar cultural background. Therefore, at a HSI, other social identities (e.g., gender, sexual orientation, religious) may be more important. Additionally, cultural values gap did not modify the strength of the relationship between cultural identity and CDSE. It is possible that a gap between parents and children on another acculturation dimension (behavior or identity, instead of values) (Schwartz et al., 2010) may be more relevant to the relationship between cultural identity and CDSE.

Limitations and Future Research

This study broadens our understanding of CDSE, social support, and cultural identity, but there are a few limitations to consider. One limitation is the assessment of both social support from family in general and from siblings in particular. As discussed earlier, there may be similarities between "family" (family in general) support and sibling support because siblings are encompassed in "family." Future research should differentiate among support provided by different family members (for example, parents, aunts/uncles, cousins). Because cultural values gap concerns the parent-child relationship, it is necessary to directly assess parental support. Therefore, future studies should measure parental support and whether cultural values gap moderates the parental support-CDSE relationship.

Cultural identity was not predictive of CDSE, but it is possible that the intersecting Latinx FGCS identity may influence students' level of CDSE. However, in our study, we did not directly measure the centrality or saliency of the Latinx FGCS identity. Identity centrality is the importance of a social identity to the individual (Ashmore, Deaux, & McLaughlin-Volpe, 2004). Although we asked participants how strongly they identified as a Latinx and as a student, we did not ask participants about the intersection of those identities: their strength of identification with a "Latinx FGCS" identity. A previous study found that managing two central identities is linked to identity interference, which in turn is associated with poorer mental health (Settles, 2004). Future research is needed to determine the mental health correlates of identifying as a Latinx FGCS.

Whereas identity centrality concerns the enduring explicit importance of a social identity, identity salience refers to the implicit importance of a social identity based on the situation or context (Ashmore et al., 2004). It is possible that the current study's findings depend on the salience of participants' Latinx FGCS identity. For example, social support might be predictive of CDSE when the FGCS identity is made salient, such as when the participant is in a classroom with mostly non-FGCS. Similarly, cultural identity might be predictive of CDSE when the Latinx identity is made salient, such as when the participant is in a classroom with mostly European-American students.

Research should also explore other predictors of CDSE. For example, when controlling for background variables, such as income or type of high school, FGCS had outcomes (for example, high degree aspiration, high internal locus of attribution to academic success) similar to that of non-FGCS (Pascarella, Wolniak, Pierson, & Terenzini, 2003).

Finally, most of the participants in this study were female, U.S.-born, and Mexican American; therefore, we could not examine gender, generational, or ethnic group differences. Relatedly, generalizations to the Latinx FGCS population are limited because the sample did not represent other gender, generational, or ethnic groups. Future studies should collect data from a more representative sample to better assess gender, generational, or ethnic group differences in CDSE and the predictors of CDSE.

Implications

Our findings have implications for future research and practice in career development. This study presents a different perspective in the understanding of career development by including individuals with multiple social identities. Variables previously found to predict CDSE (family support, ethnic identity) were not significant for this sample of Latinxs who are also FGCS. Rather, CDSE for those with multiple identities may be predicted by other variables. Because Latinx FGCS are likely to manage various identities, which may include gender, generation status, or ethnic group identification, vocational research should continue to examine the management of multiple social identities.

Additionally, ours is the first study to include cultural values gap in research about CDSE. Although previous studies have examined acculturation, other researchers have not examined the contribution of acculturative gaps to CDSE. This study's findings suggest that acculturation gaps may significantly impact the sibling support and CDSE link. Finally, our study suggests that sibling support plays an important positive role in Latinx FGCS' CDSE, specifically for those who endorse drastically different cultural values from their parents.

Within the home, families should encourage supportive sibling relationships. To better assist students, career counselors and vocational researchers should continue to embrace students in their complexity (e.g., multiple social identities). They should recognize that these students are also influenced by the environment outside of the university, such as their home.

Recommendations for universities include organizing events that promote current or prospective students to attend events, such as new student orientation, with siblings. For example, "parent weekend," a popular university event, may be expanded to a sibling or family weekend for the specific cohort group, which many college universities already do for their general student population. This way, the sibling relationship is encouraged and supported by the university. In addition, faculty, staff, and administrators can encourage students to seek social support both inside and outside of the university (siblings). Finally, universities may benefit from training faculty, staff, and administrators to support diverse students and acknowledge their multiple social identities.

Conclusion

This study offers insight into the career development of Latinx FGCS, and whether cultural values gap plays a role in social support and cultural identity's ability to predict CDSE. Contrary to previous research suggesting that social support and ethnic identity should relate to CDSE (Mejia-Smith & Gushue, 2017; Metheny & McWhirter, 2013; Schultheiss et al., 2002), neither social support (family, siblings) nor cultural identities (ethnic, national, bicultural) were significant predictors of CDSE. However, sibling support predicted CDSE for Latinx FGCS who held very different cultural values from their parents. This finding stresses the importance of sibling support in the presence of a large parent-child gap in cultural values.

A limitation of previous studies is that they primarily studied either Latinxs or FGCS, but not both; therefore, this study contributes to the understanding of those with multiple marginalized identities. This study also addresses the gap in the literature by examining relatively neglected variables (for example, sibling support, national identity, and bicultural identity) as predictors of CDSE. Further, we also examined whether acculturation gaps may influence CDSE. Our findings suggest that there are positive factors, such as sibling support, that can assist Latinx FGCS and their CDSE. Based on our findings, universities can support Latinx FGCS and promote their CDSE by encouraging sibling relationships and social support, such as with events inclusive of siblings.

References

Arbona, C. (1995). Theory and research on racial and ethnic minorities: Hispanic Americans. In F. T. L. Leong (Ed.), *Career development and vocational behavior of racial and ethnic minorities* (pp. 37–66). Mahwah, NJ: Lawrence Erlbaum Associates.

Ashmore, R. D., Deaux, K., & McLaughlin-Volpe, T. (2004). An organizing framework for collective identity: Articulation and significance of multidimensionality. *Psychological Bulletin, 130*(1), 80–114. doi: 10.1037/0033–2909.130.1.80

Betz, N. E., Hammond, M. S., & Multon, K. D. (2005). Reliability and validity of five-level response continua for the career decision self-efficacy scale. *Journal of Career Assessment, 13*(2), 131–149. doi:10.1177/1069072704273123

Betz, N. E., Klein, K. L., & Taylor, K. M. (1996). Evaluation of a short form of the career decision-making self-efficacy scale. *Journal of Career Assessment, 4*(1), 47–57. doi:10.1177/106907279600400103

Chen, X. (2005). *First-generation students in postsecondary education: A look at their college transcripts. National Center for Education Statistics.* Retrieved from http://nces.ed.gov/pubs2005/2005171.pdf

Cicirelli, V. G. (1989). Feelings of attachment to siblings and well-being in later life. *Psychology and Aging, 4*(2), 211–216. doi: 10.1037/0882-7974.4.2.211

Cobb, S. (1976). Social support as a moderator of life stress. *Psychosomatic Medicine, 38*(5), 300–314. doi:10.1097/00006842-197609000-00003

Cole, E. R. (2009). Intersectionality and research in psychology. *American Psychologist, 64*(3), 170–180. doi:10.1037/a0014564

Conger, K. J., & Little, W. M. (2010). Sibling relationships during the transition to adulthood. *Child Development Perspectives, 4*(2), 87–94. doi:10.1111/j.1750-8606.2010.00123.x

Connidis, I. A. (1992). Life transitions and the adult sibling tie: A qualitative study. *Journal of Marriage and Family, 54*(4), 972–982. doi: 10.2307/353176

Constantine, M. G., Kindaichi, M. M., & Miville, M. L. (2007). Factors influencing the educational and vocational transitions of Black and Latino high school students. *Professional School Counseling, 10*(3), 261–265. doi: 10.5330/prsc.10.3.bg613873q5104226

Crenshaw, K. (1989). Demarginalizing the intersection of race and sex: A Black feminist critique of antidiscrimination doctrine, feminist theory and antiracist politics. *The University of Chicago Legal Forum,* (1), 139–167. Retrieved from https://philpapers.org/archive/CREDTI.pdf?ncid=txtlnkusaolp00000603

Dennis, J., Basañez, T., & Farahmand, A. (2010). Intergenerational conflicts among Latinos in early adulthood: Separating values conflicts with parents from acculturation conflicts. *Hispanic Journal of Behavioral Sciences, 32*(1), 118–135. doi:10.1177/0739986309352986

Fouad, N. A., & Arbona, C. (1994). Careers in a cultural context. *The Career Development Quarterly, 43*(1), 96–104. doi:10.1002/j.2161-0045.1994.tb00851.x

Fry, R. (2002). *Latinos in higher education: Many enroll, too few graduate.* Retrieved from http://www.pewhispanic.org/files/reports/11.pdf

Fry, R., & Lopez, M. H. (2012). *Hispanic student enrollments reach new highs in 2011.* Retrieved from http://www.pewhispanic.org/files/2012/08/Hispanic-Student-Enrollments-Reach-New-Highs-in-2011_FINAL.pdf

Gloria, A. M., & Castellanos, J. (2012). Desafíos y bendiciones: A multiperspective examination of the educational experiences and coping responses of first-generation college Latina students. *Journal of Hispanic Higher Education, 11*(1), 82–99. doi:10.1177/1538192711430382

Gloria, A. M., & Hird, J. S. (1999). Influences of ethnic and nonethnic variables on the career decision-making self-efficacy of college students. *The Career Development Quarterly, 48*(2), 157–174. doi:10.1002/j.2161-0045.1999.tb00282.x

Gomez, M. J., Fassinger, R. E., Prosser, J., Cooke, K., Mejia, B., & Luna, J. (2001). Voces abriendo caminos (Voices forging paths): A qualitative study of the career development of notable Latinas. *Journal of Counseling Psychology, 48*(3), 286–300. doi:10.1037//0022-0167.48.3.286

Gushue, G. V. (2006). The relationship of ethnic identity, career decision-making self-efficacy and outcome expectations among Latino/a high school students. *Journal of Vocational Behavior, 68*(1), 85–95. doi:10.1016/j.jvb.2005.03.002

Gushue, G. V., & Whitson, M. L. (2006). The relationship of ethnic identity and gender role attitudes to the development of career choice goals among black and Latina girls. *Journal of Counseling Psychology, 53*(3), 379–385. doi:10.1037/0022-0167.53.3.379

Hackett, G., & Betz, N. E. (1981). A self-efficacy approach to the career development of women. *Journal of Vocational Behavior, 18*(3), 326–339. doi:10.1016/0001-8791 (81)90019-1

Hwang, W.-C. (2006). Acculturative family distancing: Theory, research, and clinical practice. *Psychotherapy: Theory, Research, Practice, Training, 43*(4), 397–409. doi:10.1037/0033-3204.43.4.397

Hwang, W.-C., & Wood, J. J. (2009). Acculturative family distancing: Links with self-reported symptomatology among Asian Americans and Latinos. *Child Psychiatry and Human Development, 40*(1), 123–138. doi:10.1007/s10578-008-0115-8

Kiang, L., Yip, T., & Fuligni, A. J. (2008). Multiple social identities and adjustment in young adults from ethnically diverse backgrounds. *Journal of Research on Adolescence, 18*(4), 643–670. doi: http://dx.doi.org/10.1111/j.1532-7795.2008.00575.x

Leal-Muniz, V., & Constantine, M. G. (2005). Predictors of the career commitment process in Mexican American college students. *Journal of Career Assessment, 13*(2), 204–215. doi:10.1177/1069072704273164

Lent, R. W., Brown, S. D., & Hackett, G. (1994). Toward a unifying social cognitive theory of career and academic interest, choice, and performance. *Journal of Vocational Behavior, 45*(1), 79–122. doi:10.1006/jvbe.1994.1027

Lent, R. W., Brown, S. D., & Hackett, G. (2000). Contextual supports and barriers to career choice: A social cognitive analysis. *Journal of Counseling Psychology, 47*(1), 36–49. doi:10.1037/0022-0167.47.1.36

Lent, R. W., Brown, S. D., & Larkin, K. C. (1984). Relation of self-efficacy expectations to academic achievement and persistence. *Journal of Counseling Psychology, 31*(3), 356–362. doi:10.1037/0022-0167.31.3.356

Lewin, K. (1951). *Field theory in social science.* New York: Harper & Brothers.

Mejia-Smith, B., & Gushue, G. V. (2017). Latina/o college students' perceptions of career barriers: Influence of ethnic identity, acculturation, and self-efficacy. *Journal of Counseling & Development, 95*(2), 145–155. doi:10.1002/jcad.12127

Metheny, J., & McWhirter, E. H. (2013). Contributions of social status and family support to college students' career decision self-efficacy and outcome expectations. *Journal of Career Assessment, 21*(3), 378–394. doi:10.1177/1069072712475164

Milevsky, A. (2005). Compensatory patterns of sibling support in emerging adulthood: Variations in loneliness, self-esteem, depression and life satisfaction. *Journal of Social and Personal Relationships, 22*(6), 743–755. doi:10.1177/0265407505056447

Nguyen, A.-M. D., & Benet-Martínez, V. (2007). Biculturalism unpacked: Components, measurement, individual differences, and outcomes. *Social and Personality Psychology Compass, 1*(1), 101–114. doi:10.1111/j.1751–9004.2007.00029.x Biculturalism

Nguyen, A.-M. D., & Benet-Martínez, V. (2013). Biculturalism and adjustment: A meta-analysis. *Journal of Cross-Cultural Psychology, 44*(1), 122–159. doi:10.1177/0022022111435097

Padilla, A. M. (2006). Bicultural social development. *Hispanic Journal of Behavioral Sciences, 28*(4), 467–497. doi: 10.1177/0739986306294255

Pascarella, E. T., Pierson, C. T., Wolniak, G. C., & Terenzini, P. T. (2004). First-generation college students: Additional evidence on college experiences and outcomes. *The Journal of Higher Education, 75*(3), 249–284. doi:10.1353/jhe.2004.0016

Pascarella, E. T., Wolniak, G. C., Pierson, C. T., & Terenzini, P. T. (2003). Experiences and outcomes of first-generation students in community colleges. *Journal of College Student Development, 44*(3), 420–429. doi:10.1353/csd.2003.0030

Phinney, J. S. (1990). Ethnic identity in adolescents and adults: Review of research. *Psychological Bulletin, 108*(3), 499–514. doi:10.1037/0033–2909.108.3.499

Phinney, J. S., Horenczyk, G., Liebkind, K., & Vedder, P. (2001). Ethnic identity, immigration, and well-being: An interactional perspective. *Journal of Social Issues, 57*(3), 493–510. doi:10.1111/0022–4537.00225

Rivera, F. I., Guarnaccia, P. J., Mulvaney-Day, N., Lin, J. Y., Torres, M., & Alegría, M. (2008). Family cohesion and its relationship to psychological distress among Latino groups. *Hispanic Journal of Behavioral Sciences, 30*(3), 357–378. doi:10.1177/0739986308318713

Roberts, R. E., Phinney, J. S., Masse, L. C., Chen, Y. R., Roberts, C. R., & Romero, A. (1999). The structure of ethnic identity of young adolescents from diverse ethnocultural groups. *Journal of Early Adolescence, 19*(3), 301–322. doi:10.1177/0272431699019003001

Robotham, D., & Julian, C. (2006). Stress and the higher education student: A critical review of the literature. *Journal of Further and Higher Education, 30*(2), 107–117. doi:10.1080/03098770600617513

Rodriguez, N., Mira, C. B., Myers, H. F., Morris, J. K., & Cardoza, D. (2003). Family or friends: Who plays a greater supportive role for Latino college students? *Cultural Diversity and Ethnic Minority Psychology, 9*(3), 236–250. doi:10.1037/1099–9809.9.3.236

Schultheiss, D. E. P., Kress, H. M., Manzi, A. J., & Glasscock, J. M. J. (2001). Relational influences in career development: A qualitative inquiry. *The Counseling Psychologist, 29*(2), 216–241. doi:10.1177/0011000001292003

Schultheiss, D. E. P., Palma, T. V, Predragovich, K. S., & Glasscock, J. M. J. (2002). Relational influences on career paths: Siblings in context. *Journal of Counseling Psychology, 49*(3), 302–310. doi:10.1037/0022–0167.49.3.302

Schwartz, S. J., Park, I. J. K., Huynh, Q.-L., Zamboanga, B. L., Umaña-Taylor, A. J., Lee, R. M., … Agocha, V. B. (2012). The American identity measure: Development and validation across ethnic group and immigrant generation. *Identity, 12*(2), 93–128. do i:10.1080/15283488.2012.668730

Schwartz, S. J., Unger, J. B., Zamboanga, B. L., & Szapocznik, J. (2010). Rethinking the concept of acculturation: Implications for theory and research. *American Psychologist, 65*(4), 237–251. doi:10.1037/a0019330

Settles, I. H. (2004). When multiple identities interfere: The role of identity centrality. *Personality and Social Psychology Bulletin, 30*(4), 487–500. doi:10.1177/ 0146167203261885

Settles, I. H., & Buchanan, N. T. (2014). Multiple groups, multiple identities, and intersectionality. In V. Benet-Martínez & Y. Hong (Eds.), *The oxford handbook of multicultural identity* (pp. 160–180). doi:10.1093/oxfordhb/9780199796694.001.0001

Smedley, B. D., Myers, H. F., & Harrell, S. P. (1993). Minority-status stresses and the college adjustment of ethnic minority freshmen. *The Journal of Higher Education, 64*(4), 434–452. doi:10.2307/2960051

Tajfel, H., & Turner, J. (1979). An integrative theory of intergroup conflict. In W. G. Austin & S. Worchel (Eds.), *The social psychology of intergroup relations* (pp. 33–47). Monterey, CA: Brooks/Cole.

Terenzini, P. T., Springer, L., Yaeger, P. M., Pascarella, E. T., & Nora, A. (1996). First-generation college students: Characteristics, experiences, and cognitive development. *Research in Higher Education, 37*(1), 1–22. doi:10.1007/BF01680039

Volling, B. L. (2003). Sibling relationships. In M. H. Bornstein, L. Davidson, C. L. M. Keyes, K. A. Moore, & The Center for Child Well-being (Eds.), *Well-being: Positive development across the life course* (pp. 205–220). Mahwah, NJ: Lawrence Erlbaum Associates.

Warner, L. R. (2008). A best practices guide to intersectional approaches in psychological research. *Sex Roles, 59*(5/6), 454–463. doi:10.1007/s11199-008-9504-5

Whiston, S. C., & Keller, B. K. (2004). The influences of the family of origin on career development: A review and analysis. *The Counseling Psychologist, 32*(4), 493–568. doi:10.1177/0011000004265660

Zimet, G. D., Dahlem, N. W., Zimet, S. G., & Farley, G. K. (1988). The multidimensional scale of perceived social support. *Journal of Personality Assessment, 52*(1), 30–41. doi:10.1207/s15327752jpa5201_2

6. Academic (Im)Posturing: A Critical Autoethnography of Becoming a Latinx, First-Generation College Student and Professor

Rebecca Mercado Jones

Abnormality was the price a person had to pay for her or his inborn extraordinary gift.
—Gloria Anzaldúa (1987), *Borderlands: La Frontera*

We are what we pretend to be, so we must be careful about what we pretend to be.
—Kurt Vonnegut (1962), *Mother Night*

I can vividly recall moments throughout my life when I felt truly special. Special, not in the millennial sense of the word ("we're *all* special, now here's your trophy!"), but an exception to the norm. In my childhood, I sought ways to stand out as the fourth child of five and the second girl. I always did well in school; striving to be praised by my teachers was my most important priority, and the least I could do for my hardworking, single mom. I thought of teachers as celebrities. When I encountered them doing ordinary things such as grocery shopping or walking their dogs, I was star struck. "Wow, they are just like me," I used to think. I knew I was rather weirdly obsessed with my teachers because my brothers and classmates teased me with names such as "brown noser," "teacher's pet," and "chupamedias," which they intended to be insults. But I had to stand out; I had to be the smartest student with the highest grades in the class—but especially smarter than the smart boys in my class. Because being smart was *my* thing. That I could do, even if it was just for me, and even if it didn't get me anywhere.[1]

One of these celebrity teachers guided me to Cisneros' (1991) book, *A House on Mango Street*. That was the first time I saw myself reflected in literature. It was such an existential moment, which happens for people of color much later than it does for the average White reader who is raised on "the classics." Here, Esperanza was living a life like mine, in a world that looked a lot like mine. A world where men were served first at dinner and women were taught to aspire to marrying well and bearing cute, but more importantly, hard-working and well-behaved babies. A world where there was no need to be embarrassed by the size or appearance of your house because everyone was equally as poor. On the back of the book, hidden within the author's biography is the line, "Sandra is living in New York City and she is no one's wife and no one's mother." Aha! Now, there's a life, which was entirely novel to me, but seemed worthy of my aspiration, I thought. I wanted to be that kind of special—exceptional.

This drive to be special, to be smart, to be recognized, shifted a bit when I was 14. Then, my mom died. To put it too simply and too swiftly, she died because she couldn't afford healthcare. She only worked minimum-wage jobs, somehow raising us on what she was paid working at places like Taco Bell. After that day, I was special for a whole new reason. Walking the halls of my middle school, I was the kid whose mom just died. I felt like a pariah, *la paria*. From that point on, I wanted to be exceptional for her, to be a person she would be proud of, though I'd never get the chance to hear it from her. I assume because she married at 19 (she was pregnant), had five children, was left penniless and abandoned in a state far away from her family, that she would want the opposite for me. I assume she would want me to be more like Sandra Cisneros (1991) and less like her. I'll never know for certain.

Because of the omnipotence of a school counselor, Ms. Mae Jackson, college became more than just a pipe dream. I made it. I was on my way to being more like Sandra. Once there, I was affirmed in my specialness because going to college was not what kids from my neighborhood usually did. Most of my friends never went to college, and two of my brothers didn't even finish high school. I was designed to be unusual, or so I thought. I now know, many books and years later, that feeling different from the rest of my family was part of the recipe to my success. One such book was Rubin's (1996) *The Transcendent Child*, which describes an early sense of dis-identification from one's family and provides insight into why some people transcend their past, and others do not. I would later find these insights helpful in understanding why I seemed to flourish a bit more than my brothers. However, back then, on my way to college, although I felt special, I also felt kind of lonely.

Attempts have been made to intellectualize the first-generation college student (FGCS) experience for the presumed audiences of faculty, administrators, and staff (Housel & Harvey, 2009; Orbe, 2004; Protivera McGlynn, 2011). These publications are necessary in understanding and advocating for FGCS. It is also important to know the storied nature of these experiences, specifically through first-person narration and analysis. Critical autoethnography allows the contextualization of those stories and experiences within a larger cultural context. Critical autoethnography is unique in the way it also requires the researcher to "acknowledge the inevitable privileges we experience alongside the marginalization and take responsibility for our subjective lenses through reflexivity. We write as an Other, and for an Other" (Boylorn & Orbe, 2014, p. 15). This is especially important considering how previous research on FGCS has suggested that the day-to-day experience of being a FGCS varies considerably (Orbe, 2004). In this chapter, I try my best to refrain from a conventional academic voice in lieu of a more authentic one. In doing so, I turn story into theory and theory into story. This practice ensures that I am accountable to those who need chapters like this the most— FGCS who come from a wide range of various intersecting social identities. I write as an academic "Other" for a future academic "Other" (Boylorn & Orbe, 2014).

Navigating College as a First-Generation, Latinx Student

I chose Central Michigan University the same way many FGCS choose, very simply; they offered me the best scholarship. On the big day that I moved into my all-girls dormitory, I realized very quickly that I wasn't just special—I was strange. I was strange because my *primos* moved me in, not my parents, strange because I didn't know that there was more "up north" to go than where we already were. Strange because I still had crooked teeth and a tan all year round. Strange because of my so-called "thick accent" and my work ethic. People who went to college, I learned, had two parents in one house, living grandparents, time to get drunk on a weekday, and never knew what it felt like to be embarrassed by playing aloud the music they listened to, or the food they ate, or the shoes they wore. Going to college, for them, was expected, not exceptional.

Set in the backdrop of a Predominantly White Institution (PWI), I learned I wasn't simply motivated by my desire to be special; I was an aberration—a minority. This was a new identity for me because I had always lived in predominately Black neighborhoods. I received a "minority scholarship" as a means to brighten my lily-White institution, and I borrowed the rest through loans. As a stipulation of my scholarship, I was required to "check in" with the minority student services' office. I quickly learned that I needed them and their services. I needed that office to feel human, to vent, to have a semblance of family while I was away from mine. College was a time of startling self-discoveries, as I imagine it is for most college students. I learned about consciousness, the self, and what is "Other." I acquired the code of "double consciousness" (Du Bois, 1903) and learned the language of "the white gaze" (Fanon, 1952), and I used this language and code to make sense of my experiences. I saw myself as I was, with the contrast of my old world colliding with this new world that seemingly belonged to White rich kids more than it did to me. I also began to see myself as these students saw me: worlds and identities plowing into one another. I saw myself both as kind of special and kind of strange.

I will never forget my first week of college, when I learned about how one of my White roommates saw me (let's just call her "Angie"). "I've never met anyone like you before," Angie said, timidly but with a hint of excitement. "Like me, how?" I was thinking she meant cute, sassy, with a generous pinch of hood. But Angie replied, "You know, south of the border…" she kind of whispered, loudly, the "south of the border" part, as if she suspected there was something wrong with what she was saying but she wasn't ashamed to say it, as long as she said it with a hint of tickle.

Taken aback, I asked, "What do you mean?" Her attempt to clarify only made it worse, "Well, I mean we have Mexicans in the fields and stuff where I grew up, but they aren't like *real* people." She—we—didn't last long. The four of us assigned to Sweeny Hall, room 206, did not last even a semester. Angie greeted our third roommate, Simone, and her sister on move-in day similarly, exclaiming to Simone's sister, "Wow, you're the darkest Black person I've ever seen before!" What eventually tipped the scale was Angie shouting, "Go back to Africa!" at our friend while trying to slam the door on her face.

Angie taught me a lot, and not just about White people. I had known White people all my life; after all, that's how White privilege operates (McIntosh, 1990)—but she exposed the "hidden transcripts" that White people have about me and brown families like mine—the things that most White people are too "polite" to say aloud (Scott, 1990).[2] Being born to a mom a similar shade as Beyoncé with five kids and no dad in sight, I suspected many White people had an opinion about my "broken" family, but living with the spokesperson of "the white gaze"? As I said, Angie taught me *somethangs'*.

The weird thing about Angie was that she was a self-proclaimed liberal and feminist. By my freshman year of college, I may have seen these words before, but I was unfamiliar with what they meant. Angie transferred after that first semester, but little did I know then just how many people Angie would come to represent in my life: White, liberal, and conventionally smart—but culturally illiterate. Furthermore, I also couldn't have anticipated how important those initial interactions with Angie, and with being a broke first-generation college freshman and Latinx—a term used to resist the gender binary and misogyny often imbued in some Latinx cultures (Love Ramirez & Blay, 2017)—at a PWI would come to mean in shaping my imagination, my commitments, my research, and ultimately my entire sense of being.

Early in my second year of college, I had a Peruvian professor, Dr. Sergio Chavez, who taught a notoriously easy (amongst the small but tight-knit community of Latinx students on campus) course called, "Cultures of Latin America." I studied minimally for the first exam because that's all I thought I needed. But when Dr. Chavez passed back the exams, he asked me to stay after class. Oh, shit! My stomach sank. I was confused; my perfectly average grade signified that I clearly didn't cheat. I was on pin and needles, and I couldn't focus on his lecture.

After class, he brought his face close to mine as I leaned on the doorframe so that I could smell the staleness of his coffee breath. He said, "Rebecca, you have a double whammy. You're Mexican and you're a girl—you have got to be better than the best. Because you represent me, you represent yourself, and you represent our entire community to the rest of these students."

I was 19 and dumbfounded. Moreover, that was too heavy of a burden to bear. I couldn't speak for or represent anyone, who was *I* to do so? But, in some way, he was right. I was the only Latinx in that class, and in almost all of my classes, except Spanish. In this milieu, I understood myself as being special, not just because I was smart, but I was special for being Latinx who was—surprisingly—smart.

That is what college did for me: Beyond teaching me math, science, English, college showed me who I was—to myself and to others. Through my sociology, anthropology, communication, and Spanish courses, I learned about the history, the language, the struggle, and the systematic erasure of my culture and other historically marginalized cultures. In that "Cultures of Latin America" course, I learned about my indigenous roots; as silly as it may sound, I hadn't known that Mexicans could be *indígenas*. I read ethnographies of Latin-American communities, which ignited my hunger to learn more (Collier & Quaratiello, 1994; Pozas, 1962). Then I enrolled in another popular course (again, amongst my small group of Latinx friends), "Latinos in the United States," where I learned about the Bracero Program, about the United Farmworkers, Chicana identity, about the Zoot Suit Riots, about the California walkouts of the late 1960s. Up until that point, I thought my people were ahistorical. I thought the only Mexican person who made any meaningful contribution to history was Cesar Chavez.

College gave me "a people," a legacy, a sense of pride in where I come from—in the place you'd least expect it—the Whitest place I had ever been. There, tucked away in the cornfields, with mostly White professors teaching me about racism, assimilation, and colonization, I learned about my historical self. Learning about the de(con)struction of marginalized cultures from the perspective of mostly White professors also inspired a desire to go straight to the source. I wanted nothing more than to study abroad in Mexico, to see where my grandparents left and to see myself reflected back in other students, professors, and lessons. However, I didn't have the thousands of dollars it cost, and the furthest I had ever been from Detroit was when we lived in South Carolina. I was so young then, I don't even remember it. We didn't travel—that's not a thing poor people do (Langston, 1988). So the very thought of traveling seemed like a fantasy, but "studying abroad" was a chimera.

One good thing about being as poor as I was (I was financially independent—my mother had died and legal guardianship ended at 18) was that I had access to a lot of financial aid in the form of loans. This, I now know, is a predatory trap that many low-income, FGCS fall into (Jehangir, Stebleton, & Deenanath, 2015); I, too, was not above falling into it. I had no one to advise me as the only person in my family to navigate college tuition and fees, but even if I did, these loans gave me access to something I never had before: money. So even though I couldn't afford to study abroad, I borrowed the money and went anyway. Although I'm probably still paying off that *torta* I bought in-between classes in Puebla, Mexico, it was worth it. I would have never had the opportunity to do so otherwise. Today I remain the only one of my siblings to travel to our mother country.

In Mexico, I studied my mother's tongue. I could finally describe myself in the language I was meant to speak in, but had stolen from me. As Anzaldúa (1987) would put it, my "wild tongue" was finally freed. Learning Spanish meant I had access to another reality; as the Sapir-Whorf Hypothesis suggests (Koerner, 1992), language influences our thoughts. Now, my thoughts were more expansive and at the same time more grounded. I developed a sense of awareness about how small my world was and a purpose that transcends beyond it. Finally, doing something I never believed I'd be able to do, traveling to Mexico (and by myself, to boot!), made the all the impossible seem possible. When I returned to campus in the fall, I had grown the courage and confidence to throw myself into what I thought were unobtainable opportunities, to do some really special things.

While in my undergraduate program, loans, and scholarships bought me the time to get involved in things that mattered. I joined a historically Latina sorority, Sigma Lambda Gamma; I resurrected the Latino Student Union; and I even armed a megaphone at a student protest aimed at protecting affirmative action initiatives on campus. I found myself at college. I found my voice, I learned another language, and I learned that the search for specialness that motived my actions before served as the very foundations of my identity.

I wasn't searching to be different; I was different. I was Latinx—culturally and racially different from my peers at this predominately White, middle-class institution. I was the first person in my immediate family to go to college, and so I was also different from the world where I was born. That was the loneliest realization I came to learn in my undergraduate years. I wasn't quite like my brothers and sister and cousins and my old friends anymore—I used to try to hide being a college student when I went home to visit. The less I talked about it, the easier it was for us all to forget. Being "educated" automatically translated into "You think you're better than me," no matter how I tried to spin it. I learned very quickly how to downplay success and how to code switch, "hop-scotching between different cultural and linguistic spaces and different parts of our own identities—sometimes within a single interaction" (Demby, 2013, para. 5). The way I spoke and the words I used changed depending on with whom I was speaking. About halfway through my undergraduate degree, I began to question, after this whole college thing was over, where would I go, especially if I didn't want to go back to that elusive place called "home" (Chawla & Holman Jones, 2015)?

Dr. Chavez and other professors in my undergraduate courses introduced me to the idea of graduate school, but was *I* smart enough for *graduate school*? I wanted to be a professor, just like them, but how would I get there? I now know just how critical it is for a professor to recognize a student's potential and to convince them of it. Growing up poor has a way of convincing you of what you deserve, which is always less than you actually do. My professors took that additional step to not just tell me that I was smart, but that I was also smart *enough* for graduate school, and they led me to the program that would help me to get there (Mercado Thornton, 2013; 2015a; 2015b).

Learning How to Apply to Graduate School

The program was a U.S. Department of Education's Federal TRIO Program called the McNair Scholars Program (The McNair Scholars Program, 2016). Looking back, the McNair Program was the real game changer. It was created to help first-generation, low-income, underrepresented students like me obtain doctoral degrees. It was designed specifically for minority kids like me—kids who didn't have professional parents, and didn't know why or how much that even matters. The program taught me the difference between a master's degree, a PsyD, a PhD, and an EdD. I had no idea what those acronyms meant, or that I would need one of them in order to be a professor like my celebrity heroes. The program prepped me for the Graduate Record Exam (GRE) I didn't know I had to take; encouraged me to write emails; made me press "send" to professors I wanted to study with; and helped me to craft personal statements that would open doors that I didn't know existed. I learned about teaching and research assistantships and fellowships that were specifically designed to help first-generation, underrepresented kids like me get to graduate programs like theirs.

The McNair Program, and its director, Lynn Curry, bridged gaps for me by giving me social, economic, and cultural capital that I would need in order to exist and thrive in what West (1993–1994) calls "the white bourgeoisie academic institutions" (p. 63). Academia was designed by the White bourgeoisie for the White bourgeoisie, not for broke Latinx kids. I had already gotten a hint of that in undergrad, and another heavy dose awaited me in graduate school. Programs like the McNair Scholars Program help students like me to elbow our way into a system that wasn't designed for us. Beyond ensuring us access to basic information required to make it to graduate school, like GRE preparatory classes and ways to hunt for graduate school funding, Lynn arranged for us to do things I thought were reserved for rich White folks, like yoga and canoeing. I remember she made us dress up in our finest clothes and forced us to learn dining etiquette. At the start of it, I was perturbed. I thought, "I know how to eat and to keep my elbows off tables, geez…." By the end, I remember feeling stung by deep inadequacy. Poor people know they are poor—that is no mystery to anyone who has ever been poor—but to learn about how class membership and consciousness affects someone in the most insidious ways remains a constant enigma for me. It is one thing to read about Bourdieu's (1979) concepts of social, economic, and cultural capital, and it's another to uncover how those traits, behaviors, and knowledge take shape in your life—and more importantly, how that lack of capital keeps you from ever being inside of spaces and information you don't even know you need.

In the McNair Program, I also had a formal mentoring relationship with a communication faculty member. I had had many informal mentoring relationships in my life, teachers and professors who liked me. However, this formal mentoring relationship, which required that I explicitly ask someone to be my mentor, was instrumental to securing a spot in a graduate program. Dr. Lesley Withers was, in many ways, very different from me. She was White, from Maine, and she loved sci-fi. She also believed in my ability to do original research. I didn't, but she did. She encouraged me to think creatively about how I could transform my passions into one specific research question. She held my hand through a totally foreign process. I did not attend the type of rigorous university, nor was I in the type of major, that prepares its students to do original research. Hell, I didn't even own a computer then. Dr. Withers helped me to design the study, recruit participants, and find meaning in a bunch of numbers. On a Saturday, in her casual clothes, Dr. Withers came to the Grawn Computer Lab, where I wrote to explain what the squiggly lines and math signs meant. I would not have written my proudest work without her. I would not have had that formal, explicit, positive mentoring experience without the McNair Program requiring me to do so.

The most paramount thing the McNair Scholars Program gave me was the confidence to apply to a doctoral program right out of my undergraduate program. I didn't think I was ready then, and I probably never would have applied to a doctorate program if it weren't for the GRE training, the research skills, the formal mentorship—the social, economic, and cultural capital the McNair Scholars program gave me. Still to my amazement, they let me in. At 22 years old, three months fresh from graduation, I was back in the classroom at Ohio University. This time, I faced the rows, standing in front of them instead of sitting in them.

Navigating a Doctoral Program

All doctoral students in my communication program had to take three graduate classes while teaching two classes. I was simultaneously juggling living away from my family for the first time, being a female instructor of color at 22 to mostly White students, being the only Latinx in my graduate cohort, trying to read hundreds of pages per week, writing papers longer than anyone wants to read, and existing more than 100 miles away from a decent *taco de lengua*. Doctoral programs are challenging for everyone, that's a fact. For me, the program was challenging in so many intersecting ways.

I was the subject of the philosophical racial, economic, and gender inequality that my cohort and I read about daily. When we read about hypothetical inequality—I saw my mother's story, I recalled moments in my childhood, I pictured my brothers' struggles. In my health communication courses, we read and discussed a book entitled, *The Silicone Breast Implant Story: Communication and Uncertainty* (Vanderford & Smith, 1996). Members of my cohort were getting impassioned about sexism and the systematic injustices that women with implants face, and I just couldn't. "Yo, implants are an elective, cosmetic surgery," I argued. "At least these women have health insurance or the means to receive surgery. People die because they don't have access to healthcare...." Like my mom, I wanted to say, but didn't. When you're already on the outside, you don't do the kicking yourself. The reaction was appalling. One classmate exclaimed, "Breast implants can save someone's life; you don't know how badly someone struggles with body image!" She was right; I had no clue what it meant to want breast implants so badly I would die.

The following year, in my advanced feminist theory course, we studied the break that distinguishes the second wave of feminism from the third wave (Grant, 1993). I thought back to that conversation on breast implants—systems of oppression are truly blind to one another (Crenshaw, 1991). I also think about that split every time a White woman lectures a woman of color about "intersectional feminism." There's a ton of that in graduate school, and in academia, in general.

The first week of my doctoral program, I overheard a new colleague complain about how her family had to spend "yet again, another summer in the Keys," because that's where her family's beach house was. What in the? People actually own beach houses? Like real people? Own "beach" houses? In the Florida Keys? That was another one of those existential moments when I realized my place in the universe—not just that I am poor, but out-of-touch-with-reality-poor. These were the kinds of people I was made to discuss economic inequality with for four years.

There, in my doctoral program, I felt alone. I was the only person of color in my cohort. I wrestled with imposter syndrome— the belief that you are not smart enough to be where you are and that you have fooled everyone who thinks otherwise (Clance & Imes, 1978). I constantly questioned, am I smart enough? Should I be postponing making "real money" in order to help my family? Would I be able to survive a dissertation? Would I get a tenure-track job (in a decent place, not too far from home)? Life seemed shaky and uncertain, and I was homesick.

When I went home, though, I was even lonelier. I'd go out with my old friends (if they could find a sitter) and by 11 p.m., I'd find myself passed out in the backseat. I couldn't hang with them, and that is what there is to do for fun in Detroit. My friends and family still boast about my "big bad master's degree." There's no point in trying to clarify that I have a PhD; that's never received in the way I intend, so it's better to just to go with it.

Half of the students who start a doctoral program don't complete it (Cassuto, 2013), and I wonder how much higher the rate is for FGCS and/or students of color. Oddly though, I would also cite my family and friends as the reason I finished. I wanted to show my younger *primas* and my friends' kids that there's more in life than what is in front of you. I come from generation after generation of teenage mothers. I wanted them to see something different, something special, and I believe education is the way.

Between the loneliness of my doctoral program and the strange familiarity of my old home in Detroit, I found a fit. My doctoral advisor, Dr. Devika Chawla, led me to Anzaldúa (1987), Hill Collins (2000), and Fanon (1952). They helped assuage being Other by teaching me what it means to be so. Much like when I read *A House on Mango Street*, and about the historical accomplishments of Mexicans, it was gratifying to see myself and similar experiences reflected back in "canonical" literature. When Anzaldúa (1987) wrote about living life in the margins, permanently in between cultures, it brought me life! My father was White, my mother was Mexican, my skin was fair for a "half-breed," and I always felt like so, *como un mestizaje*, like Anzaldúa (1987). Because my father left when my siblings and I were very young, we were raised to think of our culture as Mexican, though I never looked so. My *hermanos* and cousins always joked that I was "the dumpster baby" because I wasn't as dark as them. I, too, felt as though I existed on a border and in the shadows. There, in the pages of *Borderlands: La Frontera*, I was coaxed to tolerate the ambiguity within myself, accept a plural sense of self, and embrace this new mestiza consciousness that Anzaldúa (1987) advocated.

Hill Collins (2000), on the other hand, made me feel "sum type of way."[3] I was forced to look at my own reflection critically—but not in ways that I was used to or comfortable with. I was forced to confront the privilege that my ethnically ambiguous skin color gave me. Being my family's "dumpster baby" might also be the very reason I had access to opportunities they were denied. I now understood my identity as marginal and not as special and that I had access to rights and opportunities that my undocumented family members didn't have, like receiving federal loans to go to college and graduate school. Reading *Black Feminist Thought* gave me qualms with feminism legitimacy (Hill Collins, 2000). Yes, I benefit from the liberating force of feminism—Anzaldúa (1987) exposed and situated the machismo culture I was reared with—but could I still be a feminist if I wanted to be a wife and mom someday? Hill Collins' (2000) "standpoint epistemology" introduced me to the notion of intersectionality and how complex and nuanced identity is—a concept that had been discussed earlier by Crenshaw (1991). Hill Collins (2000) uncovered that I had been sold a particular brand of feminism, White feminism, which constrained my understanding. She and Anzaldúa introduced me to "theories of the flesh" (Moraga & Anzaldúa, 1983). My doctoral program, and Dr. Chawla specifically, gave me the foundation upon which my intellectual career would be raised: the theories of intersectional feminism and the notions of identity politics, colonization, narrative, and performance.

Much of graduate school, for me, was also about learning how to pretend to be a faculty member. I taught, I read, I wrote, I did service. The real scuffle was really trying to convince students (and my colleagues and even myself at times) that I had the same qualifications as someone who looked the part: old White dudes who wore tweed jackets with elbow patches. I will never be that, nor do I want to be. As Lorde (1984) famously put it, "the master's tools will never dismantle the master's house." However, graduate school helped me gain power and access to learn who the master is and what he does. Even more paramount, I learned his performance.

Learning How to Posture as a Professor

By the time I was finishing my dissertation and on the job market for tenure-track positions, I had a lot of exposure to different types of professors. As a student of communication and now a scholar of performance,[4] I had a habit of noticing how we "do" human behavior. Most, although not all professors, enact these consistent quirks, I discerned. It was as if there is this secret script that academics have to learn in order to perform.

The academic performance seems to involve a claw gesture with an index finger and a thumb, and the professor twists this claw back and forth while he or she talks. Professors often turn statements into questions, by attaching the word, "right?" at the end. Female professors don't change their names when they get married because that would signal they are not "real" feminists. When professors discuss summer plans, they include traveling to another country, but they mention it casually as if they are as familiar with the place as they are with the grocery store. But not just any grocery store—professors shop at artisanal, small grocery stores that have things like Fair Trade whole coffee beans and gluten-free crackers from Great Britain. When one finally becomes a professor, never again can they eat at McDonald's or any fast food—in fact—they have to act like they're disgusted by it. Bonus if they become vegetarian, but not vegan, because being vegan isn't "sustainable" enough. Professors have to say simple things in ways that make them sound more complicated than they actually are, like "the ways in which" instead of "the way" or "problematic" instead of "it's a problem." Being a professor has a whole dialect and way of being—a very tightly-controlled, exclusive script.

The professor script illustrates the powerful ways that race, gender, and class matter, even when and where they are not supposed to, like the supposedly liberal spaces of academia (Correspondents of the New York Times, 2005; Allen, 2011). Academia is not the antidote to Foucault's (1978/1990) "network of power relations," which professors teach their students about. It is the very reflection of that network. Learning how to be a professor, for me, has been observing and decoding how White, middle- and upper-class people live, work, think, eat, and teach.

Once I secured a tenure-track position, I reasoned, I would never act like that. I would never do the claw, and nothing would come between me and Taco Bell; I was raised on cinnamon twists. However, before I could resist the social forces of assimilation within academia, I had to get my foot through the door. So I played the game; I wore the Hillary Clinton pantsuit and my most "conservative" earrings and shoes, I spoke as "professionally" as I could muster, and I even threw in some highly skilled and thoroughly timed faux laughs. It must have worked, because I secured a tenure-track job just as I was finishing my dissertation.

Being a First-Generation, Latinx Professor

As a first-generation, Latinx assistant professor at Oakland University, I continue to battle all of the struggles I have discussed: the double isolation, imposter syndrome, subtle racism, classism, and even some overt discrimination. Just as the title of the book suggests, I, too, am *Presumed Incompetent* (Gutiérrez y Muhs, Niemann, Gonzáles, & Harris, 2012) all too often by my colleagues and students. During the first few weeks of class, I had to do a tremendous amount of academic posturing in order to earn the respect that is simply given to older and Whiter faculty members. In a conversation with one of my colleagues, I expressed some guilt about being hired over an adjunct faculty member who had been teaching at the university for a number of years. In an attempt to assuage that guilt, she assured me that I was "well-qualified" for the position and not the "affirmative action hire or anything." I had never suspected that I was, until then.

When I found the text *Presumed Incompetent*, I was partly relieved and partly enraged by the fact that the struggles I had faced were so widely shared by other female faculty of color (Gutiérrez y Muhs, et al., 2012). Thirty chapters articulated the anguish that I had experienced with students, colleagues, the tenure and promotion process, and just the field of academia in general. When Niemann (2012) cautioned that faculty of color are "vulnerable to the effects of tokenism, racism, stigmatization and stereotype threat" (p. 351), I could recall countless moments in my academic career that so perfectly exemplified all of those concepts. I realized it's not just me, it's not something I'm doing wrong, nor is it that I don't belong; it's the result of a profession that has yet to forcefully confront White male supremacy and elitism, although the liberal bastions think they have (Chang, 2012).

What is special about me, what makes me even more of a "minority" and "marginal," is the very fact that *I* am here and writing this chapter, as a college professor. According to the Census' Report on Educational Attainment, I'm part of less than five percent of Latinas who have an advanced degree (Ryan & Bauman, 2016). I would argue that small number is not so much an illustration of a culture that "doesn't value education," but more emblematic of a culture that is preoccupied with fighting for basic human rights. Recently I read that only six percent of college faculty are Black and Latinx (House, 2017). I have also been the youngest tenure-track faculty member in my department for the past six years. I am a first generation, low-income, college student of color who made it all the way to and through a PhD program, *gracias a Dios* (and countless others)!

I am also a living reminder that the McNair Scholars Program helps change the lives of first-generation, low-income, underrepresented students everyday.[5] It is important to understand that TRIO Programs and other programs funded by the Department of Education are under siege. Elected officials must work to save such important programs that help people like me academically succeed.

Advice to Students From and On the Same Path

Now that I'm here, it would be negligent not to share my experiences and lessons, in my own code, with other students who come from similar modest roots. I wish I had known that being kind of lonely and feeling like an imposter was part of the deal in academia (Boyd, 2012). Family and friends might not understand nor support your decision to commit yourself to education. From my own experiences as a FGCS and coming from a mostly poor Mexican-American family, I learned that getting a degree didn't count as "hard work," nor is my success as valued because I will never make any "real money." I cannot afford to "take care of" the expenses of the elderly in my family or sponsor relatives in Mexico to come to the United States, like is culturally expected of those who "make it." In contrast, degrees never leave you or lay you off. *Pero por otro lado*, it is also important to remember the academic world was built for and by the White bourgeoisie, as West (1993–1994) puts it. If you're neither, learn to take comfort in solitude, books, and knowledge.

Lately, I've noticed a trend in complaints between and amongst my academic colleagues about how "entitled" our students are. These same colleagues question why I haven't bought a house yet or why I don't send my baby to daycare full time. One of my colleagues advised me to "just borrow $30,000 dollars or so for a down payment from your parents" to afford a house. Middle- and upper-class White people get to find solidarity, unified by a sense of entitlement. The higher up I went in my education, the more "special" I was and the more insular my world became, and this is a reality for most professors of color and FGCS. I draw comfort, however, from the recognition that it was harder and lonelier for the Black and brown women in academia who came before me, like my celebrity heroes, Gloria Anzaldúa (1987) and Patricia Hill Collins (2000).

If there exists a community designed to support you on your campus—a minority student services' office, a TRIO program like the McNair Scholars Program or Upward Bound, a historically Black or Latinx or Asian Greek organization, or a resource group for faculty of color—seek them out and lean on them. The American myth of meritocracy brainwashes us to believe idea that one earns their wealth and income through one's own hard work and sheer determination, which research has continuously debunked (Langston, 1988; Correspondents of the New York Times, 2005). No one becomes successful all on his or her own. Those who have been able to find a sliver of success like myself know we owe it to our mentors to reach the hand back and help others up, *P'adelante!*[6]

The sacrifices made and the dedication that Ms. Jackson and Lynn Curry, Drs. Chavez, Withers, and Chawla invested in me doesn't end with me. Whenever I have a student of color or a student who has identified themself as a FGCS, I make it a priority to tell them that I'm invested in their success. I could never be as bold with a student as Dr. Chavez was with me, and I regret that because of the impact he had on the course of my undergraduate career. However, I do keep in the forefront of my mind those whom I am accountable to, with, and for, and they are the reason that I perform all of the "invisible labor" that faculty of color often have to do (Williams June, 2015). In academia, invisible labor is all the extra work that professors of color do that doesn't count or isn't valued by the institution, like writing letters of recommendation, informally mentoring students, or excessive contact hours. I try to be especially available and attentive (before, during, and after class) to my students of color who might be FGCS and/or from a working-class background because they might need me to be available for the personal and the academic constraints they experience. I oftentimes remind those students that they, too, aren't just special because they are "minorities," but because of all they have to learn and potentially overcome in order to be inside and stay in the college classroom.

The final thing that I advise students who might be from or on a similar path is to know that you are also accountable to you. Some of what I claimed within these pages might seem to suggest that first-generation, underrepresented students have to impersonate the White bourgeoisie in order to thrive in academia (West, 1993–1994). That isn't so—you don't have to pretend to be someone you are not. *Sin embargo*, for the sake of transparency and critical reflexivity, I did have to learn the game in order to play. I had to learn what the academic script was and how to identify it in order to have the opportunity to subvert it. By knowing what the academic script is, I saved myself from slipping into behaviors and languages that serve to exclude or isolate working-class brown folks. This book and others like it are powerful reminders for first-generation faculty of color to be authentic about where we began and how we speak and write, whom we want to reach, and where we would like to see academia go (Gutiérrez y Muhs et al., 2012; Jehangir et al., 2015).

I am special, not in the way it signifies in the era of the notorious millennial, but in the way one imagines academia. As a first-generation, low-income, Latinx college student turned college professor, my image and narrative is not as common as I would like it to be. Although I'd never be audacious enough to call myself a "celebrity" like I did my own professors, I do think responsibly about my potential to be so for students. I believe it is my burden and privilege to represent what it means to be a working-class, first-generation academic, and Latinx in a space where there are so few of us. It is my responsibility to fight for similar opportunities, resources, and experiences for the students who come from similar "special" backgrounds.

Notes

1. For a deeper discussion on how personal narratives resist the infiltration of neoliberal ideologies in academia, see Jones and Calafell (2012).
2. This is a reference to Scott's (1990) notion of the "hidden transcript." In his monograph, "Domination and the Arts of Resistance," Scott exposes the notion of a private dialogue that the powerful have about their practices and goals, which allow them to maintain their power. Conversely, he discusses the way that the subordinate class uses a private code to mock the ruling class and as a means to invoke everyday resistance. I try to subvert traditional academic texts by inserting my own subjective code as a means to disrupt the monotony of academic convention.
3. This is a reference to a hip hop song, "Type of Way" (Lamar, 2013). This song purposely resists naming feelings to demonstrate the complexity and rawness of emotions one feels when encountering difficult situations like the ones Rich Homie Quan identifies within the lyrics.
4. For more information about performance studies, see *The Sage Handbook of Performance Studies,* edited by Madison and Hamera (2006) and Conquergood (2002).
5. Any first-generation college student who is interested in a PhD program should look for a McNair Scholars Program (see www.ed.gov/programs).
6. Mentoring is thoroughly explored as a salient factor in ensuring the success of female faculty color in the edited book, *Presumed Incompetent* (Gutiérrez y Muhs et al., 2012).

References

Allen, B. J. (2011). *Difference matters: Communicating social identity.* Long Grove, IL: Waveland Press.

Anzaldúa, G. (1987). *Borderlands: The new mestiza.* San Francisco, CA: Aunt Lute Books.

Bourdieu, P. (1979). *Distinction: A social critique of the judgment of taste.* Boston, MA: Harvard University Press.

Boyd, B. A. (2012). Sharing our gifts. In G. Gutiérrez y Muhs, Y. F. Niemann, C. G. González, & A. P. Harris (Eds.), *Presumed incompetent: The intersections of race and class for women in academia* (pp. 277–282). Louisville, CO: University Press of Colorado.

Boylorn, R. M., & Orbe, M. P. (Eds.). (2014). *Critical autoethnography: Intersecting cultural identities in everyday life.* Walnut Creek, CA: Left Coast Press.

Cassuto, L. (2013, July 1). Ph.D. attrition: How much is too much? *The Chronicle of Higher Education.* Retrieved from http://www.chronicle.com/article/PhDAttrition-How-Much-Is/140045/

Chang, G. (2012). Where's the violence?: The promise and perils of teaching women of color studies. In G. Gutiérrez y Muhs, Y. F. Niemann, C. G. González, & A. P. Harris (Eds.), *Presumed incompetent: The intersections of race and class for women in academia,* (pp. 198–218). Louisville, CO: University Press of Colorado.

Chawla, D., & Holman Jones, S. (Eds.) (2015). *Storying home: Place, identity, and exile.* London: Lexington Books.

Cisneros, S. (1991). *The house on Mango Street.* New York, NY: Vintage Contemporaries.

Clance, P. R., & Imes, S. A. (1978). The imposter phenomenon in high achieving women: Dynamics and therapeutic intervention. *Psychotherapy Theory, Research & Practice, 15*(3), 241–247. http://dx.doi.org/10.1037/h0086006

Collier, G. A., & Lowery Quaratiello, E. (1994). *Basta! Land & the zapatista rebellion in Chiapas.* Oakland, CA: Food First Books.

Conquergood, D. (2002). Performance studies: Interventions and radical research. *TDR: The Drama Review, 46*(2), 145–156.

Correspondents of the New York Times. (2005). *Class matters.* New York, NY: Times Books.

Crenshaw, K. (1991). Mapping the margins: Intersectionality, identity politics, and violence against women of color. *Stanford Law Review, 43*(6), 1241–1299.

Demby, G. (2013, April 8). How code-switching explains the world. *National Public Radio.* Retrieved from http://www.npr.org/sections/codeswitch/2013/04/08/176064688/how-codeswitching-explains-the-world

Du Bois, W. E. B. (1903). *The souls of black folk.* New York, NY: Bantam Classic.

Fanon, F. (1952). *Black skin, white masks.* New York, NY: Grove Press.

Foucault, M. (1978/1990). *The history of sexuality.* New York, NY: Vintage Books.

Grant, J. (1993). *Fundamental feminism.* New York, NY: Routledge.

Gutiérrez y Muhs, G., Niemann, Y. F., González, C. G., & Harris, A. P. (Eds). (2012). *Presumed incompetent: The intersections of race and class for women in academia.* Louisville, CO: University Press of Colorado.

Hill Collins, P. (2000). *Black feminist thought.* NY: Routledge.

House, J. (2017, November 27). How faculty of color hurt their careers helping universities with diversity. *Diverse Issues in Higher Education.* Retrieved from http://diverseeducation.com/article/105525/

Housel, T. H., & Harvey, V. L. (2009). *The invisibility factor: Administrators and faculty reach out to first-generation students.* Boca Raton, FL: BrownWalker Press.

Jehangir, R. R., Stebleton, M. J., & Deenanath, V. (2015). *An exploration of intersecting identities of first-generation, low-income students (Research Report No. 5).* Columbia, SC: University of South Carolina, National Resource Center for The First-Year Experience and Students in Transition.

Jones, R. G., & Calafell, B. M. (2012). Contesting neoliberalism through critical pedagogy, intersectional reflexivity, and personal narrative: Queer tales of academia. *Journal of Homosexuality, 59*(7), 957–981. http://doi.org/10.1080/00918369.2012.699835

Koerner, K. E. F. (1992). The Sapir-Whorf Hypothesis: A preliminary history and a bibliographical essay. *Journal of Linguistic Anthropology, 2*(2), 173–198. https://doi.org/10.1525/jlin.1992.2.2.173

Lamar, D. (2013). Type of way. *On still going in: Reloaded.* New York, NY: Def Jam Records.

Langston, D. (1988). Tired of playing Monopoly? In J. Cochran, D. Langston, & C. Woodward (Eds.), *Changing our power: An introduction to women's studies* (pp. 338–343). Dubuque, IA: Kendall Hunt Publishing Company.

Lorde, A. (1984). The master's tools will never dismantle the master's house. In C. Moraga & G. Anzaldúa (Eds.), *This bridge called my back: Writings by radical women of color* (pp. 94–101). New York, NY: Kitchen Table Press.

Love Ramirez, T., & Blay, Z. (2017, April 7). Why people are using the term 'Latinx.' *Huffington Post.* Retrieved from http://www.huffingtonpost.com/entry/whypeople-are-using-the-term-latinx_us_57753328e4b0cc0fa136a159

Madison, S. D., & Hamera, J. (Eds.) (2006). *The Sage handbook of performance studies.* Thousand Oaks, CA: Sage Publications.

McIntosh, P. (1990). White privilege: Unpacking the invisible knapsack. *Independent School, 49*(2), 191–196.

Mercado Thornton, R. (2013). First, second, third person speaking: A generational approach to understanding immigration. *Journal of Latino/Latin American Studies, 5*(1), 2–11. doi: 10.18085/llas.5.1.t552h54237402535

Mercado Thornton, R. (2015a). Co-authoring lives: A tale of two friends. *Departures in Critical Qualitative Research, 4*(4), 33–51. doi: 10.1525/dcqr.2015.4.4.33

Mercado Thornton, R. (2015b). Motown magic and/in haunted hollers: From one Othered America to another. In Devika Chawla & Stacey Holman Jones (Eds.), *Stories of home: Place, identity, exile* (pp. 85–104). Lanham, MD: Lexington Books.

Moraga, C., & Anzaldúa, G. (Eds.). (1983). *This bridge called my back: Writings by radical women of color.* New York, NY: Kitchen Table Press.

Niemann, Y. F. (2012). The making of a token: A case study of stereotype threat, stigma, racism, and tokenism in the academe. In G. Gutiérrez y Muhs, Y. F. Niemann, C. G. González, & A. P. Harris (Eds.), *Presumed incompetent: The intersections of race and class for women in academia* (pp. 336–355). Louisville, CO: University Press of Colorado.

Orbe, M. P. (2004). Negotiating multiple identities within multiple frames: An analysis of first-generation college students. *Communication Education, 53*(2), 131–149. doi: 10.1080/0363452041000168240 1

Pozas, R. (1962). Juan the Chamula: An ethnological re-creation of the life of a Mexican Indian. (L. Kemp, Trans.). Berkeley, CA: University of California Press.

Provitera McGlynn, A. (2011). *Envisioning equity: Educating and graduating low-income, first-generation, and minority college students.* Madison, WI: Atwood Publishing.

Rubin, L. (1996). *The transcendent child: Tales of triumph over the past.* New York, NY: Basicbooks.

Ryan, C. L., & Bauman, K. (2016). *Education attainment in the United States, 2015: Population characteristics, current population report.* Washington, DC: United States Census Bureau. Retrieved from https://www.census.gov/content/dam/Census/library/publications/2016/demo/p20 -578.pdf

Scott, J. C. (1990). *Domination and the arts of resistance.* New Haven, CT: Yale University Press.

The McNair Scholars Program. (2016). Embrace his legacy. Create your own. Retrieved from http://mcnairscholars.com/

Vanderford, M. L., & Smith, D. H. (1996). *The silicone breast implant story: Communication and uncertainty.* Mahwah, NJ: Lawrence Erlbaum Associates.

Vonnegut, K. (1962). *Mother night.* New York City: Gold Medal Books.

West, C. (1993–1994). The dilemma of the black intellectual. *The Journals of Blacks in Higher Education, 2*(Winter), 59–67.

Williams June, A. (2015, November 8). The invisible labor of minority professors. *The Chronicle of Higher Education.* Retrieved from https://www.chronicle.com/article/The-Invisible-Labor-of/234098

Section Two: Considering Invisible Marginalities

7. "If We Had Used Our Heads, We Would Be Set." Intersections of Family, First-in-the-Family Status, and Growing Up in Working-Class America

Teresa Heinz Housel

I want to be able to say, as so many single mothers have told me, that I knew they would be fine, that the children were my life, my joy, all I'd ever need. If the kids remember that time at all, I'm sure they would see me as full of strength, love, and courage. I had to be, for them. But in truth, I have never been so scared and unsure of the future as I was then. My only guidance was that small inner voice.
—Michael Evangelista (2003, p. 66), a single father of three

Introduction

Because my father, Clifford Heinz, passed away in October 2005, I cannot ask him what it was like to single-handedly raise two daughters. However, one of my earliest memories suggests that he would have shared Evangelista's (2003) perspective. In this childhood memory, my 3-year-old self crept past my parents' opened bedroom door at dusk. Peering inside, I glimpsed my father's outlined body as he knelt before the bed, hands clasped in silent prayer.

I didn't know it at the time, but my 34-year-old father was desperately trying to save everything that was collapsing around him. His tire company employer's impending strike would cause him to declare bankruptcy and lose our family home the next year. Meanwhile, my equally young mother had recently left my father to pursue an affair with a married man. She took almost everything in the house with her. She left the sofa, television and stereo, and my parents' bed that my father, older sister, and I slept on every night.

It is almost unfathomable to reconcile this memory with the adult I am today. As a lecturer at a major New Zealand research university, my similarly professionally-employed spouse and I live in a quiet suburb in one of the most beautiful places in the world. My life's script predicted otherwise, but through hard work, the kindness of mentors, careful decision-making, and a lot of luck, I am here.

This essay examines the complex intersections between my identities as a first-generation college student (FGCS) (or first-in-the-family student) who was also the daughter of a single father in a rural working-class family during the 1970s and '80s. Drawing from Dykins Callahan's (2008) critical autoethnography of her experiences as a poor and White first-generation student, this essay approaches my family's everyday practices as "'cultural performances'" that "constitute ways of being in communities in specific historical and sociocultural moments" (Denzin, 2003, p. 265, quoted in Dykins Callahan, 2008, p. 353). Critical autoethnography "allows narrative explorations of an individual's lived experiences within the contexts of her cultural and historical movement, revealing power struggles within that culture and reflexively engaging the individual's participation in maintaining or opposing those power relations" (Dykins Callahan, 2008, p. 353). In this way, this methodology helps pinpoint the intersections between my intersecting identities as a FGCS in larger cultural-historical contexts. This essay acknowledges that people's identities are fragmented, complex, and overlapping. Although not all identities may be salient in a person at any given time, they nonetheless influence each another across time and place.

To examine my intersecting identities, this essay first discusses my family's educational and financial background in light of how the post-World War II economic boom impacted many White working-class families in America. At the same time, the country's rapidly increasing divorce rate in the late 1960s and '70s, alongside gender-role shifts as many women entered the workforce, meant that more fathers gained child custody than ever before. As a FGCS daughter of a working-class single father, my father had little support in a culture that marginalized single fathers and their children. This emotional isolation, coupled with my family's working-class orientation and lack of higher education, both predicted and shaped my lack of middle-class social and cultural capital as a FGCS at an elite private liberal arts college.

Blue Collar Families With Middle-Class Dreams in Post-World War II America

My older sister sometimes remarks that it's a good thing I don't remember my parents' divorce. In one of my few memories from 1975, I entered my parents' bedroom and nearly walked onto glass shards from broken framed family photos that blanketed the floor. My mother cowered in a corner, crying, while my father held her. My parents had been fighting again about money and her on-going affair, and in white-hot anger they flung everything they could grab at each other.

Not until many years later did I understand what enormous financial anxieties they faced in the mid-1970s' economic downturn. When my parents married in the mid-1960s, their economic futures looked bright in booming post-war America. Neither parent attended college, but they didn't have to because many White high school graduates could easily find a well-paying factory job with insurance benefits and pension (Cherlin, 2014). In contrast, recent studies on single fathers report that single fathers without college degrees have significantly lower incomes and less assets than college-educated parents (Zhan & Pandey, 2004, p. 669). After graduating high school and completing military service, my father found a stable, full-time unionized job at The Goodyear Tire & Rubber Company in Akron, Ohio in the mid-1960s. He used a VA loan to purchase a modest ranch-style home in a quiet rural area in northeastern Ohio. My parents fully expected that my mother would stay home with the children while my father earned a comfortable living wage.

My parents joined many of their peers in quickly acquiring material possessions in their aspirational emulations of middle-class America (Schor, 2003). As Schor (2003) points out, by the 1970s television became an important source for information and consumer cues as it portrayed the "lifestyles of the rich and upper middle class," and inflated "the viewer's perceptions of what others have" (p. 185). This conspicuous consumption negatively impacted the working- and lower-classes, who devoted increasing amounts of their wages to goods and services as their struggled to achieve the "good life," or "a comfortable, middle-class standard of living" (Schor, 2003, p. 184). Over the next few years, like many young couples from poorer backgrounds (hooks, 2000), my parents purchased shiny new things—cars, a color television, furniture, and stereos—in the consumer-driven society of post-War War II America. My father's factory initially pay sustained them, but by the 1970s, the purchasing power of real wages (after inflation has been taken into account) were flat or falling as the costs of housing, healthcare, and education also increased in America (Desilver, 2014; Schor, 2003, pp. 184, 186; Tupy, 2016). When my father's wages no longer paid their bills, they financed expenses for dining out, gas, department stores, and furniture with credit cards, which flooded the market in the 1960s and '70s, with low-income households as an easy marketing target (Greenbaum & Rubinstein, 2011; Schor, 2003, p. 187). I can still recall my father's description of his wallet bulging with credit cards. To help maintain this consumption and meet rising living costs, the number of women entering professional and blue-collar jobs rapidly increased between 1970 and 1982 (Guilder, 1986; Hacker, 1984). My mother mirrored this trend when she began waitressing at a truck-stop restaurant in the early 1970s. Meanwhile, my father pursued many money-making schemes: selling baseball cards at flea markets, stuffing envelopes, and trying to sell tiny pink plastic elephants that walked when you pulled a string. Their paycheck-to-paycheck habits that became permanent caused us all chronic anxiety and instability.

Because I rarely saw my mother after their divorce and my father passed away, I only know fragments of their relationship's demise. My adult self surmises my father's double factory shifts, frequent arguments over money, and little quality time together led my mother to be charmed by a charismatic married man who frequented the restaurant. By early 1976, she and the new man left their respective families to marry, leaving my father to start his new life as a single father with two young daughters in a near-empty house.

The Rise of Single-Father Families in America in the 1970s

Most states today have sex-blind custody laws (Grant, 1994), which help ensure that children are "placed with the parent who has the time, stability, and desire to be a responsible parent and good role model" (Grant, 1994, p. 16). Divorces were rare before the late nineteenth century, but fathers nearly always gained custody because children were considered his legal property (Grant, 1994). Fathers also often assumed care in earlier times because of maternal mortality. They usually had assistance from extended family, so it was rare that they parented alone (DeFrain & Eirick, 1981; Mendes, 1976). By the early twentieth century, both the courts and social services favored maternal custody. Organisations such as children's aid societies argued that it was in the children's best interests to live with their mother, and that fathers should gain custody only if the mother died or was too mentally or physically ill to parent (Grant, 1994).

When my father won custody in 1976, he joined a minority of divorced American fathers with custody at that time (custody defined as having primary responsibility for the children a majority of the time) (Greif, 1992, p. 565). There were fewer than 350,000 single-father families in the United States in the 1960s (Meyer & Garasky, 1993). In 1970, single-mother families comprised nearly 90% of the American single-parent population (Gillenkirk, 2000, p. 18), while there were 393,000 single fathers raising at least one child under age 18 (Kramer, Myhra, Zuiker, & Bauer, 2015, p. 23). However, traditional two-parent married households constituted 81% of all American households in 1970 (Kramer et al., 2015, p. 23).

No doubt reflecting the low numbers of American single fathers, research about them was scarce prior to the late 1990s. Eggebeen, Snyder, and Manning (1996) point out that studies historically included small, non-random convenience samples (Gersick, 1979; Risman, 1986, 1987; Risman & Park, 1988), samples in small geographic regions such as cities (Mendes, 1976), or larger samples involving support-group participants (Greif, 1985a). These primarily exploratory, descriptive studies mostly examined parenting styles (Bronte-Tinkew, Scott, & Lilja, 2010; Risman, 1986; Risman & Park, 1988), or why the fathers received custody (Greif, 1985a).

Though their numbers were still low compared to single-mother families, American single-father families increased in the 1970s (Eggebeen et al., 1996). Between 1970 and 1978, the number of single fathers (including widows) increased to 423,000 (U.S. Census Bureau, 1978; U.S. Census Bureau, 1970). This figure tripled to 1,351,000 by 1990 (Greif, 1992, pp. 565–566), and quintupled by 2003 (U.S. Census Bureau, 2003). As a comparison, between 1970–1990, the percentage of single mothers dropped to 86%, while the percentage of single fathers increased by about one-third to 14% (U.S. Department of Commerce, 1990). The number of children being raised by single fathers nearly tripled to 1,993,000 between 1970–1990, while the number of children raised by single mothers doubled to 13,874,000 (U.S. Department of Commerce, 1991). The statistics reflect how the number of single-father families has been increasing at a faster rate than single-mother families since 1970 (Bianchi, 1995; Brown, 2000; Zhan & Pandey, 2004;).

Key factors influenced the increasing rate of single fathers in the 1970s. Primarily, the U.S. experienced a dramatic increase in divorce rates in the 1970s with the introduction of no-fault divorces and reduced social stigma of divorce (DeFrain & Eirick, 1981; Eggebeen et al., 1996; History Cooperative, 2015; Zhan & Pandey, 2004). The changes to family structure created a new generation of so-called latchkey children in the U.S. like my sister and I

(Wallace, 2016). Non-marital childbearing also became more common in the 1970s and 1980s (Eggebeen et al., 1996).

Changing conceptions of fatherhood further influenced these trends. In contrast to the stereotype of the distant, breadwinning father of the 1960s and earlier, Baby Boomer fathers displayed greater interest in emotional nurturing and actively participating in their children's everyday activities (Napier, 1991). At the same time, women had more non-maternal options such as a career to define themselves, and public stigma decreased for non-custodial women (Greif & Pabst, 1988). Political movements for gender equality and gender-free laws in deciding custody arrangements also made it easier for American men to gain custody (Bartz & Witcher, 1978; Coles, 2009; De-Frain & Eirick, 1981; Keshet & Rosenthal, 1976; Mendes, 1976).

With such social and political changes in 1970s' American society, fathers like mine received custody because judges deemed them to be the best parents (DeFrain & Eirick, 1981, p. 266; Ziol-Guest, 2009). My mother's life with her new partner was unstable at best. My sister tells me that we stayed with one of his ex-wives for a while. At one point, she moved my sister and I into an apartment that they shared. I slept on a plastic lawn chair because they had little furniture. My sister missed so much school that she nearly repeated a grade. Her new partner also soon turned out to be mentally and physically abusive.

Although family courts in the 1970s were more amenable to awarding custody to fathers, courts still favored the mother (Mendes, 1976; Meyer & Garasky, 1993, p. 85). In the context of Mendes' (1976) study on custody-seeking fathers, my father was an "aggressive seeker" because he obtained custody by "determined and forceful action" (p. 309). My father bitterly fought for custody. My father's experience mirrors Gersick's (1979) early comparison study of divorced custodial and noncustodial fathers, which found that custodial fathers "had often been motivated to seek custody because of feeling wronged or betrayed by the wife" (see Coles, 2015, p. 153). Furious that my mother cheated and recognizing that her new partner was abusive, my father waged an extended court battle over many months and hired a private detective to find my sister and me. The progressive judge was so persuaded by the case's intensity that he interviewed my 10-year-old sister about where she wanted to live. He awarded my father custody, telling my mother that her situation was no place to raise children, but my father received no child support or alimony.

Shortly after my father passed away, my sister and I found a diary that he kept during the custody battle. He apparently followed his attorney's advice to detail my mother's actions for court evidence. As I read the entries, I was astounded to realize that my father navigated the agonizing legal process on his own. The custody-seeking fathers in Crowley's (2006) study turned to fathers' rights support groups when their custody cases and complex family law overwhelmed them; however, my father had no community or institutional support. At one point, he approached my grandfather, who advised him to "keep it together and don't start drinking."

Interestingly, Mendes (1976) suggests that aggressive seekers like my father tend to be strongly motivated by their own traumatic childhood experiences (p. 309), and many are better fathers that those who are "assenters" (Hanson, 1985), or who end up with the children because the mother didn't want custody. My father endured his own parents' bitter divorce in the 1940s, and was raised by his grandmother after his mother abandoned the family. When I once asked him why he fought so hard for custody, he told me that he "wanted to give us a home." He knew what it is like not to have one.

Financially devastated by Goodyear's strike and the court costs, my father lost our house to foreclosure in 1977. We moved to an apartment nearby for a few years until he financially regrouped. I have a few memories of the well-kept brick duplex and the kindly elderly couple who lived near door. In June 1979, when we moved from the apartment to a modest rural ranch home where I mostly grew up, around one in every 10 single parents was a male (DeFrain & Eirick, 1981, p. 265).

Navigating Family and Education on Our Own

It is tempting to solely frame my educational experiences by my FGCS identity. Researchers identify how FGCS frequently lack reading, writing, and oral communication skills, which can translate into poor retention rates once they arrive at college (Reid & Moore, 2008; Ryan & Glenn, 2002/2003). FGCS take part in fewer extracurricular organizations, campus cultural programs, internships, and career networking activities than their peers from middle- and upper-class economic backgrounds (Glenn, 2004; Moschetti & Hudley, 2008). FGCS typically have lower levels of parental involvement in their education and carry the burden of financial worries (Bui, 2002; McCarron & Inkelas, 2006). Moreover, many FGCS feel socially, ethnically, and emotionally marginalized on campus (Bui, 2002; Francis & Miller, 2008; Lundberg, Schreiner, Hovaguimian, & Miller, 2007).

I encountered similar challenges as I journeyed from my small town's local public schools to a highly selective private college. Like many FGCS, I largely navigated the path to college on my own as I took college preparatory classes, applied to colleges and arranged campus visits, and completed financial aid forms. Because I was a stubborn and resourceful student, I largely overcame many of my initial academic adjustments to Oberlin College's rigorous courses within a couple semesters, but my transition to the school's upper-middle-class, intellectual culture was more jarring and continued in waves with new situations.

While being first-generation certainly impacted my college experience, coming from a single-father family was the most influential framework through which I perceived and lived my education. I was always acutely aware that we were different from other families. Teachers and other parents just didn't know how to interact with us. In first grade, a well-meaning teacher announced in front of the class that I could make a card for my father while the others wrote Mother's Day cards. My friends' parents wouldn't let their daughters spend the night in a home without a female adult present. Classmates snickered at the contents of my packed lunches, which included submarine sandwiches and chocolate bars that my father purchased at a local convenience store on the way home from work. Later on, in college, I rarely discussed my family with classmates because I was so tired of explaining why my mother didn't raise me.

Not only did my classmates and teachers treat me differently, but I also *felt* different. As Nieto (1982) points out, "The role of single father in contemporary American society is one for which norms, values, and performance expectations are still lacking" (p. 474). This was especially true in the 1970s and early 1980s. At this time, social, psychological, and financial support from government agencies targeted single mothers, whose situation was "more readily accepted and less likely to be viewed as aberrant" (Nieto, 1982, p. 474). It was also far more common for boys to live in father-only families (Meyer & Garasky, 1993). Mendes (1976) argues that single fathers need individual and family counselling, and on-going social support to manage the household, discipline children, and confront sexual development (especially for daughters). My father had no institutional support other than our church, which offered kindness and occasional meals, but really didn't know how to relate to his situation.

As I place my family's situation in its larger cultural-historical context, without question we possessed privilege in being part of White majority culture and having a stably employed father. Like many White single-father families, and particularly those with slightly older fathers (near and above age 40) who worked full time, we were not poor, unlike many female-headed families and single mothers in a society with gender-based labor discrimination (Bianchi, Subaiya, & Kahn, 1999; Kramer et al., 2015; Meyer & Garasky, 1993, p. 450; Ziol-Guest, 2009; Zhan & Pandey, 2004). Single-mother families also face other structural and individual challenges such as non-enforcement of child support and inadequate public benefits (McLanahan & Booth, 1989; McLanahan & Sandefur, 1994). Custodial fathers prior to the 1980s tended to have higher educations and incomes, prestigious jobs, and were White and middle-aged (Meyer & Garasky, 1993, p. 74). My father didn't attend college, but he worked full-time at his unionized job with generous health care benefits and pension.

My Whiteness also gave me educational privilege. Lillard and Gerner (1999) point out that "educational attainment provides the central vehicle through which upward mobility can occur," though "educational researchers have long been concerned about the extent to which higher education has been accessible to all students regardless of socioeconomic and racial characteristics" (p. 706). My small country schools were free from violence such as gangs, and although I felt socially ostracized, I didn't endure institutionalized racism. I could freely participate in extra-curricular activities, compete in acting and speech contests at other schools, attend summer academic camps for gifted students, and visit a nearby private liberal arts college's cultural events without fear of racial harassment or discrimination. Although I frequently felt emotionally and socially alone, my place in larger White majority culture made my access to education easier.

Through the framework of being raised by a single father, I approached my education with scrappy grit that mirrored my father's endurance through a hard custody battle and raising daughters alone. Our aloneness, in fact, gave me the resilience that I needed to educationally succeed. We had mostly teenaged babysitters until we moved to our rural home in 1979, just before I entered second grade. Like many children of single fathers, I spent many hours alone after school and during summers while my father worked (De-Frain & Eirick, 1981, p. 267; McLanahan & Casper, 1995; Mendes, 1976). Similar to Greif's (1985b) findings, I got ready for school on my own from a very young age. After school and on weekends, my father tasked my sister with "parentifying" responsibilities of cooking, cleaning, and babysitting me (Greif, 1992, p. 571; Greif, 1985c). Our father was usually alone, too: Other than his bowling league, he had little or no social life (DeFrain & Eirick, 1981, p. 266). He also dated infrequently. Although Bronte-Tinkew et al. (2010) suggest that unpartnered single fathers can devote more attention to their children, my father was often overwhelmed with working double shifts while managing the household (DeFrain & Eirick, 1981, p. 268).

Being without parental supervision might have propelled me into school absenteeism and other misbehaviors, as often occurs with children of single-father families (Bronte-Tinkew et al., 2010; Carlson & Corcoran, 2001; Demuth & Brown, 2004; Downey, Ainsworth-Darnell, & Dufur, 1998). In my case, our rural location combined with my grit, aloneness, and natural curiosity to be catalysts for learning. I had few or no avenues to get into trouble because farms and few neighbors surrounded us. If the situation helped create or suited my personality, I don't know for certain, but I intellectually thrived in the quiet environment without a mother to monitor my activities. I was an introverted, highly imaginative, and sensitive child, so I used the time alone to do schoolwork. I discovered books after a friend's mother took me to get a public library card. Shortly thereafter, I realized that I loved to write stories, too. I spent many humid summer days at our kitchen table writing the stories down into books that I hand-stitched together. With my father often away at work, no mother to structure activities, few neighbor friends, and countless hours to think, my mind became my best friend.

Educational Attainment of Children From Single-Father Families

Of the research dedicated to single-parent families, some studies examine children's educational outcomes. As single parents became common in the 1970s and 1980s, researchers began to examine family composition's impact on educational attainment (Haveman & Wolfe, 1994; Krein & Beller, 1988; McLanahan & Sandefur, 1994). Children from single-parent homes tend to have weaker future opportunities because they lack economic and social resources available in two-parent homes (McLanahan & Sandefur, 1994; Zhan & Pandey, 2004). These disparities exist between children of divorced and married parents across different income levels. Additionally, many welfare recipients are minority FGCS with divorced parents and low-income homes (Education Resources Institute, 1997, pp. 9, 12). Haveman and Wolfe (1994), similarly, found that the longer children are raised in a single-parent home, and particularly single-father families, the less likely they are to graduate from high school (see also Bronte-Tinkew et al., 2010). Children from single-parent homes are less likely to attend college, and particularly selective colleges, due to fewer financial resources and lack of parental involvement, among other factors (Lillard & Gerner, 1999).

A small subset of single-parent research examines children's educational attainment in single-father families. The single father's level of education is associated with higher income, positive child-rearing practices (Wright & Wright, 1976; Scheck & Emerick, 1976), and the child's future educational and occupational attainment (Blau & Duncan, 1967; Featherman & Hauser, 1978; Sewell & Hauser, 1975). Early studies on single fathers included small samples and no comparison groups, were exploratory, heavily qualitative and descriptive, and focused on single fathers who have been traditionally White, divorced (occasionally widowed), highly educated, and high-income with prestigious careers (Coles, 2015). These studies suggest that custodial fathers had the financial resources to battle the mother-biased courts. More recently, Zhan and Pandey's (2004) quantitative analysis of data from the 1993 Panel Study of Income Dynamics, a national survey that has followed 5,000 American families since 1968, similarly found that single fathers are more educated and have college degrees, have higher incomes, receive less child support and public assistance, and are more likely to be White (Zhan & Pandey, 2004, pp. 666–667). However, Hilton and Desrochers (2000) discuss how fathers with primary custody often experience high stress when they assume unfamiliar roles such as childcare that the mother may have previously handled (p. 60). Constant stress in homes disrupted by divorce can lead to children's poor educational outcomes (McLanahan, 1988).

Like many single parents, my father anxiously tried to be "provider, caretaker, and homemaker" (Hilton & Desrochers, 2000, p. 63; see also Hill & Hilton, 1999; Risman, 1987), and this anxiety transferred onto me. Unlike historically White single fathers with higher incomes and educations, my working-class father struggled to maintain our home and other expenses on his factory wage. My father's financial worries combined with his multiple familial roles to create many disagreements at home. We bickered because I did not understand why I had to bring store-bought cookies to class for my birthdays, while my classmates brought homemade baked goods. I hated that other parents wouldn't allow my friends to spend the night at my house, and transferred my anger onto my father. We argued about money, too: Starting in junior high, I needed transportation to after-school activities, but we only had one car that he used for work. In my junior year of high school, my father lost our home to foreclosure after his company had a partial shutdown and he fell behind on bills. I managed to sustain my grades as I moved between friends' homes to finish the school year. We found an apartment by my senior year, but at times I studied by candlelight because my father could not pay the electric bill. My father often rued his marriage's breakdown and the loss of his brief hold on the American Dream. "If we had used our heads, we would be set," he always remarked, shaking his head wearily as he remembered their home that would have been paid off years ago. Typical of many children raised within on-going stressful environments with family structure instability, or who have parents who ruminate and exhibit other anxious behaviors, I developed nervous tendencies that manifested as anxiety as an adult (Bronte-Tinkew et al., 2010, p. 1124; Musick & Mare, 2006).

Though my family's emotional and financial challenges correlated with the single-father research's findings, my educational attainment in being from a working-class family far exceeds their predictions. Some researchers suggest that children from single-custodial-father families across income levels tend to be less likely to graduate high school and have lower school engagement than children raised with single mothers or two parents (Downey et al., 1998; Garasky, 1995). For example, Ziol-Guest (2009) found that compared to married parents, single fathers spend less on their children's education, toys and publications, and more on eating out, tobacco, and alcohol.

My experience was quite different. My father did not know how to help me apply for college, complete financial aid forms, or choose high school and college courses, but his encouragement translated into a home filled with books, magazines, newspapers, and encyclopedias. In fact, he always encouraged me to test out my ideas, such as forming a community writers' group while I was still a teenager and contacting the local newspaper editor to ask for a job writing monthly youth columns. Few studies have historically examined single-fathers' parenting behaviors or involvement because they mostly focus on the effects of the children's separation from the mother (Bronte-Tinkew et al., 2010; Grief, 1985b). However, Hilton and Devall (1998) argue that single fathers tend to be more adventurous parents than their single-mother counterparts because they "allow their children to participate in the activities of their peers and try activities on their own" (cited in Bronte-Tinkew et al., 2010, p. 1110). Mirroring this research, my father encouraged me to go after my goals, no matter how far-fetched. His support translated into financial support even though money was usually tight. Hilton and Desrochers (2000) discuss how many single parents can't afford to invest in their children, such as through summer camp and club activities (p. 64). When I asked my father if I could attend summer sports camps and academic institutes for gifted students, he always found the money, somehow.

My father's willingness to provide educational resources at home and support extra-curricular opportunities encouraged me to learn. Many researchers indicate that having emotional and cognitive stimulation in the home, and having educational items such as books help predict positive school readiness, cognitive outcomes, and years of educational attainment (Teachman, 1987). Even if single fathers do not spend as much as married fathers on educational resources, previous research suggests that they have spent more time than married biological fathers and stepfathers in helping their children with homework, reading to their children, and taking part in leisure activities (Cooksey & Fondell, 1996; Hawkins, Amato, & King, 2006). These activities are in addition to the father's performance of traditionally mother-led roles, such as talking about the children's social life and problems (Hawkins et al., 2006). Constant parental encouragement is crucial for educational attainment regardless if the child has single or partnered parents. Saracho (2007) points out that when parents tell their children that they expect them to academically succeed, discuss school, and also make books and other reading material available at home, they communicate their value for education. These interactions are especially important for adolescents, when children might engage in misbehaviors such as taking drugs and truancy (Bronte-Tinkew et al., 2010). However, single fathers who exhibit parental involvement can mitigate the negative effects of living in a single-parent home (Bronte-Tinkew et al., 2010, p. 1111; Fass & Tubman, 2002).

Research on single fathers' involvement in their children's education confirms my experiences. Santos and Alfred (2016) used qualitative interviews to examine Latino single fathers' involvement in their children's literacy development. The fathers all balanced full-time work with caregiving and kept various literacy materials in the home, ranging from pamphlets, library books, to video games. The researchers found the fathers had varying amounts of time for their children's reading and learning while they juggled many roles as single parents. Despite the father's challenges, the fathers engaged in activities that supported their children's learning (Santos & Alfred, 2016, p. 13). Similarly, after work my father always brought home daily three newspapers for me to read. He also subscribed to many news, nature, and cultural magazines. By sixth grade, as I ate my dinner of instant ramen noodles alone after school, I read the newspaper before moving on to library books and then schoolwork. My home's rich linguistic environment communicated that learning was both fun and never-ending. I carried this enthusiastic passion for learning into my education at a highly rigorous college, where I performed well and held leadership roles in several campus media organizations.

Opportunities for Future Research on Single Fathers and Educational Attainment

Our family's experience reflects the need for further research as single-father families continue to increase in America. In contrast to the 1970s and earlier, fathers are now much more likely to obtain custody (Garasky & Meyer, 1995; Seltzer, 1990). Single-father families are now among the fastest growing types of families in the U.S. (Ziol-Guest, 2009, pp. 23–24). As of 2011, there were 8.6 million single-mother families, and 2.6 million households were single-fathered ("Introduction," 2016).

As their numbers increase, the racial and ethnic composition of American single-father families is also changing. Most researchers have only examined White single fathers because most have been historically White (Coles, 2002, p. 413). Cultural and media stereotypes of African-American men as absent or deadbeat fathers have limited researchers' attention to the increasing numbers of African-American single-father families. However, recent studies focus on African-American and Latino single fathers (Eggebeen et al., 1996; Coles, 2002, 2009; Santos & Alfred, 2016). Adolescents in single-father families are now more likely to be African American or belong to another minority group than children in other types of family structures (Eggebeen et al., 1996, p. 1109). African-American single fathers tend to be unemployed, less educated, have low income, and are more likely to receive public assistance than married fathers (Brown, 2000).

In addition to the changing composition of single-father families, single fathers who have never been married are increasing (Zhan & Pandey, 2004), while single-father families resulting from the mother's death have nearly disappeared (Eggebee et al., 1996, p. 451). Single men can now also legally adopt children (typically older children), although such adoptions by gay or straight men comprise a small percentage of single fathers (Coles, 2015, p. 145). Perhaps reflecting the change from the past majority of single fathers who were White and higher-income, fewer single fathers now are financially privileged, and they are increasingly younger and have lower incomes (Eggebeen et al., 1996; Zhan & Pandey, 2004).

The recent single-father research raises questions about how the demographic composition of single-father families with FGCSs are likewise changing. If families headed by younger, lower-income, non-college-educated, and non-White single fathers are increasing, how do these family demographics impact the children's preparation, transition into, and performance in college? Based on the single-father research, I recognize that my father was unusual for the resources, time, and emotional support that he devoted to my education. Future research could compare educational attainment for children from White and non-white single-father families with lower incomes, lower education levels, rural or urban backgrounds, and with younger fathers, or a combination of any of these demographics. In addition, future research is needed to examine the complex intersections between different identities of FGCSs from single-father families. Orbe's (2004, 2008) research on FGCSs negotiation of different identities discusses how identities have contrasting saliencies across situations. Reflecting this point, my first-generation status may have led me to be unsure how to choose college classes, but my single-father family and working-class background felt more salient during school breaks when I brought college classmates home and felt embarrassed by our atypical family structure and small apartment in a rural town. Now, as an adult and faculty member, I no longer experience the jarring juxtaposition in bringing friends or colleagues to my family's home, but I am nonetheless always keenly aware that my path to this place heavily credits a dedicated single father who was far ahead of his time.

Figure 7.1: The author and her father, Clifford Heinz (1941–2005), on the day she received her PhD in Communication and Culture from Indiana University in 2005. Photo credit: Timothy Housel.

Conclusion

As I explored the growing body of research on single fathers for this essay, I was astounded at my father's courage and resilience. When interpreted through critical autoethnographic inquiry, my lived experiences are both products and reflections of specific cultural and historical moments. My experiences also reveal disruptions to gender norms in the 1970s and '80s as my father single-handedly raised two fearless, strong daughters (Dykins Callahan, 2008, p. 353).

In my home in New Zealand, I have a cardboard box containing items that my sister and I removed from my father's house after he died. Among these items is a wooden cigar box that my father kept in his top-right desk drawer. I never explored the box's contents during his lifetime because I somehow knew it was like a diary, a private place for his thoughts alone.

After he passed away, I quietly spent an afternoon carefully pulling out its contents one-by-one. I discovered a tightly-packed stack of mementoes that reflected his unwavering support for us: newspaper clippings of school honor rolls, school portraits, holiday cards we had given him, certificates for academic awards. The items were organized in order from most recent (the local newspaper clipping of my engagement announcement, published shortly before he became ill) to earliest (primary school-related items). I sat for a long time in my study that day, holding the items on my lap, contemplating the paths my life could have taken if my father hadn't fought so hard for custody or given us constant encouragement.

A childhood friend recently commented about my upbringing: "The odds were stacked so high against you." They certainly were, but as a daughter who was the first in her family to attend college, knowing that my single father fought so hard to raise my sister and me on his own pushed me to academically succeed. As Mendes' (1976) early study of single fathers points out, "the parent-child relationship which has the best chance of succeeding is one in which the child was initially wanted" (p. 311). In the case of my sister and me, we weren't just wanted—our father tried his absolute hardest with the tools he had to gift us the conditions in which to thrive.

Author's Note: This essay is dedicated to my father, Clifford Heinz (1941–2005). Even though my single father raised two daughters, this essay focuses only on my experiences because my sister's story is hers to tell.

References

Bartz, K. W., & Witcher, W. C. (1978). When father gets custody. *Children Today, 7*(5), 2–6, 35.

Bianchi, S. M. (1995). The changing demographic and socioeconomic characteristics of single parent families. *Marriage and Family Review, 20*(1–2), 71–97.

Bianchi, S. M., Subaiya, L., & Kahn, J. R. (1999). The gender gap in the economic well-being of non-resident fathers and custodial mothers. *Demography, 36*(2), 195–203. doi: https://doi.org/10.2307/2648108

Blau, P., & Duncan, O. D. (1967). *The American occupational structure.* New York: Wiley.

Bronte-Tinkew, J., Scott, M. E., & Lilja, E. (2010). Single custodial fathers' involvement and parenting: Implications for outcomes in emerging adulthood. *Journal of Marriage and Family, 72*(5), 1107–1127. doi:10.1111/j.l741-3737.2010.00753.x

Brown, B. V. (2000). The single-father family: Demographic, economic, and public transfer use characteristics. *Marriage and Family Review, 29*(2–3), 203–220. doi: https://doi.org/10.1300/J002v29n02_12

Bui, K. V. (2002). First-generation college students at a four-year university: Background characteristics, reasons for pursuing higher education, and first-year experiences. *College Student Journal, 36*(1), 3–11.

Carlson, M. J., & Corcoran, M. E. (2001). Family structure and children's behavioral and cognitive outcomes. *Journal of Marriage and Family, 63*(3), 779–792. doi: https://doi.org/10.1111/j.1741-3737.2001.00779.x

Cherlin, A. J. (2014). *Labor's love lost: The rise and fall of the working-class family in America*. New York, NY: Russell Sage Foundation.

Coles, R. L. (2002). Black single fathers: Choosing to parent full-time. *Journal of Contemporary Ethnography, 31*(4), 411–439. doi: https://doi.org/10.1177/0891241602031004002

Coles, R. L. (2009). Just doing what they gotta do: Single black custodial fathers coping with the stresses and reaping the rewards of parenting. *Journal of Family Issues, 30*(10), 1311–1338. doi: https://doi.org/10.1177/0192513X09339290

Coles, R. L. (2015). Single-father families: A review of the literature. *Journal of Family Theory & Review, 7*(2), 144–166. doi: https://doi.org/10.1111/jftr.12069

Cooksey, E. C., & Fondell, M. M. (1996). Spending time with his kids: Effects of family structure on fathers' and children's lives. *Journal of Marriage and the Family, 58*(3), 693–707. doi: https://doi.org/10.2307/353729

Crowley, J. E. (2006). Organizational responses to the fatherhood crisis: The case of fathers' rights groups in the United States. *Marriage & Family Review, 39*(1–2), 99–120. doi: 10.1300/J002v39n01_06

DeFrain, J., & Eirick, R. (1981). Coping as divorced single parents: A comparative study of fathers and mothers. *Family Relations, 30*, 265–273. doi: https://doi.org/10.2307/584140

Demuth, S., & Brown, S. L. (2004). Family structure, family processes, and adolescent delinquency: The significance of parental absence versus parental gender. *Journal of Research in Crime and Delinquency, 41*(1), 58–81. doi: https://doi.org/10.1177/0022427803256236

Denzin, N. (2003). Performing [auto] ethnography politically. *Review of Education, Pedagogy, and Cultural Studies, 25*(3), 257–278. doi: https://doi.org/10.1080/10714410390225894

Desilver, D. (2014). *For most workers, real wages have barely budged for decades*. Retrieved from http://www.pewresearch.org/fact-tank/2014/10/09/for-most-workers-real-wages-have-barely-budged-for-decades/

Downey, D. B., Ainsworth-Darnell, J. W., & Dufur, M. J. (1998). Sex of parent and children's well-being in single-parent households. *Journal of Marriage and the Family, 60*(4), 878–893. doi: https://doi.org/10.2307/353631

Dykins Callahan, S. B. (2008). Academic outings. *Symbolic Interaction, 31*(4), 351–375. doi: https://doi.org/10.1525/si.2008.31.4.351

Education Resources Institute, & Institute for Higher Education Policy. (1997). *Missed opportunities: A new look at disadvantaged college aspirants.* Boston, MA and Washington, DC: Author.

Eggebeen, D. J., Snyder, A. R., & Manning, W. D. (1996). Children in single-father families in demographic perspective. *Journal of Family Issues, 17*(4), 441–465. doi: https://doi.org/10.1177/019251396017004002

Evangelista, M. (2003). Phoenix Rising: The making of a single father. *Mothering, 116*, 66.

Fass, M., & Tubman, J. (2002). The influence of parental and peer attachment on college students' academic achievement. *Psychology in the Schools, 39*(5), 561–573. doi: https://doi.org/10.1002/pits.10050

Featherman, D. L., & Hauser, R. M. (1978). *Opportunity and change.* New York: Academic Press.

Francis, T. A., & Miller, M. T. (2008). Communication apprehension: Levels of first-generation college students at 2-year institutions. *Community College Journal of Research and Practice, 32*(1), 38–55. doi: https://doi.org/10.1080/10668920701746688

Garasky, S. (1995). The effects of family structure on educational attainment: Do the effects vary by the age of the child? *The American Journal of Economics and Sociology, 54*(1), 89–105. doi: https://doi.org/10.1111/j.1536-7150.1995.tb02633.x

Gersick, K. E. (1979). Fathers by choice: Divorced men who receive custody of their children. In G. Levinger & O. Noles (Eds.), *Separation and divorce* (pp. 307–323). New York: Basic Books.

Gillenkirk, J. (2000). A revolution in American fathering. *America, 183*(14), 18–21.

Glenn, D. (2004, September 3). For needy students, college success depends on more than access, study finds. *The Chronicle of Higher Education, 51*(2), p. A41.

Grant, A. H. (1994). Paternal custody. *The Single Parent, 37*(4), 16–20.

Greenbaum, H., & Rubinstein, D. (2011). *The cardboard beginnings of the credit card.* Retrieved from http://www.nytimes.com/2011/12/04/magazine/the-cardboard-beginnings-of-the-credit-card.html

Greif, G. L. (1985a). Single fathers rearing children. *Journal of Marriage and the Family, 47*(1), 185–191. doi: https://doi.org/10.2307/352081

Greif, G. L. (1985b). *Single fathers.* New York: Lexington Books, Free Press.

Greif, G. L. (1985c). Children and housework in the single father family. *Family Relations, 34*(3), 353–357. doi: https://doi.org/10.2307/583573

Greif, G. L. (1992). Lone fathers in the United States: An overview and practice implications. *British Journal of Social Work, 22*(5), 565–574.

Greif, G. L., & Pabst, M. S. (1988). *Mothers without custody.* New York: Lexington Books, Free Press.

Guilder, G. (1986). Women in the work force. *The Atlantic.* Retrieved from https://www. theatlantic.com/magazine/archive/1986/09/women-in-the-work-force/304924/

Hacker, A. (1984, December 9). Women vs. men in the work force. *New York Times.* Retrieved from http://www.nytimes.com/1984/12/09/magazine/women-vs-men-in-the-work-force.html?

Hanson, S. M. H. (1985). Single custodial fathers. In S. M. H. Hanson & F. W. Bozett (Eds.), *Dimensions of fatherhood* (369–392). Beverly Hills, CA: Sage.

Haveman, R., & Wolfe, B. (1994). *Succeeding generations: On the effects of investments in children.* New York: Russell Sage Foundation.

Hawkins, D. N., Amato, P. R., & King, V. (2006). Parent–adolescent involvement: The relative influence of parent gender and residence. *Journal of Marriage and Family, 68*(1), 125–136. doi: https://doi.org/10.1111/j.1741-3737.2006.00238.x

Hill, L. C., & Hilton, J. M. (1999). Changes in roles following divorce. *Journal of Divorce and Remarriage, 31*(3–4), 91–114. doi: 10.1300/J087v31n03_06

Hilton, J. M., & Desrochers, S. (2000). The influence of economic strain, coping with roles, and parental control on the parenting of custodial single mothers and custodial single fathers. *Journal of Divorce & Remarriage, 33*(3–4), 55–76.

Hilton, J., & Devall, E. (1998). Comparison of parenting and children's behavior in single-mother, single-father, and intact families. *Journal of Divorce and Remarriage, 29*(3–4), 23–54.

History Cooperative. (2015, 29 May). *The history of divorce law in the USA.* Retrieved from http://historycooperative.org/the-history-of-divorce-law-in-the-usa/

hooks, b. (2000). *Where we stand: Class matters.* New York, NY: Routledge.

Introduction. (2016). In K. L. Swisher (Ed.), *Single-parent families: Opposing viewpoints in context* (pp. 7–9). San Diego, CA: Greenhaven Press.

Keshet, H. F., & Rosenthal, K. M. (1976). Single parent families: A new study. *Children Today, 7*(3), 13–17.

Kramer, K. Z., Myhra, L. L., Zuiker, V. S., & Bauer, J. W. (2015). Comparison of poverty and income disparity of single mothers and fathers across three decades: 1990–2010. *Gender Issues, 33*(1), 22–41. doi: https://doi.org/10.1007/s12147-015-9144-3

Krein, S. F., & A. H. Beller. (1988). Educational attainment of children from single-parent families: Differences by exposure, gender, and race. *Demography, 25*(2), 221–234. doi: https://doi.org/10.2307/2061290

Lillard, D., & Gerner, J. (1999). Getting to the Ivy League: How family composition affects college choice. *The Journal of Higher Education, 70*(6), 706–730. doi: https://doi.org/10.1080/00221546.1999.11780805

Lundberg, C. A., Schreiner, L. A., Hovaguimian, K., & Miller, S. S. (2007). First-generation status and student race/ethnicity as distinct predictors of student involvement and learning. *NASPA Journal (Online), 44*(1), 57–83.

McCarron, G. P., & Inkelas, K. K. (2006). The gap between educational aspirations and attainment for first-generation college students and the role of parental involvement. *Journal of College Student Development, 47*(5), 534–549. doi: https://doi.org/10.1353/csd.2006.0059

McLanahan, S. (1988). Family structure and dependency: Early transitions to female household headship. *Demography, 25*(1), 1–16. doi: https://doi.org/10.2307/2061474

McLanahan, S., & Booth, K. (1989). Mother-only families: Problems, prospects, and politics. *Journal of Marriage and Family, 51*(3), 557–580. doi: http://dx.doi.org/10.2307/352157

McLanahan, S., & Casper, L. (1995). Growing diversity and inequality in the American family. In R. Farley (Ed.), *State of the union: America in the 1990s: Vol. 4. Social trends* (pp. 1–45). New York: Russell Sage.

McLanahan, S., & Sandefur, G. (1994). *Growing up with a single parent: What hurts, what helps.* Cambridge, MA: Harvard University Press.

Mendes, H. A. (1976). Single fatherhood. *Social Work, 21*(4), 308–312.

Meyer, D., & Garasky, S. (1993). Custodial fathers: Myths, realities, and child support policy. *Journal of Marriage and Family, 55*(1), 73–89. doi: https://doi.org/10.2307/352960

Moschetti, R., & Hudley, C. (2008). Measuring social capital among first-generation and non-first-generation, working-class, white males. *Journal of College Admission, 198* (Winter 2008), 25–30.

Musick, K., & Mare, R. D. (2006). Recent trends in the inheritance of poverty and family structure. *Social Science Research, 35*(2), 471–499. doi: https://doi.org/10.1016/j.ssresearch.2004.11.006

Napier, A. (1991). Heroism, men and marriage. *Journal of Marital and Family Therapy, 17*(1), 9–16. doi: https://doi.org/10.1111/j.1752-0606.1991.tb00857.x

Nieto, D. S. (1982). Aiding the single father. *Social Work, 27*(6), 473–478. doi: https://doi.org/10.1093/sw/27.6.473

Orbe, M. P. (2004). Negotiating multiple identities within multiple frames: An analysis of first-generation college students. *Communication Education, 53*(2), 131–149. doi: 10.1080/0363452041000168240l

Orbe, M. P. (2008). Theorizing multidimensional identity negotiation: Reflections on the lived experiences of first-generation college students. In M. Azmitia, M. Syed, & K. Radmacher (Eds.), *The intersections of personal and social identities. New Directions for Child and Adolescent Development, 120*, 81–95. doi: https://doi.org/10.1002/cd.217

Reid, M. J., & Moore, J. L. (2008). College readiness and academic preparation for postsecondary education: Oral histories of first-generation urban college students. *Urban Education, 43*(2), 240–261. doi: https://doi.org/10.1177/0042085907312346

Risman, B. J. (1986). Can men mother? Life as a single father. *Family Relations, 35*(1), 95–102. doi: https://doi.org/10.2307/584288

Risman, B. J. (1987). Intimate relationships from a microstructural perspective: Men who mother. *Gender and Society, 1*(1), 6–32. doi: http://dx.doi.org/10.1177/089124387001001002

Risman, B. J., & Park, K. (1988). Just the two of us: Parent-child relationships in single-parent homes. *Journal of Marriage and Family, 50*(4), 1049–1062. doi: https://doi.org/10.2307/352114

Ryan, M. P., & Glenn, P. A. (2002/2003). Increasing one-year retention rates by focusing on academic competence: An empirical odyssey. *Journal of College Student Retention, 4*(3), 297–324. doi: https://doi.org/10.2190/KUNN-A2WW-RFQT-PY3H

Santos, R. A., & Alfred, M. V. (2016). Literacy, parental roles, and support systems among single Latino father families. *Journal of Research and Practice for Adult Literacy, Secondary, and Basic Education, 5*(3), 5–17.

Saracho, O. N. (2007). Hispanic families, as facilitators of their children's literacy development. *Journal of Hispanic Higher Education, 6*(2), 103–117. doi: https://doi.org/10.1177/1538192706299009

Scheck, D. C., & Emerick, R. (1976). The young male adolescent's perception of early childrearing behavior: The differential effects of socioeconomic status and family size. *Sociometry, 39*(1), 39–52. doi: https://doi.org/10.2307/2786590

Schor, J. B. (2003). The new politics of consumption: Why Americans want so much more than they need. In G. Dines & J. Humez (Eds.), *Gender, race, and class in media* (pp. 183–195). New York: Sage.

Seltzer, J. A. (1990). Legal and physical custody arrangements in recent divorces. *Social Science Quarterly, 71*(2), 250–266.

Sewell, W. H., & Hauser, R. M. (1975). *Education, occupation and earnings: Achievement in the early career.* New York: Academic Press.

Teachman, J. D. (1987). Family background, educational resources, and educational attainment. *American Sociological Review, 52*(4), 548–577. doi: https://doi.org/10.2307/2095300

Tupy, M. (2016, January 19). *Cost of living vs. wage stagnation in the United States, 1979–2015.* Retrieved from http://reason.com/archives/2016/01/19/cost-of-living-vs-wage-stagnation-in-the

U.S. Census Bureau. (1970). Washington, D.C.: Government Printing Office.

U.S. Census Bureau. (1978). Washington, D.C.: Government Printing Office.

U.S. Census Bureau. (2003). *America's families and living arrangements* (Current Population Reports Series P20–553). Washington, DC: Government Printing Office.

U.S. Department of Commerce. Bureau of the Census. (1990). *Household and family characteristics; March 1990 and 1989* (Series P-20. No. 447). Washington, DC: US Government Printing Office.

U.S. Department of Commerce. Bureau of the Census. (1991). *Marital status and living arrangements: March 1990* (Series P-20. No. 450). Washington, DC: US Government Printing Office.

Wallace, K. (2016, March 30). From '80s latchkey kid to helicopter parent today. *CNN.* Retrieved from https://edition.cnn.com/2016/03/30/health/the-80s-latchkey-kid-helicopter-parent/index.html?no-st=1523152067

Wright, J. D., & Wright, S. R. (1976). Social class and parental values for children: A partial replication and extension of Kohn's thesis. *American Sociological Review, 41*, 141–161.

Zhan, M., & Pandey, S. (2004). Postsecondary education and economic well-being of single mothers and single fathers. *Journal of Marriage and Family, 66*(3), 661–673. doi: 10.1111/j.0022–2445.2004.00045.x

Ziol-Guest, K. M. (2009). A single father's shopping bag: Purchasing decisions in single-father families. *Journal of Family Issues, 30*(5), 605–622. doi: https://doi.org/10.1177/0192513X08331022

8. Living With Anxiety as a First-Generation College Student: Intersections of Mental Health and the First-Generation College Student Experience

Andrea L. Meluch

When I entered college more than a decade ago, I was excited, nervous, and ready to distance myself from my family. I know that, like most college students, I wanted to enter a new world of possibility where I could pursue my interests, find new friends, and decide who I was as an individual. Although I was able to accomplish these goals, I also encountered personal obstacles that I had not anticipated when I first entered college. As a first-generation college student (FGCS), I knew that I was entering a world that was going to be very different from the one with which I was accustomed. However, what I did not know until college was how difficult it would be to be a FGCS living with anxiety.

I was diagnosed with anxiety during my early college years and I continue to manage my anxiety now as a full-time academic. Experiencing anxiety firsthand as a FGCS has made me acutely aware of the intersections of mental health and being a FGCS. At many points in my academic journey, I have felt very much feel like I was alone in navigating my way through higher education. Today, as a health communication scholar, first-generation academic, and now adult living with anxiety, I feel uniquely positioned to bring attention to the often-isolating experience of being a FGCS living with a mental health issue. My personal narrative as a FGCS living with mental health issues can hopefully help those in the higher education community to better understand this marginalized experience that unfortunately so many FGCS experience.

As I begin this discussion, I acknowledge that I am a cisgender White woman who has a middle-class lifestyle. I have experienced much privilege in my academic and personal life that many other FGCS and academics do not share. For example, my parents' hard work provided me with the opportunity to attend good primary and secondary schools where I excelled academically. I received substantial academic scholarships during my time as an undergraduate and, later, graduate assistantships and stipends as a graduate student. I also have had good health insurance throughout my life and have always had access to mental health resources and services that many FGCS may not have. However, my mental health challenges and academic life have often created a blend of obstacles that have been at times difficult to manage.

My goal in writing this chapter is to explain in my own words the isolating experience of being a FGCS living with anxiety. In particular, I will highlight the stigmatized nature of mental health and the increasing frequency of mental health issues diagnosed among college students and academics. I will then present my own personal narrative as a FGCS and later graduate student and academic living with anxiety. I will further draw attention to my experiences of personal shame, social isolation, and stigmatization of mental health.

Stigma and Mental Health

Although they are receiving increasing attention and sensitivity, mental health issues are still highly stigmatized (Sartorius, 2007). For those experiencing depression and anxiety, shame, social isolation, and marginalization are common consequences accompanying mental health issues. For some, the stigma can be just as debilitating as the mental health issue itself (Sartorius, 2007).

Stigma is defined as an "attribute that is deeply discrediting" (Goffman, 1963, p. 3). Goffman's foundational work, *Stigma*, defines stigma as the personal characteristics of an individual (such as illness and sexual orientation) that are in some way viewed by the wider population as disgraceful or shameful. Stigmas are socially constructed (Smith, 2011). As such, stigma is rooted in the relationships between individuals; in this way, stigma is experienced by changes in the interactions that people who are stigmatized have with others. The experience of stigma among individuals often occurs through labeling, stereotyping, and discrimination (Smith, 2011). Examples of stigmatized health conditions include mental illness (Eisenberg, Downs, Golberstein, & Zivin, 2009a; Mak, Poon, Pun, & Cheung, 2007; Sartorius, 2007) and HIV/AIDS (Mahajan et al., 2008), among many others.

Mental health issues have been a focal issue in the study of stigma since Goffman's (1963) early work. More recently, researchers examining the associations between stigma and mental health have examined how stigmatized identity can influence likelihood to seek resources (Corrigan, 2004; Eisenberg et al., 2009a; Stebleton, Soria, & Huesman, 2014). For example, Eisenberg et al. (2009a) examined the help-seeking behaviors and perceived stigma among 5,555 students from 13 universities in the United States. The researchers found that perceptions of public stigma (or the negative stereotypes and discrimination the public has toward mental illness) were significantly associated with not seeking help (therapy, medication, other sources of social support). Both this study and others demonstrate the negative effects of stigma toward mental illness. In particular, this research is relevant in the college setting because of the increased number of mental health issues experienced by college students.

Prevalence of Mental Health Issues Among College Students

Mental health receives significant attention today from colleges and universities because of its prevalence among college students. "Mental health issues" is a broad term used to refer to mental illnesses such as depression, post-traumatic stress disorder (PTSD) and other anxiety disorders, substance abuse, eating disorders, and suicidal ideation. According to the National Alliance on Mental Health (NAMI, 2012), mental health issues affect 73% of all students at some point during their college career. The Association for University and College Counseling Center Directors found that anxiety is the most common mental health issue for college students, with 47.3% of college students included in their survey experiencing some level of anxiety (Reetz, Krylowicz, Bershad, Lawrence, & Mistler, 2015). Depression, relationship problems, and suicidal ideation follow behind anxiety as the predominant mental health concerns that college students report (Reetz et al., 2015).

Other researchers report that mental health issues, including depression and substance abuse (such as alcoholism), have increased among adults, including college-aged individuals, in the U.S. in recent years (Compton, Conway, Stinson, & Grant, 2006). As such, college students are not alone in experiencing increases in managing mental health issues. Recent research has also found that increased communication technology usage and information overload among college students have led to more symptoms of depression and stress (Thomée, Eklöf, Gustafsson, Nilsson, & Hagberg, 2007; Thomée, Härenstam, & Hagberg, 2011). Finally, following the economic downturn of 2008, many college students are facing increasing social pressures to be successful and, simultaneously, to manage greater financial burdens associated with the high cost of college (Flatt, 2013; Watkins, Hunt, & Eisenberg, 2011). Thus, many factors are associated with the increases in mental health issues among college students in recent years.

Colleges and universities are especially concerned about mental health and students, as mental health issues often lead to academic problems (Eisenberg, Golberstein, & Hunt, 2009b; Stebleton & Soria, 2013). Eisenberg et al. (2009b) examined the association among mental health issues, such as depression and anxiety, and academic outcomes, such as grade point average (GPA) and dropout rates. The researchers surveyed a random sample of 2,798 students from a large public university. They found that depression is a significant predictor in obtaining a lower GPA and a higher probability of dropping out of college. Further, Eisenberg et al. (2009b) also noted that students with co-occurring depression and anxiety are more likely to have a lower GPA. Finally, they also found that eating disorders are related to lower GPAs among students.

Although mental health issues have the likelihood of negatively affecting academic performance among all college students, FGCS struggling with mental health issues may be more at-risk for negative academic outcomes than their non-first-generation peers. FGCS are already less likely to graduate when compared to their non-first-generation peers (Engle & Tinto, 2008). The combination of first-generation status among college students and mental health issues poses particularly difficult academic and personal obstacles (Stebleton & Soria, 2013; Stebleton, Soria, & Huesman, 2014). FGCS are more likely to experience feelings of depression and not have a strong sense of belonging when compared to their non-first-generation peers (Stebleton & Soria, 2013; Stebelton et al., 2014). Thus, FGCS often experience both mental health issues (Engle & Tinto, 2008) and negative academic outcomes (Stebleton & Soria, 2013; Stebleton et al., 2014) at increased levels when compared to their non-first generation peers.

Feelings of depression among FGCS can negatively impact academic success (Stebleton et al., 2014). In their study, Stebleton et al. (2014) compared sense of belonging, mental health status, and use of mental health services between first-generation and non-FGCS. The researchers found that FGCS report higher levels of depression and stress, and have a lower sense of belonging when compared to non-first-generation students. Further, Stebleton et al. (2014) found that FGCS experiencing depression and other mental health issues are less likely to use counseling services at their university or college. Other research has found that despite the increased use of counseling centers on college campuses in general, many FGCS are not aware of the mental health services available through their college campuses (Watkins et al., 2011). In particular, Watkins et al. (2011) noted that Hispanic FGCS are less likely to discuss mental health and associated treatment options within the Hispanic community.

Likewise, African-American FGCS may also be at a disadvantage in seeking out mental health services in university settings due to long-held stereotypes (Masuda, Anderson, & Edmonds, 2012). Specifically, African-American individuals may feel greater stigmatization when they experience mental health issues because they also internalize other negative stereotypes regarding the African-American community (Williams & Williams-Morris, 2000). These findings indicate that FGCS who experience mental health issues may not be aware of counseling services available to them and/or may not feel comfortable using these services because of the stigma that accompanies mental health issues.

Although mental health issues among FGCS are well-documented (Flatt, 2013; Engle & Tinto, 2008; Stebelon et al., 2014), little research has examined the personal stories of these students. Scholarly literature can provide greater insight into how mental health issues in academia can become less stigmatized through sharing the voices of FGCS experiencing mental health issues. As a now-academic and FGCS who has experienced mental health issues, I believe my personal narrative is particularly relevant to literature examining issues of stigmatization of mental health issues for FGCS, social isolation as a FGCS experiencing mental health, and the associated shame surrounding mental health issues in the working class.

My Experience as a First-Generation College Student Living With Anxiety

I have been living with anxiety for as long as I can remember. As an adolescent, I would worry incessantly. I would worry about my grades and not being seen as good enough by my family and teachers. Throughout college I experienced panic attacks, sleepless nights, and a constant feeling of being on edge. Living with anxiety as a FGCS created additional challenges beyond managing the anxiety itself. These additional challenges included feeling withdrawn from my peers because of my mental health issues; feeling unable to seek help from various on-campus resources; and overwhelming feelings of embarrassment because of my perceived inadequacies. Over the course of my four years pursuing my undergraduate degree and six years pursuing my graduate degrees, at times my mental health issues felt like my biggest challenge. At other times, they subsided and allowed me to focus on my studies, personal life, and goals.

I grew up in a suburb of Cleveland, Ohio. My father worked for a local utility company and my mother was a homemaker. I was the oldest of three children—two girls and one boy. When I was a senior in high school I started applying to colleges. As neither of my parents had attended college, the process was overwhelming. I was always a smart kid in school, but I was by no means a valedictorian. Although my parents encouraged me to apply for scholarships to local colleges, they stopped short of encouraging me to go away to college. My parents were concerned about the financial implications of living away at college and believed I was better suited to attend college while living at home. Thus, when I was awarded a full-tuition academic scholarship to the local state school, this solidified my decision to live at home.

Being a FGCS on an academic scholarship made my family extremely proud of me, but also made me feel that there were high expectations that I needed to live up to. My experiences were similar to research that suggests that college students feel an increased pressure to be successful today (Watkins et al., 2011). I self-imposed high expectations from the beginning of my college career onward. For example, I knew before entering college that I would pursue graduate work, so I pushed myself to achieve high grades in all my classes. Wanting to do well in college in order to get into graduate school is not an uncommon experience; however, having anxiety made these pursuits a struggle from the beginning. During my freshman year, I researched admission requirements for various graduate programs, and then would spend hours thinking about what I needed to do over the next three years to meet those requirements. I would focus so much on my future academic pursuits that I often lost sight of my present challenges.

During my first year of college, I felt extremely isolated as a commuter student and a FGCS. It also did not help that I did not understand why I was so panicky about school. If I had an exam coming up in a class, I would spend more time worrying about the exam than actually studying. I would lose sleep going over in my head what would happen if I failed the exam, and subsequently lost my scholarship. I would spend my day feeling tightness in my neck and shoulders and sometimes find it difficult to breathe. I did not realize then that I was experiencing mild to moderate symptoms of anxiety. Many of my symptoms (restlessness, muscle tension, difficulty controlling worry) were early signs of anxiety (National Institute of Mental Health, 2016). Further, being female and exposed to the stressors accompanying being a FGCS heightened my risk of experiencing anxiety (National Institute of Mental Health, 2016). I honestly thought for the entire first year of college that the way I felt was what college was supposed to be like. My mother, in particular, told me that college is supposed to be "hard." As such, I equated my experiences of anxiety with what I thought was normal experiences of college-related stress.

One spring afternoon during my first year of college, I was driving home from campus and talking on my cellphone to my best friend from high school. We were talking about our classes and I mentioned that I had an exam coming up the next week. All of a sudden I felt completely paralyzed. I told my friend I needed to hang up and pull off the road because I could not focus. As I pulled off the road into a gas station, I felt the surrounding world close in on me. It became difficult for me to breathe. Blackness started to enter my field of vision from the perimeters, as if the world around me were starting to close in. As my breaths became more labored, I began to feel like I was floating. I had experienced other panic attacks throughout high school, but never while driving and one that made me feel unsafe.

Throughout my sophomore and junior years of college, I decided to start seeing a therapist. I had health insurance that covered some costs associated with seeking therapy. At the time I started therapy, I was aware that my university had a free counseling center. However, I chose to use a counselor in a private practice closer to my home. My decision to seek a counselor outside of my college, despite the associated costs, was largely because I did not want anyone, especially my friends or professors on campus, to see me walking into the counseling center at school.

Coming from a working-class background, I was extremely self-conscious about looking weak or like I could not handle the stressors of life. I felt that counseling was something to be ashamed of. In particular, I felt that at school my friends, classmates, and professors would view me as vulnerable if they knew that I went to a counselor. Further, I found it very difficult to share my need for counseling at home. My parents assumed that college was supposed to be hard and did not necessarily believe that therapy had helpful properties in the way I believed it did. Deep down, I knew at the time that seeking counseling was essential for me. I was unable to manage my anxiety on my own and my family did not understand this struggle. Coming from a working-class background made me hyperaware of the "pull yourself up by your bootstraps" mentality. However, that mentality did not help me in the way that I needed. Thus, within my home life, I felt uncomfortable sharing any of the daily mental health struggles I experienced. Like many individuals from a working-class background, I perceived a public stigma regarding counseling (Golberstein, Eisenberg, & Gollust, 2008). Researchers have found that college students are likely to self-stigmatize their mental health issue because of the public stigma surrounding mental health, and that these perceptions can influence willingness to seek counseling (Vogel, Wade, & Hackler, 2007). As such, perceived stigmatization because of mental health issues in the working-class can be a barrier for many individuals, myself included, in seeking counseling services.

When I started counseling in the fall of 2007, I was fairly certain that seeking counseling would discredit my academic and social reputation. At the beginning of my sophomore year, I was doing well in all my classes, inducted into the honor society, worked for the school newspaper, and joined a sorority. I had truly worked hard throughout my freshman year to make friends and be involved on campus, and I was cautious to lose or diminish any of my new relationships. However, I constantly felt like I was hiding a part of myself from my new friends. I made the decision to disclose my mental health issues to a new college friend and the stigma attached to mental health issues and counseling was confirmed to me.

One evening I was hanging out with a new college friend. We were watching a television show and talking about school. When the main character on the television show went to see a counselor, we started to talk about mental health. I then told her that I had started to see a counselor. I could see that she was surprised. My friend exclaimed that she thought counseling was a "sham." I immediately became very defensive. She tried to backtrack on what she had said, but I still knew at that point that she did not think counseling was valuable. After that conversation, I chose not to mention my mental health struggles to friends from college. This decision followed me into graduate school.

During my sophomore year in college, I continued to go to therapy, but I found myself struggling academically for one of the first times in my life. I always excelled academically in high school and my first year of college. I finished my freshman year with a 4.0 GPA and felt that all my worry and nervousness was worth the successful academic outcomes. However, my sophomore year of college was a different experience altogether. I took an advanced English course required for my major and felt as if I had started spinning out of control. I was constantly thinking about this class. I would read the material, but I would feel like nothing had sunk in. It was almost like my mind would go blank, and the harder I tried to focus, the less I could concentrate. I made notecards for the class, but I would find myself unable to scrounge up the willpower to look at them.

After more than a month of struggling with this class, I decided to withdraw from it. I felt like a complete failure because I could not pull myself together in the class. When I submitted the withdraw request, I started to cry. It was the first time in my life that I truly felt like I could not keep anything together. The rest of that semester continued to be a struggle. I still maintained a high enough GPA to keep my scholarship, but it was the only semester in my entire college career (including my six years in graduate school) that I earned a "B." I realize how ridiculous it sounds that a "B" was a low point for me, but in my mind a "B" was basically a failing grade.

I talked with my therapist about my low points during that semester and did not feel any ability to pick myself back up and continue moving along. I also did not feel like I was able to tell anyone about my mental health, least of all my professors. Today I understand that if a student is struggling with mental health, they should seek assistance from resources on campus and consider informing their professors. However, when I was a student struggling to keep myself together, I felt that if my professors saw me as being anything less than perfect, then I was going to lose everything I was working toward.

Throughout my college experience, my parents understood that I was not dealing with normal levels of stress. However, they also did not understand why I needed to go to therapy for as long as I did. They believed that after a few sessions I would be cured. The anxiety I experienced, coupled with the fact that my parents were unable to fully understand the pressures of being in college, created a lot of tension in our relationship. During college, I found that I wanted to distance myself from my family and become my own person. However, I also constantly wanted to live up to being a successful daughter. Having mental health issues seemed, to me at least, like I was not a daughter of whom they could be proud. This made me feel like I needed to get even more distance from them so that I could figure out who I was and what I wanted out of life.

After my particularly difficult sophomore year of college, therapy helped me start to be able to better manage my anxiety. In therapy I was able to address and deal with issues of shame regarding my anxiety and the stressors that I experienced as a FGCS. I found that through these conversations I felt less alone in my struggles, and that it was okay to be open about my experiences of anxiety and important to seek help. In my junior and senior years of college, I excelled academically and felt happy in my personal life. I still had some challenges, but for the most part I felt that I was able to manage my anxiety. It also helped that my junior year of college I started dating my now-husband. For the first time in a long time, I felt I could be open with someone about my mental health and seeking therapy. The ability to be completely honest about my mental health issues with someone close to me made me feel as if a huge weight had been lifted off my shoulders. Whereas at school and at home I felt that I needed to hide my mental health issues, in my relationship with my now-husband, I could be open and not feel embarrassed about the fact that I was not the perfect student or daughter that I so desperately wanted to be.

After I graduated with my undergraduate degree, I immediately entered graduate school. When I decided to go on to graduate school I was managing my anxiety well. I had decided my senior year to stop going to therapy because I was doing so well. I was finally sleeping well and did not feel tense all of the time. Although being in high stress situations in school had always been a trigger for me, it did not dawn on me that my anxiety would likely become a huge challenge for me throughout graduate school.

My graduate experiences as a FGCS living with anxiety shared many similarities with my undergraduate life. Graduate school was very much a roller coaster for my mental health. I started and stopped therapy throughout graduate school and began taking medication to help better manage my anxiety. Much of my anxiety worsened around high stress periods, including writing my master's thesis, applying to doctoral programs, taking comprehensive exams, and completing my dissertation.

Throughout graduate school I truly had a toxic belief that I needed to keep all my personal mental health struggles hidden. In academic settings, we prize our cognitive capacities, and anything that threatens those capacities is extremely damaging to our reputations. However, keeping my mental health struggles to myself was more damaging than opening up to my peers. In actuality, I found that when I was open with my peers about my mental health struggles, many of them were experiencing similar issues, including anxiety and depression.

My anxiety reached a tipping point when I was finishing my dissertation and navigating the academic job market. The combined intense stress of working on my dissertation in addition to the uncertainty and difficulty accompanying the academic job market left me barely functioning at certain points. It was at this point in my life that I could no longer hide my anxiety. I was in many ways forced to be open about my struggles with my family, friends, peers, and mentors.

I have found it beneficial to speak up about my experiences living with anxiety to individuals in my personal and professional life. After some conversations with a fellow graduate student, we decided to start an online support group for advanced graduate students and junior academics to talk about everything from career stressors to mental health in academia. By opening up about my experience, I found that many of my academic peers were experiencing similar challenges, but did not have a safe outlet to talk about them. In addition, opening up to my family about my anxiety and what I viewed as my weakness was in many ways cathartic. I no longer felt like I had to keep up the appearance of being the person who could handle everything. Instead, I was honest about my struggles with anxiety and the fact that my anxiety was not caused by being particularly stressed while finishing graduate school, but only amplified because of the stressful circumstances.

Conclusion and Future Thoughts

Living with anxiety was a struggle for me during my entire adolescence and now in my adult life as well. As a FGCS and now-academic living with anxiety, I find that my family often has difficulty understanding my experiences that are so different from their own. Having chosen to pursue academia as a career, I have had, like so many others, to learn to navigate a world that my family knows very little about (Barney Dews & Law, 1995; Welsch, 2004).

My experience as a first-generation academic continues to be both exciting and taxing. My passion for pursuing knowledge and pushing my understanding of the social world to greater depths has also created many stressors that have at times left me feeling alone and lost. I have also often found myself managing my stressors on my own without any assistance from family, friends, professors, or counselors for fear of being stigmatized. As an academic, it is often difficult to speak up about any part of my identity that can make me perceived as weak or less committed to my scholarly pursuits.

Similar to our students, academics commonly experience anxiety and related mental health issues. Thought pieces and blogs increasingly examine the issue of anxiety in higher education (Shaw & Ward, 2014; Walker, 2015). However, despite the increasing recognition of the problem, the fact remains that having anxiety, or any other type of mental health disorder, often leaves the individual feeling as if she or he is living with a mark of weakness that could jeopardize one's career goals. In addition, living with anxiety as a first-generation academic has often left me feeling not well understood by those closest to me, including parents, siblings, and friends.

I wish I could end this chapter by saying that I have some significant advice to impart from my experiences, but the fact is that everyone experiences and manages mental health issues a little differently. My experience has been that living with mental health issues is a day-to-day challenge. Some days, weeks, and years are easier than others. However, for me anxiety is constantly the lingering worries in the back of my head that I am not capable of doing the things that I have set out to do. Sometimes the anxiety wins and I lose sleep and feel completely hopeless and upset. Seeking therapy, being open to those around me, and working with my physicians and counselors have provided me with tools for managing my anxiety. However, just because these resources have worked for me does not mean that they are right for others experiencing similar issues.

Sharing my story as a first-generation academic with mental health issues has not been an easy task. However, I believe sharing my story is important because it is a similar experience that many other first-generation undergraduate and, especially, graduate students also experience. FGCS are at an increased risk for experiencing mental health issues, social isolation, and negative academic outcomes (Eisenberg et al., 2009b; Stebleton & Soria, 2013). Further, students of color who are FGCS are less likely to seek resources for mental health issues (Masuda et al., 2012; Watkins et al., 2011). To improve the experience for all FGCS experiencing mental health issues, more research is needed to help lessen the stigma associated with this experience. Today, as a professor I regularly engage with FGCS who encounter the same struggles I experienced and often do not come from a background of understanding or acceptance. However, when my students, especially first-generation students, disclose their mental health issues to me, I find it crucial to first let them know that they are not alone in their struggles. I then to refer them to the mental health resources we have on campus. We must tell FGCS that they are in no way inferior because of their personal struggles with mental health and that there are many resources available.

References

Barney Dews, C. L., & Law, C. L. (Eds.). (1995). *This fine place so far from home: Voices of academics from the working class*. Philadelphia: Temple University.

Compton, W. M., Conway, K. P., Stinson, F. S., & Grant, B. F. (2006). Changes in the prevalence of major depression and comorbid substance use disorders in the United States between 1991–1992 and 2001–2002. *The American Journal of Psychiatry, 163*(12), 2141–2147. doi: 10.1176/ajp.2006.163.12.2141

Corrigan, P. (2004). How stigma interferes with mental health care. *American Psychologist, 59*(7), 614–625. http://dx.doi.org/10.1037/0003-066X.59.7.614

Eisenberg, D., Downs, M. F., Golberstein, E., & Zivin, K. (2009a). Stigma and help seeking formental health among college students. *Medical Care Research and Review, 66*(5), 522–541. doi: 10.1177/1077558709335173

Eisenberg, D., Golberstein, E., & Hunt, J. B. (2009b). Mental health and academic success in college. *The B.E. Journal of Economic Analysis & Policy, 9*(1), 1–35. doi: https://doi.org/10.2202/1935-1682.2191

Engle, J., & Tinto, V. (2008). Moving beyond access: College success for low-income, first-generation students. Washington, DC: The Pell Institute. Retrieved from http://files.eric.ed.gov/fulltext/ED504448.pdf

Flatt, A. K. (2013). A suffering generation: Six factors contributing to the mental health crisis in North American higher education. *College Quarterly, 16*(1), e-publication. Retrieved from http://collegequarterly.ca/2013-vol16-num01-winter/flatt.html

Goffman, E. (1963). *Stigma: Notes on the management of spoiled identity.* Englewood Cliffs, NJ: Prentice-Hall.

Golberstein, E., Eisenberg, D., & Gollust, S. E. (2008). Perceived stigma and mental health care seeking. *Psychiatric Services, 59*(4), 392–399. doi: 10.1176/ps.2008.59.4.392

Mahajan, A. P., Sayles, J. N., Patel, V. A., Remien, R. H., Sawires, D. J., Ortiz, D., ... Coates, T. (2008). Stigma in the HIV/AIDS epidemic: A review of the literature and recommendations for the way forward. *AIDS, 22*(Suppl 2), S67–S79. doi: 10.1097/01.aids.0000327438.13291.62

Mak, W. W. S., Poon, C. Y. M., Pun, L. Y. K., & Cheung, S. F. (2007). Meta-analysis of stigma and mental health. *Social Science & Medicine, 65*(2), 245–261. doi: 10.1016/j.socscimed.2007.03.015

Masuda, A., Anderson, P. L., & Edmonds, J. (2012). Help-seeking attitudes, mental health stigma, and self-concealment among African American college students. *Journal of Black Studies, 43*(7), 773–786. doi: https://doi.org/10.1177/0021934712445806

National Alliance on Mental Illness (NAMI). (2012). College students speak: A Survey report on mental health. Arlington, VA. Retrieved from www.nami.org/namioncampus

National Institute of Mental Health. (2016). *Anxiety disorders.* Retrieved from https://www.nimh.nih.gov/health/topics/anxiety-disorders/index.shtml

Reetz, D. R., Krylowicz, B., Bershad, C., Lawrence, J. M., & Mistler, B. (2015). *The Association for University and College Counseling Center directors annual survey.* Retrieved from http://www.aucccd.org/assets/documents/aucccd%202015%20monograph%20-%20public%20version.pdf

Sartorius, N. (2007). Stigma and mental health. *The Lancet, 370*(9590), 810–811. doi: 10.1016/S0140-6736(07)61245–8

Shaw, C., & Ward, L. (2014, March 6). Dark thoughts: Why mental illness is on the rise in academia. *The Guardian.* Retrieved from https://www.theguardian.com/higher-education-network/2014/mar/06/mental-health-academics-growing-problem-pressure-university

Smith, R. A. (2011). Stigma, communication, and health. In T. L. Thompson, R. Parrott, & J. F. Nussbaum (Eds.), *The Routledge handbook of health communication* (2nd ed., pp. 455–468). New York: Routledge.

Stebleton, M. J., & Soria, K. M. (2013). Breaking down barriers: Academic obstacles of first-generation students at research universities. *The Learning Assistance Review, 17*(2), 7–19.

Stebleton, M. J., Soria, K. M., & Huesman, R. L. (2014). First generation students' sense of belonging, mental health, and use of counseling services at public research universities. *Journal of College Counseling, 17*(1), 6–17. doi: 10.1002/j.2161–1882.2014.00044.x

Thomée, S., Eklöf, M., Gustafsson, E., Nilsson, R., & Hagberg, M. (2007). Prevalence of perceived stress, symptoms of depression and sleep disturbances in relation to information and communication technology (ICT) use among young adults—An explorative prospective study. *Computers in Human Behavior, 23*(3), 1300–1321. doi: 10.1016/j.chb.2004.12.007

Thomée, S., Härenstam, A., & Hagberg, M. (2011). Mobile phone use and stress, sleep disturbances, and symptoms of depression among young adults—a prospective cohort study. *BMC Public Health, 11*(66), 1–11. doi: https://doi.org/10.1186/1471-2458-11-66

Vogel, D. L., Wade, N. G., & Hackler, A. H. (2007). Perceived public stigma and the willingness to seek counseling: The mediating roles of self-stigma and attitudes toward counseling. *Journal of Counseling Psychology, 54*(1), 40–50. doi: http://dx.doi.org/10.1037/0022-0167.54.1.40

Walker, J. (2015, November 12). There's an awful cost to getting a PhD that no one talks about. *Quartz.com.* Retrieved from https://qz.com/547641/theres-an-awful-cost-to-getting-a-phd-that-no-one-talks-about/

Watkins, D. C., Hunt, J. B., & Eisenberg, D. (2011). Increased demand for mental health services on college campuses: Perspectives from administrators. *Qualitative Social Work, 11*(3), 319–337. doi: https://doi.org/10.1177/1473325011401468

Welsch, K. A. (Ed.). (2004). *Those winter Sundays: Female academics and their working-class parents.* Lanham, MD: University Press of America.

Williams, D. R., & Williams-Morris, R. (2000). Racism and mental health: The African American experience. *Ethnicity & Health, 5*(3–4), 243–268. doi: https://doi.org/10.1080/713667453

9. Navigating Multiple Marginalized Identities: Experiences of an Emancipated First-Generation Transgender Foster Care College Student

Jacob O. Okumu and Kay-Anne P. Darlington

College students can claim first-generation status if none of their parents or guardians received a bachelor's degree (Choy, 2001). Research shows that at least one in six college students considered as first generation in the United States is not only from a low-socio-economic background, but is also less academically prepared for college and significantly unlikely to persist to graduation (Davidson, 2016; Jehangir, Stebleton, & Deenanath, 2015). On the other hand, the foster care system in the U.S. is a structure where governmental authority assumes temporary responsibility for minors who have been removed from their primary care-givers and placed under protection and nurturance of the state court and child welfare jurisdiction until they emancipate or age out. An individual "ages out" or emancipates from foster care when they are legally released from state court and child welfare jurisdiction (commonly at age 18 in the U.S.), after it has been established as impossible to reunite the child with the biological family or find an alternative permanent placement (Okumu, 2014). Based on 2016 estimates, 431,467 children were in foster care system in the U.S. (U.S. Department of Health and Human Services, 2017). Additionally, 250,248 children exited foster care during the 2016 fiscal year, 20,532 of which were emancipated/aged out (U.S. Department of Health and Human Services, 2017). Although there is a dearth of national-level research about the post-foster care experience for those who age out of the system, a recent study by the Columbia Law School (2016) confirms that one in four youth who age out of the foster care system in New York City are likely to spend time in a homeless shelter.

College students with experiences in the foster care system share characteristics with first-generation college students (FGCS). For example, like FGCS, foster care youth often report that few people in their lives expected them to attend or succeed in college (Okumu, 2014). Also, both groups of students are likely to experience inadequate guidance and support in preparing for and navigating higher education (Okumu, 2014; Dworsky & Pérez, 2010; Price, 2008). Unfortunately, the research on foster care youth is sparse. To our knowledge, there has not been a comparative scholarship of demographic factors that impact foster care youth transitioning into college.

Many programs on campuses aim to meet the developmental needs of students who self-identify as lesbian, gay, bisexual, transgender, or queer (LGBTQ). In many instances, these student populations are stigmatized for presenting identities and social roles that do not conform to conventional gender expectations (Lombardi, 2009; Nuru, 2014). These students' needs and issues are often looked at from the perspective of their LGBTQ identity or their first-generation experience or (much less likely) their foster care experience. As a result, there is little room for specifically addressing the unique needs and experiences of those who have foster care experience, are LGBTQ, and are FGCS. Indeed, on most college campuses, the services for each of those groups are fragmented and unintegrated. Such constraints present innumerable challenges as students navigate gender identity, conflicting self-concepts, the enactment of self, and the role of oneself in relation to others. This facilitates the further marginalization of this group of students who have foster care experience, are FGCS, and who identify as LGBTQ. Though there is some research on transgender and other LGBTQ students in college (Beemyn, Curtis, Davis, & Tubbs, 2005; Griner et al., 2017; Oswalt & Lederer, 2017), no researchers have yet examined the intersections of LGBTQ identity, foster care experience, and FGCS.

In this chapter, we explore the story of Malika (a pseudonym), who not only identifies as first-generation former foster care youth, but also as transgender female. Drawing from previous research on transgender identity (Booth, 2011; Grossman & D'Augelli, 2006; Lombardi, 2009), we use the term *transgender* as an umbrella word that refers to an individual who self-identifies with a gender that diverges from the conventionally socially acceptable gender roles, expectations, norms, and identity as dictated by assigned birth or biological sex and external genitalia. This term also includes those who identify as transsexuals, as well as those who have undergone or are in the process of hormone treatment and sex reassignment to align their bodies with their preferred gender.

Drawing from the research context on transgender identity, this chapter's authors examine a first-generation, transgender emancipated foster care student's intersecting developmental identities as constituents of a communication process by which self-concepts, self-understanding, and enactments of the self are infused through interpersonal relationships with others in a college environment. In other words, how does the intersectionality of Malika's different life-stories and voices impact her identity formation and reshape how she engages with a college campus environment?

Theoretical Framework—The Communication Theory of Identity

The Communication Theory of Identity (CTI) is based on the assumption that communication, our relationships, and our communities are central components in our identity development (Hecht, 1993; Hecht, Jackson, & Ribeau, 2003; Hecht, Warren, Jung, & Krieger, 2005). In that context, individuals internalize various social relations and roles through communication. Those identities are, in turn, enacted as social behavior through communication. In being dynamically dialectical, CTI focuses more on mutual influences between identity and communication, and subsequently conceptualizes identity as communication rather than as a product of communication or vice versa (Hecht et al., 2003).

CTI identifies four loci of identity that intersect at multiple levels: personal, relational, enacted, and communal. At the personal level, our identity includes our thoughts, feelings, self-concept, and sense of well-being. However, within identity's relational frame, we also interact with others and express who we are through verbal and non-verbal messages. The relational frame of our identity focuses on how our identity emerges through our interactions with others, as well as how those interactions construct their own identities (Hecht et al., 2003). The third frame of our identity, the enactment of identity to others, focuses on messages that individuals send that express their identity. In other words, we interact with others and express who we are through our verbal and nonverbal cues (Hecht & Faulkner, 2000). Our identity expressions therefore exist on the enacted level, where they are influenced by our relationships.

However, we also have identities that transcend our individuality and our one-on-one enactments in relationships. We are members of various affiliations representing communal frame of reference that bind us together by way of histories, collective memories, rituals, and practices. This constitutes *the communal locus of our identity*. This frame constitutes the fourth location of identity and occurs in the context of a larger community. It represents a shared identity of all its members (Hecht, 1993).

CTI integrates the self, relationships, society, and communication as intersecting loci for identity. In as much as these loci of identity are inseparable and complementary, understandings of identity may shift among and between different levels and contexts. As a result, we have to negotiate tensions between different layers to conceptualize our identity (Hecht et al., 2005; Wadsworth, Hecht, & Jung, 2008). Nonetheless, all four frames assist us in better understanding of ourselves and others as we experience our social world (Hecht et al., 2005).

Malika Shares Her Story as a Marginalized Transgendered Foster Care Youth

Malika is a 21-year-old college student who self-identifies as a transgender Black female enrolled in a mid-size four-year public university in the Midwest region of the U.S. She was placed into the foster care system after legal and medical authorities in her home state deemed her biological mother as incapable of caring for her due to several mental health-related complications. She lived in six foster care placements and attended five different schools over eight years.

While transitioning into college, she has felt alienated not only as a foster youth, but also as the only non-White transgender student in her class:

> I sometimes get internally confused and forget whether or not I am male or female emotionally and even cognitively. Sometimes I'm not even sure what roles my mind, body, and heart play in my life. For instance, at first, I used to paint my nails and then.... Whenever I anticipate handshakes I used to hide them. My boobs were beginning to grow and my voice was becoming softer and yet I was still very muscular and walked like a well-built man just about to pounce on someone. Once, I wore some lipstick in the morning, then took it out before I left my dorm room. For a while afterwards, I decided to put on lipstick only at night. My roommate also do not understand what foster care means.

Malika's foster parents sent her to the university assuring her that the institution was *a diverse* community. Nonetheless, during her first week in college, she could not see anyone who looked like her. She was the only Black transgender student in her engineering class and the only one with experiences from the foster care system. Many of her peers avoided interacting with her because of her mixed-race and transgender identity. She could not even have a consistent peer for some group assignments.

When Malika began her freshman year, she arrived with a strong personal drive, determination, yet had great anxiety and uncertainty. She had just been dropped off by the Independent Living manager of her immediate former foster care home with all her belongings in trash bags. She didn't have her biological parents for support, or any life skills preparation or even college survival advice manual. The manager just said farewell to her with the phrase, *"Now begins a new chapter of your life. I wish you well."* She had aged-out of the foster care system and was on her own.

She immediately felt different from her peers as she passed them saying final goodbyes to their parents, who had helped settle into their freshman residential halls. As a result, she admitted that she very rarely discloses her identity as transgender or former foster care youth:

> I do not think a lot about being first-generation, transgender or emancipated foster care college student. I do not go around telling my peers that I was in foster care or I am transitioning or stuff like that. Aah…I never told anyone this… but when I was in high school, my foster home was in a farm in the middle of nowhere. I never used to hang out with my friends! You know as a senior in high school, you get invited to movies and parties and so on. I could not do any of that. You know…someone invites you out and offers to drive you in their car and then you say, wait a minute; we need to run a background check on you first! I wanted to be around people! I wanted communication and interaction with other normal people so bad. I needed that connection with my peers without background checks! Then you have boobs growing and yet you look like a man! How do you share stuff like that with people?

Malika therefore felt that she would be alienated and isolated if she disclosed some aspects of her identities. She felt that some of her peers and instructors would not understand her.

By the third week of freshman year, Malika began to have interpersonal relationship challenges with her roommates. The roommates branded her as antisocial because she mostly kept to herself and did not join them in their house parties. Little did they know that she was on six different antidepressants, and had begun to struggle academically and socially despite her best efforts. She began to spiral into depression and had no one to talk to because she had not developed help-seeking skills. After deliberations with the residence hall director, Malika relocated to another residence hall and placed in a single dorm room, and she loved it until loneliness crept in.

She first attempted suicide four months into her freshman year. According to Malika, the loneliness and alienation she experienced was the biggest contributing factor to her suicide attempt. She couldn't interact with others on her residence hall floor section because she felt depressed, and she no longer had roommates for interaction. That semester, Malika ended up in a local hospital and was hospitalized for a week.

In her first two years in college, she would be hospitalized another eight times, her medications changed twelve times, and her grades tumbled despite her best efforts. She felt alone on campus, in her classes. However, it was during the college's family-themed weekends where she was forced to see others with relatives that hurt the worst. She had no connectedness to anyone she would call family. None of her foster parents attended college, so they also could not understand her experience.

Malika came back to campus from the last hospitalization only to realize that she had an appointment with the Center for Student Conduct (Judiciaries). She was subsequently placed on disciplinary probation for an attempt to self-harm. Nonetheless, she remained in good standing for the rest of that year and followed approved student conduct protocol. During this probationary time, Malika was sexually assaulted. She reported the case, but as she was still biological male and in her mind, males do not get raped, she decided to drop it.

Later that year, she had a few more hospitalizations as she and her mental health professionals labored to find the right combination of psychotropic medications. However, she just went along with whatever medical recommendation they suggested even though she did not feel she needed it. Malika notes that this was similar to her experience in foster care: follow the psychotropic medical regimen without question for fear of losing privileges. As a foster care child, Malika stated that compared to her foster care placements, she nonetheless felt at home in the hospitals. She believed that she was in good company with others who shared her predicaments and life experiences. The hospital environment helped her feel removed from the stressors of society and able to make friends with others who understood what it was like to be suicidal, raped, abused, neglected, a social outcast, or clinically depressed.

During one Thanksgiving holiday, she stated that she awoke and observed that everybody was leaving, going to their parents, had their folks coming to pick them up. There she was again with nowhere to go. She was the only person left in her residence hall. It was just a day or two, but it made her so lonely and rejected. This experience negatively impacted Malika's ongoing evolving process of developing a positive sense of personal identity. The experience was also worsened by her perceived negative image of a foster care child in the wider community. She stated that as she transitioned into college, she never told her peers that she was an emancipated foster youth because of her negative past experience of being viewed as delinquent.

During Malika's junior year, she was placed in gender-neutral housing on campus and reports that she loved it there. She had been working with her medical professionals transitioning into being female. At this time, a campus-wide housing crisis forced students to double or triple up, but Malika was restricted to her single room and an entire hallway with four empty rooms. Midway through that semester, a new student joined the gender-neutral housing section, but was placed in an empty room in another hallway. That meant that Malika was the only student on campus with her own bathroom and hallway with four empty rooms. Malika felt like she was being isolated from the community setting. She raised the concern to the university om-budsman and the director of the LGBTQ center, stating that she would like to have a roommate or at least students assigned to her hallway because lone-liness was detrimental to her personal growth and college experience. The two university officials referred her back to the residential housing director, but all that Malika got from residential housing officials was: *"We can revisit this conversation at a later date."* It was never revisited. By the end of that semester, Malika decided to move off campus because she could not continue to deal with the roommate restrictions, isolation, and marginalization.

Conceptualizing Malika's Intersecting Identity via Personal Locus

Through the personal locus, Malika's identity consists of her sense of self-being. It entails her thoughts, feelings, self-concept, and sense of well-being. In other words, Malika as an individual is the focus of her identity in which feelings about herself and her self-understanding shape how she identifies. As a first-generation student, Malika stated that being the first one to go to col-lege is constantly in her mind, enhances her image about herself and her self-esteem, and is always a key motivating factor for her success while in college.

> Once you are emancipated [from foster care] it is like going through another death. You find yourself out there with no legal guardians. It is tough! Additionally, I am a first-generation college student and a piece of me always desires to go back to my biological parents even though their parental rights are legally terminated and ask, "Are you proud of me, are you really proud of me?" However, I just have to learn that not everyone will necessarily be proud of me and my accomplishments. I have to learn that I was not going to make everyone happy. I wanted to come to college and build my skills so that when I start having children, I can in turn provide them with the stability I never had.

As a transgender queer student, the personal frame relates to Malika's evolving internal sense of gender identity and how it fuses or interacts with other identity loci. In other words, it involves her individual sense of being female, male, or identifying outside traditional gender roles and norms. When asked about how conscious she was about being transgender queer, she stated that in the beginning it was an immense struggle negotiating the tension between what she felt inside and what others observed. This struggle is especially difficult because she has to make personal meaning of the dynamics of physically and emotionally transitioning from male, boyfriend, and heterosexual to female, girlfriend, and queer. Using the same personal frame to conceptualize Malika's identity transitioning to college as an emancipated foster youth, the experience of emancipation entailed assuming and developing a new sense of being and identity. She conceptualizes this new personal sense of being in the following manner:

> Coming from care and joining college, I am beginning to realize that you can be everything you want to be…and not just simply a label forced upon you. It is fine to sound educated. I just wanted to be able to change the stigma of foster children. We are not ghetto. We are not hoodlums. Not all of us steal. We do not rob people. We are not angry people. We were just placed in a situation and a system that we had no control over and now that I have control over my life, I want to be able to show the next generation, my own children that you can have control over your life. You just have to make those changes. You have to be committed to yourself and be committed to these changes. Sometimes people forget that we [foster care youth] need to be treated as decent people! We have always been "caseloads"! More and more I am realizing that we are more than caseloads. We are now decent people with actual names and feeling, adults, and scholars, not just a caseload! College for me was the time to cease to be a caseload. I am beginning to realize that it is time to take out the trash. My past and experiences in the foster care system is the garbage. My future is the treasure. It is time to take out the trash in my life. Once I take out the trash, I do not have to worry about anything else. I become clean and presentable. I can better myself. I can desire more that makes my life worth living. I can achieve more for myself than what the foster care system has constantly told me I cannot do. I had noticed that I had developed attachment to laundry and garbage bags, something that I had not been aware of until I came into college for the transitional program then had to move into regular housing. College experience is beginning to teach me that it is time to take out the trash in my life.

Malika's status as a first-generation, transgender, and emancipated foster care student together also intersected as a salient feature of her personal identity frame. This intersection stemmed from the different challenges she experienced transitioning into college compared to her peers with no similar personal identity loci. She felt not only alienated with very little or no support transitioning into college as a former foster youth, but also as a transgender student who is also first generation. She offered the following example to underscore the privileges that her peers consciously or unconsciously benefit from, and which heavily contributes to her feelings of isolation and dejection:

A lot of us do not have families that come up to visit from time to time. I had to learn not to be envious. I kind of felt left out and it painfully reminded me of what I did not have and perhaps will never have. I had to struggle not to be jealous of people who had stable families and connection to their families. There is nothing I can do to change this. I am beginning to realize that I am on this college campus for a reason. I am here to better myself. I have not had a family this far and perhaps I do not need one now.

In a follow-up interview regarding her experiences transitioning to college, she emphasized that those identities were central to her personal frames of identity:

I realize that when there is an event to go to on campus, or if we have a break, my friends tell me, "Oh, you know what? My dad will pick me up, or my mom or grandma or boyfriend or girlfriend will drop off the food and bring me stuff, send me money or pay for my books!" Here I was, still working on whether I am a female who has always been a female or a male convinced that he needs to be a female. I have never thought of anyone picking me up or someone dropping off my food! For me it was about how and when I was going to get my food, not who will bring my food! So, when they were talking about these, I began to realize that oh gosh, I am not just a college student, I have to figure out on how to take care of so much stuff! No one will be there to take care of me and other stuff that I need! Everything in college was going to be on me! I know I am of legal age, but it is different when you feel like one and have to act like one! Maybe, this explains why most of my closest friends are older! I have learnt to take care of myself. I cannot afford to depend on somebody else! My closest friends are older because they get that.

However, it is important to note that Malika's intersecting identities are not always salient and central to her personal frames of identity. She mentioned that most times when she is asked how she would self-identify, she takes a moment and examines the context before responding:

In high school, whenever I told folks that I am in foster care, they would react, "Oh my gosh, here is another pathetic troubled charity case!" Some people treat us or see us like being delinquent, trouble makers, and hoodlums! As I transition into college, I know that my previous life in foster care may seem really hard but I have managed to walk around not feeling pity for myself for having been in foster care. I walk straight and say to myself that it could have been much worse. Yes, we have been hurt before but that is not what we are. We are equally smart and we can be who we want to be in life. We have made it to college just like you have! And so, I simply blend in! I just go with what the majority of other kids say. Just imagine when they see me with painted nails and growing boobs and see no parents or siblings visiting during family weekends?

In the light of the above, we argue that while exploring the dynamics of salient intersecting personal frames of identity, the loci are likely to be situational and contingent on specific life situations that often trigger greater consciousness in specific loci of identity.

Enacted and Relational Frame of Malika's Identity

The intersecting nature of Malika's identities made it difficult for us to thematize how her identity presented through the four separate sections according to the CTI theory. As a result, we discuss her intersecting identities by comparing and contrasting the frames that occur in the college campus environment in the context of the CTI loci of Malika's identity. That being said, we also affirm that we reveal our identity to others through the enacted locus of identity (Hecht et al., 2003). However, for Malika, disclosing her identities as a first-generation, transgender, and emancipated foster care individual seems to be situated in the context of other loci of identity.

Malika's Identity Enactment on a Campus Environment

While on campus, Malika's intersecting identities were mostly enacted at her discretion, depending on her situation because there were no overt personal identifying indicators. It seems as if being first generation was her primary reason for enrolling into a campus program that provided additional services to FGCS. Identifying primarily as a FGCS was also the initial motivational impetus and central to her self-concept and success on campus. It also enabled her to not feel embarrassed to have come from a family with no college degree or not valuing college education. Additionally, she explained that she often felt out of place as a transgender, first-generation student from foster care. She stated:

> Teachers on this campus come across like they are used to having students coming from straight, well-off families, self-driven, better prepared, open to expressing who they are freely. You want to tell the teachers things but they simply have no time to listen. You want to explain why your grades are coming down or how you feel about your body or your mind. You want to tell them, "This is where I came from" and "That's why I am having so many struggles," but there is like this big wall. Who then do I turn to? How am I supposed to relate with my teachers if I cannot share something about myself? How can I share my true identity?

In the light of the above, this case study confirms that within the enacted loci, identity messages are situational and relative to the timing, context, and relationship with the other (Hecht & Faulkner, 2000). For Malika, it was easier to reveal her transgender and foster-care background identity once she was certain that her peers or instructors would be understanding and empathic to her background and experiences. As she stated:

I know that I need to get away from what others want me to be. But, I do reveal my inner self to others if and when I feel safe and secure. I have always tried to fit in, wanting to be what others would like me to be. I am trying to take in the most difficult parts of me…meaning those parts of my identity that do not conform to what others believe is the right way to be…. to fit so I can become more of myself. The other one is meeting other people with foster care experience, people with similar background.

In addition to her above self-reflections, Malika was also dismayed by what her peers often took for granted based on their privileges as being heterosexual, having parents with college experiences, and having never had any foster care experiences. She noted:

For my peers, it has just been parties and going out, drinking and smoking weed, and having girlfriends! I also find that in some of my initial classes in college, other students and my teachers simply don't get it! They do not get it that some families have to struggle even to get food! They take everything for granted. Their parents get them everything. Books, help them with homework… everything. I feel like I am much more independent! When I hear some of my friends having problems and they just simply say, "That you know what, I just have to call my mom and she will fix it!" And I am just like what would you do without your mom, what would you do without your parents?

Additionally, Malika found herself often very frustrated with her peers, and at times, shared briefly with them how fortunate they were relative to her situation. This created tension in her intersecting identities as she attempted to balance between what her peers and teachers expected her to be, her attempts to be what others expected of her, and what she identified internally. More often than not, she reported that she felt pressured to enact identity frames to which she did not internally self-identify, leading to her relegating certain behaviors to the private arena where she felt safe and true to herself:

At some point, I couldn't wait to be by myself in my dorm room and dress the way I like without feeling judged by my peers. I just wanted to be me. When I'm alone in my room, it was ok to do my nails, wear some pretty dress, wear my lipstick…and just be me with nobody to judge me.

Personal-Relational-Communal Identity Dynamics

The above identity dynamics also led to discrepancies between Malika's personal identity and how others perceived her (Jung & Hecht, 2004). She realizes that she had to learn to fight against the negative images and lack of knowledge her friends have about her identities.

Most of my peers do not understand what it's like to be raised in an abusive home, to be the first one in college and struggling with gender identity and transitioning! Feeling comfortable with your gender is not a mortal sin. They have no idea of pain, hurt, and hunger. All they do is to feel pity for you! Whenever I mention that I have been to foster care, their reaction makes you feel less accomplished in life. It is like the most embarrassing thing in life! I mean…I do not need any pity! I am who I am. I am strong. I can survive and succeed.

The above experiences from personal and relational loci also impacted how she lived the *communal frame* of identity. This was especially aggravated by the fact that on campus (to her knowledge) there were no people with whom she had a shared identity of being transgender, first generation, and from the foster care system. She missed the experience of the communal loci of her intersecting identities while transitioning into college. Furthermore, her three identities did not have salient visible markers to make it easier for individuals who share her experiences to come together and share their life experiences and voices in a communal setting.

Concluding Remarks and Implications for Practice

The above case study indicates three specific areas of consideration. The centrality of Malika's intersecting identities as first generation, transgender, and former foster care youth were largely influenced by situational contexts. Her different identities appeared to be more salient when they intersected with other aspects of her life experiences while transitioning into the college campus environment such as medical history, lack of family ties, socio-economic challenges, and gender. Her story also reveals a sense of the dynamics of privilege associated with being heterosexual, and having connectedness to a family that also went to college.

Malika's story also reveals that students are likely to reveal and enact their identities with and among those who also share their life experiences. Educators must therefore need to be aware of the marginalized and challenging intersecting identities that students bring to college, and take time to listen to students as they grow and develop.

Although some institutions are intentionally responding to the developmental needs of underrepresented and often underserved college students, these efforts do not seem to have obvious positive impacts. Malika's experiences reveal the complexity of negotiating multiple intersecting identities and the marginalization of some college students with these identities. Educators and university administrators need to extend the discourse on diversity in all possible fronts. One way of consolidating that effort is to marshal faculty and staff to revamp and transform their curriculum, pedagogy, and student developmental interventions so they include the connectedness of the discourse of privilege and diversity enacted in various identity negotiations.

Malika's story affirms the need for faculty and staff to be aware of the invisible, and often ignored emerging loci of the dynamics of privilege. For example, a faculty member may give an assignment that requires students to write about their Thanksgiving experience with their family, without considering the possibility that some students have never had that experience. Other faculty members at times assume we are only she or he. Faculty and staff therefore need to incorporate a more nuanced approach that goes beyond issues of culture, difference, and the interplay of power. This approach will empower educators to be genuine advocates for holistic student growth, developmental needs, and success in a college campus environment.

In the light of Malika's story, Easton (2012) rightly states:

> No matter how much you may know in your head that you and your people are victims of a system that you did not create, it doesn't really matter if you are taking the grenades. You must react to stay alive…I am entrapped in this system where things beyond my control happens, and the only thing I can do is to try my best to be successful in spite of the macrostructural problems that impact me on this microlevel (Easton, 2012, p. 162).

The marginalized intersectional identities and voices in our respective communities need a channel to raise their concerns. You and I are and can be those channels and voices.

Last but not least, educators need to be sensitive to students' less visible identities in order to meet their needs. This entails intentionally observing and listening to the verbal and non-verbal cues that students communicate in various campus contexts. If we only focus on the salient identity markers, then our curriculum, pedagogy, and student developmental initiatives will continue to privilege certain students over others and subsequently further marginalize those who already feel marginalized.

References

Beemyn, B., Curtis, B., Davis, M., & Tubbs, N. J. (2005). Transgender issues on college campuses. *New Directions for Student Services, 111,* 49–60. https://doi.org/10.1002/ss.173

Booth, E. T. (2011). Queering queer eye: The stability of gay identity confronts the liminality of trans embodiment. *Western Journal of Communication, 75*(2), 185–204. doi: 10.1080= 10570314.2011.553876

Choy, S. P. (2001). *Findings from the condition of education 2001: Students whose parents did not go to college: Postsecondary access, persistence, and attainment* (NCES 2001–126). U.S. Department of Education, National Center for Education Statistics. Washington, DC: U.S. Government Printing Office.

Columbia Law School. (2016, July). *Aged out/cast out: Solutions to housing instability for aging out foster youth in New York.* Retrieved from http://www.law.columbia. edu/sites/default/files/legacy/files/public_affairs/2016/july/aged_out-cast_out-_ mhls-arc_housing_report_july_2016.pdf

Davidson, J. V. T. (2016). *Paths of academic resilience: The educational stories of first-generation, low-income students and the processes that led to their experiences of success in the first year of college.* (Doctoral dissertation). Retrieved from Proquest dissertations & theses A&I. (18882677052)

Dworsky, A., & Pérez, A. (2010). Helping foster youth graduate from college through campus support programs. *Child and Youth Services Review, 32*(2), 255–263. http:// dx.doi.org/10.1016/j.childyouth.2009.09.004

Easton, S. (2012). On being special. In G. Gutiérrez y Muhs, Y. F. Nieman, C. G. Gonzalez, & A. P. Harris (Eds.), *Presumed incompetent: The intersections of race and class for women in academia* (pp. 152–163). Boulder, CO: University Press of Colorado.

Griner, S. B., Vamos, C. A., Thompson, E. L., Logan, R., Vázquez-Otero, C., & Daley, E. M. (2017). The intersection of gender identity and violence: Victimization experienced by transgender college students. *Journal of Interpersonal Violence*, 1–22. doi: 10.1177/0886260517723743

Grossman, A. H., & D'Augelli, A. R. (2006). Transgender youth: Invisible and vulnerable. *Journal of Homosexuality, 51*(1), 111–128.

Hecht, M. I. (1993). 2002—A research odyssey: Toward the development of a communication theory of identity. *Communication Monographs, 6*(1), 76–82. http://dx.doi. org/10.1080/03637759309376297

Hecht, M. L., & Faulkner, S. L. (2000). Sometimes Jewish, sometimes not: The closeting of Jewish American identity. *Communication Studies, 51*(4), 372–287.

Hecht, M. L., Jackson II, R. L., & Ribeau, S. A. (2003). *African American communication: Exploring identity and culture.* Mahwah, NJ: Lawrence Erlbaum Associates.

Hecht, M. L., Warren, J. R., Jung, E., & Krieger, J. L. (2005). A communication theory of identity: Development, theoretical perspective and future directions. In W. B. Gudykunst (Ed.), *Theorizing about intercultural communication* (pp. 257–278). Thousand Oaks, CA: Sage.

Jehangir, R. R., Stebleton, M. J., & Deenanath, V. (2015). *An exploration of intersecting identities of first-generation, low-income college students* (Research Report No. 5). Columbia, SC: University of South Carolina, National Resource Center for The First-Year Experience and Students in Transition.

Jung, E., & Hecht, M. L. (2004). Elaborating the communication theory of identity: Identity gaps and communication outcomes. *Communication Quarterly, 52*(3), 265–283. doi: 10.1080= 01463370409370197

Lombardi, E. (2009). Varieties of transgender/transsexual lives and their relationship with transphobia. *Journal of Homosexuality, 56*(8), 977–992. doi: 10.1080=00918360903275393

Nuru, A. K. (2014). Between layers: Understanding the communicative negotiation of conflicting identities by transgender individuals. *Communication Studies, 65*(3), 281–297.

Okumu, J. O. (2014). Meaning-making dynamics of emancipated foster care youth transitioning into higher education: A constructivist-grounded theory. *Journal of The First-Year Experience & Students in Transition, 26*(2), 9–28.

Oswalt, S. B., & Lederer, A. M. (2017). Beyond depression and suicide: The mental health of transgender college students. *Social Sciences, 6*(1), 20. doi: 10.3390/socsci6010020

Price, D. (2008). *Campus support initiative management information system review and recommendation.* Indianapolis, IN: DVP Praxis.

U.S. Department of Health and Human Services. (2017). *The AFCARS report: Preliminary FY 2016 estimates as of Oct 20, 2017.* Retrieved from https://www.acf.hhs.gov/sites/default/files/cb/afcarsreport24.pdf

Wadsworth, B. C., Hecht, M. L., & Jung, E. (2008). The role of identity gaps, discrimination, and acculturation in international students' educational satisfaction in American classrooms. *Communication Education, 57*(1), 64–87. doi: 10.1080=03634520701668407

10. *I Belong Here, Too*

Danica A. Harris

Introduction

First-generation college students (FGCS) are often described as students whose parents did not attend or complete a four-year degree from a university (Davis, 2010). FGCS experience a number of limitations prior to entering college, including lack of assistance with the logistical tasks involved in registering for college, to the undoubtedly missing role-modeled examples for what college life will be like. The lack of support FGCS experience permeates the high school and college experience. Previous research on FGCS highlights that these students tend to produce lower SAT scores, think about college later in their high school years, and overall choose less selective colleges (Orbe, 2004). Some of these factors may be linked with various cultural backgrounds of FGCS wherein they may come from family systems that prioritize family obligations to the detriment of academic responsibilities or college planning (Dennis, Phinney, & Chuateco, 2005). Depending on the roles FGCS fill in their lives outside of school, they may find that they have little time or energy to dedicate to forging forward in college because they are already in a disadvantaged position for navigating the unknown landscape of higher education. The complexities around college continue once FGCS are able to enter the academy, as they often struggle with how to choose a major, and then how to navigate the college experience. Overall, students require intentional support from their family systems and educational professionals to smoothly transition into college. For FGCS, support may look different from their peers with familial roots in higher education.

I know this struggle. As someone who has newly finished her PhD in counseling psychology, I easily recall my experiences as a FGCS, and it is not without pain that I share those experiences in this essay. The existing literature on FGCS highlights that they often have a minimum of one other marginalized identity, thus further impacting their ability to succeed in college (Dennis et al., 2005). As a woman with a working-class identity, I have often experienced the profoundly lacking financial stability needed to achieve in college. Financial instability continued to impact my student experience well into graduate training, and now as I establish myself as an emerging professional. The struggles of FGCS stem from historical contexts created for only a small subset of the population to succeed, and this history impacts FGCS to this day.

In this essay I discuss my hard-fought battle to get an education and to find my own place in an academic environment. Drawing from the research on FGCS, I examine how my experiences mirrored the academic, emotional, cultural, and financial struggles that these students frequently encounter in college. During the second half of the essay, I draw on my psychology training to discuss common psychological and other challenges that FGCS experience. I offer practical recommendations that mental health workers, faculty, and administrators can use to effectively assist FGCS in their care. Finally, I conclude by enumerating the importance of having an empowerment-based approach to help build resiliency and a sense of belonging in FGCS on our campuses.

A Changing Landscape: Higher Education After World War II

Before World War II, graduates from elite universities and colleges in the United States were White affluent men being groomed to assume their powerful fathers' roles when they stepped down from their family businesses and enterprises (Ryan & Sackrey, 1996). These college students usually studied traditional disciplines such as language, mathematics, literature, and history, the same ones their fathers had studied before them. Education's role was to enhance historical and rhetorical knowledge, rather than teaching students a new skill set, or preparing them for a particular career: These students majored in pose and power. Ryan and Sackrey (1996) assert that universities were historically inaccessible to individuals who held marginalized identities, thus contributing to the ever-growing gap between the haves and the have-nots.

In 1944, the U.S. instituted the Servicemen's Readjustment Act, commonly known as the G.I. Bill of Rights (Bound & Turner, 2002). This legislation, and subsequent G.I. Bills passed in 1952 and 1966, led to a dramatic increase in men seeking higher education after World War II. According to historians, this legislation may be responsible for the changing landscape of American higher education. Specifically, 20 million veterans' education were subsidized by these three bills, which afforded working- and lower-middle-class students the ability to attend college in mass numbers for the first time in American history (Davis, 2010). In addition to the G.I. Bills, the National Defense Education Act offered prospective students loans with both long-payback periods and subsidized interest rates. Along with grants offered to deserving individuals, these loans afforded families the ability to consider higher education as a potential option in hopes of changing their own destiny (Ryan & Sackrey, 1996).

The time period immediately following World War II brought great shifts to the American sociocultural landscape, wherein the modernization of agricultural practices and the industrialization of places that had been rural before the war now afforded mobility and created new opportunities for the non-elite to establish themselves in ways that shifted their own identities (Ryan & Sackrey, 1996). Rather than continually focusing on traditional disciplines, many universities began to capitalize on the shifting societal dynamic by offering courses that included professional and vocational training (Ryan & Sackrey, 1996). Although this shift in course offerings was a more inclusive change, it certainly did not welcome all individuals into the academy with open arms. If you were to survey college students in present day, or better yet, if you were to survey ethnic/racial/class or other minority high school students in 2017, you would likely find a commonly-held belief that college is a choice for some and not others. These exclusionary criteria may have changed; more students have the ability to attend college now, and perhaps even have more flexibility in their study area. However, there is still a somewhat unspoken set of criteria that keep some students from entering and succeeding in college (Davis, 2010). Moreover, what was once viewed as educational opportunity, a way for the middle class to find their way into the professions previously held by only the elite, has now shifted into a necessity, wherein job opportunities for the under-educated and working class are increasingly scarce. At the same time, supporting a family with less than a college education is more and more difficult (Lazerson, 1998).

I Had Not Been Taught to Go to College

Despite the goal of affording entering students with advancement opportunities and new on-the-job skills, institutions of higher education tend to further limit FGCS by not fully addressing their specific needs. Institutions also frequently do not appropriately attend to the cultural variables that often intersect with the students' first-generation identities (Stephens, Fryberg, Markus, Johnson, & Covarrubias, 2012). As a high school student reaching my final days before graduation, I remember feeling at a complete loss for what my future would hold. After hearing my peers talk about college applications for a year, and watching them fill with joy when they bought new bedding for their dorm rooms, I knew I needed to quickly figure out options for myself so I could also imagine life beyond my high school's four walls.

After graduation, I started taking classes at the local community college. I remember walking onto campus a week before classes started, with plans to register for my first semester. I spent the summer working more than full-time hours so I could save to pay for the roughly $100 fee associated with each course. Growing up poor, I knew to always understand my financial obligations on the front end. I also knew I would need to continue working full time while beginning at the community college, so I planned a schedule where I could go to school each weekday morning until noon, and then work my full-time job from 1–9 p.m. each evening. I was already accustomed to little sleep, as I worked two jobs during high school, so I knew I would stay up and work on assignments once my workday was over.

I felt excited as I approached the doors of the community college campus near my house. However, the excitement turned into fear as I entered a crowded atrium and came face-to-face with students talking to their parents and friends. Suddenly, I felt so alone. I had imagined that community college would be more comfortable for someone like me; someone who had never imagined that attending a four-year university could be in her future. Alas, as I walked into the community college, this campus that I had passed nearly every day as I drove from my high school campus to my after-school job, I felt immediately out of place, with no sense of where to begin. I wanted to belong among these students; I wanted to be accepted; I wanted to accept myself. I was unsure where to start, who to ask for help, and I ended up minutes later sitting in my car, crying. I had not been taught to go to college. I quickly found myself with a vast amount of desire to achieve, but with no true blueprint for how to do so. In that moment, I recall feeling a rush of shame and an immediate sense of not belonging.

I felt left out on that community college campus because even a college designed for transitional and under-represented students is not truly designed with them in mind. The cultural norms of middle- and upper-class students differed from mine, and the messages I received both from my family, and seemingly the universe, were that I did not belong in college. On that day, I not only faced the typical anxieties and difficulties that non-FGCS encounter, but like many other FGCS also confronted my general lack of knowledge about secondary education (Pascarella, Pierson, Wolniak, & Terenzini, 2004).

What I have learned from my experience is that colleges and universities, and by extension, the high schools that prepare students for higher education, do a disservice to under-represented students. FGCS miss out on the cultural norms and folklore passed down from parents who attended college (Stephens et al., 2012). As with any sub-group, colleges and the educated within them have a special sort of language, one that affords students with an easy transition if they are equipped to translate the code (Davis, 2010). Davis (2010) states that the culture of college, specifically learning how to get around campus, paying fees, knowing what materials to take to class, and completing many other routine tasks, are largely unclear to FGCS, thus serving as a cultural limitation before ever setting foot on campus. This limitation, coupled with the fact that first-generation students are less likely to join student organizations, study for long hours, and engage with faculty likely means that they will feel poorly equipped to handle academics after beginning college (Orbe, 2004).

My Working-Class Family and Lack of a College Road Map

Growing up in a working-class family has impacted every experience of my life. In fact, my youth taught me much about how the world works, especially about who gets ahead and who is left behind. I witnessed power disparity within my home, but more importantly I felt a sense of powerlessness every time I stepped out into the world. As a child, I was not taught to consider what I wanted to be when I grew up; rather, my family focused on how I could use my hands instead of my head. This always felt off to me. I knew that I was capable of more, but my family gave me the daily reminder that simply wanting things to be different would not change my life's course.

My parents had not gone to college, and only my mother had earned her high school diploma. Attending an affluent high school, where teenagers drove luxury cars to school and students could readily apply to any college of their choice, made my last two years of high school nearly unbearable. My parents often spoke of their desires for me to have a life unlike theirs, one where I could feel independent and successful. However, my parents taught me values that seemed to oppose their desires for my success: I was explicitly taught to be interdependent, flexible to others' needs, and was shown the importance of being part of the collective community (Stephens et al., 2012). This left me entirely unaware what independence looked like, and how to obtain it. My parents themselves were not independent. They relied heavily on each other and our family system to make ends meet, and in the process of surviving, any conversations about my future, or college, were left unspoken.

I was a high-achieving student and loved school, and my thirst for knowledge is something I carry with me to this day. After a school assembly one day, where various colleges set up tables in my high school's student union, I went home with emerging interest in my future. I recall my mother's expression when she told me that there was no college fund for me after I inconsiderately asked her about how they were going to support my desire to go to college. The truth was, and remains, that my parents wanted me to go to college, and their silence around the topic of my future was not because they did not care, it was because they did not know how to have the conversation (Covarrubias & Fryberg, 2015). My parents' own inadequacies about their lack of education and financial stability quickly seeped into my own experience, and soon, I felt just as unprepared as my parents to talk about my future or educational desires (Padgett, Johnson, & Pascarella, 2012). My mom and dad felt proud of my academic ability, but I believe they did not know how to handle my achieving nature. The truth was that college was never on the table for anyone in my family. Most of my dad's family holds less than a high school education. Members on both sides of my family were more likely to join the military to escape their working-class background then ever step foot on a college campus. Similar to other marginalized identities, first-generation students' options are limited from birth. Although I hold significant privilege related to my Whiteness, I carry with me the sometimes-hidden oppression that comes from being a working-class and first-generation college person (Gutiérrez y Muhs, Niemann, González, & Harris, 2012). People have expected me to fit in; people have expected me to find my own place, and it has felt difficult over the years to explain to them just how I do not belong at all.

Throughout my time in high school and college, I easily recall the lack of knowledge that administrators, teachers, and support staff displayed when talking to me about my potential to enroll in college, let alone how I would navigate its complexities if I got there. During a conversation with my high school dean during my junior year, she asked why I did not want to attend college. She noted my aptitude and high test scores, and flippantly stated that I could be anything I wanted to be, and that I was too smart to miss out on college. Eighteen years later, I remember the pain I felt as she spoke these words. Instead of sharing my fear and pain with her, I replied that college was not for me.

This was the truth. College was not for me. Having a dad with a seventh grade education and a mom whose ability to assist with my homework ended in middle school created a situation where no amount of my hard work prepared us for registering for college, let alone planning or paying for an academic degree. My parents' lack of advanced education left them without the words to help me understand my status relative to my peers (Covarrubias & Fryberg, 2015). I was unable to explain the truth to the well-intentioned people who wanted to help because I felt unaware of the exact hurdles I would face in trying to get into college. I only knew that money would always be a struggle.

Besides this, though, I did not know how to handle authority once I got to college. I would not understand how or where to file for the financial aid I undoubtedly needed. I would not know how to engage with my more privileged peers. Generally, I would not know what I did not know, and that one aspect alone was terrifying (Davis, 2010). Nevertheless, I knew I had to create some sort of change for my future, so obliviously I continued.

Somehow I managed to find the courage to walk back into that community college campus, and register for 15 credit hours. I mistakenly saw college as my ticket out, lacking the mature understanding of having to complete college and then also create a future for myself if I was able to make it to graduation. Thinking back, it was probably a good thing that I lacked the awareness of the struggles, pain, and heartache ahead of me, or when I returned to the car in tears, I likely would have driven off. I remember the academic advisor asking me what I wanted to major in when I transferred to a university, and I probably laughed as I told her I had no clue. Having no clue was only part of the problem, though; the rest of the problem was me and the circumstances I was born into. What the advisor, my high school dean, and the joyous students registering for college with their parents and friends in tow did not know about me was that this was likely my last stop. I saw an associate's degree in my future, at best.

Not unlike other FGCS, filled with determination and dedication to their studies (Covarrubias & Fryberg, 2015), I soldiered on through my first year of classes, while barely surviving my paycheck-to-paycheck lifestyle. When I moved out at 18, which was the age I was expected to launch into adulthood, my financial literacy was poor, and my ability to juggle adult responsibilities took a toll on my academics to the point where college removed itself from my life. My working-class background taught me that when times get tough, I must get tougher, and while I worked to survive, I was unable to plan for my future. FGCS often come from families who either identify as working-class, or who struggle to maintain financial stability. In my case, my parents similarly were unable to contribute to my education when I needed them most (Stephens et al., 2012). When faced with needing to work more hours to pay for the unexpected college costs, such as having to purchase Scantrons and a parking pass, it was seemingly easy to justify the messages I had internalized about my ability to succeed. I felt like an imposter every day in my classes, and I lost the internal struggle with myself on the day I decided that my pre-determined narrative already had the ending written (Davis, 2010).

Because FGCS often have limited access to quality education, students who desire higher education may have to seek alternative options. Consequently, FGCS have a greater likelihood in seeking briefer schooling, or vocationally-focused programs (Stephens et al., 2012). Consistent with my working-class roots, my best bet for a different future seemed predictably outlined with a trade school education and manual labor job. At 19, while working an unreasonable number of hours per week, I took out a loan and enrolled in a trade school where I earned an esthetician's license.

Initially, this trade felt like my ticket to freedom. My background led me to believe that success was exclusively linked to hard work, so I advocated for myself and persevered. After a failed marriage, a back-and-forth move across the country, and finally landing a highly-desired education job in the skin care field, I felt like I had made something of myself. However, even though I advanced at work and enjoyed my job, I was still unsatisfied.

FGCS often find themselves in a new bind after completing their education (Ryan & Sackrey, 1996). They are again faced with navigating an environment that was not built for them. They enter a workforce based on the same middle- and upper-class values that left them and their needs out of the conversation in the first place. After a few years working in skin-care education, I began to see the irony in where I ended up; I was indeed in a learning environment. With each passing year I felt emptier, and longed to finish what I started eight years before at that community college. I was extremely hopeful that in the years since I last stepped foot on that community college campus, I had changed in some way. If I was to take a second chance at education and it failed, there would certainly not be a third chance.

When I met my now-husband, his educational privilege greatly impacted me. He had a master's degree in information security and was only the second person I had ever known with that education level. I remember going out with his friends and hearing college stories, and I cringed, just hoping that no one would ask about my college experience. The older I got, the greater my lack of education impacted me. I started to resent everything about my upbringing, including my parents. I experienced profound conflict with my family as I shared my disappointment with them. They wanted me to accept my fate, the fate they, too, had to accept when they realized their own options were limited much earlier (Covarrubias & Fryberg, 2015). I was another statistic, another girl born into a class she could not see her way out of, another college dropout, another person limited by her circumstances and not her potential.

Then Everything Changed

With my husband's financial and emotional support, I returned to college to complete my bachelor's degree. Once I made the decision to return to school, I knew that I needed to finish what I started at the community college where I first felt alone and out of place. This time, however, my husband came with me to help me navigate the process of speaking to an advisor and securing financial aid. I am a strong woman, very assertive in most aspects of my life, but on this day, I needed someone who had been there and who had achieved their goals to show me how to go to college. Despite having achieved a reasonable amount of status in my current job, and despite my high academic marks in grade school, I still felt unsure of myself as a student. The college cultural landscape still felt White, affluent, and elite to me (Stephens et al., 2012).

Nevertheless, this FGCS held her head high, this time walking out of the building with tears of joy rather than pain. I quickly completed my associate's degree by taking 21 credit hours a semester, and advanced to Texas Woman's University to pursue a BA in psychology. I was one of the roughly 50% of students entering a two-year college in the early 2000's who identify as a FGCS, and I joined just over a third of students entering into a four-year university who were also the first in their families to go to college (Pascarella et al., 2004).

When I called my parents to tell them about my decision to return to school, they did not understand. I had a job that paid the bills, what else did I want? After many comments about how psychology is not a real major, and their cautioning me about how hard it would be to defy my current destiny, I simply told them that I had to give myself a chance to change. As a FGCS, I was prone to feeling guilty, and in particular I struggled with the sense that I had left my family behind (Covarrubias & Fryberg, 2015). Quickly, I felt like I did not have a place to belong. My family rejected my desire to return to college in my late twenties. They felt sure based on their own experiences that even if I was able to finish college, that my career options were limited; after all, I would always be just a poor girl. The academy did not feel like home, either. Although I often felt in awe of my course material and cherished each day I made the forty-minute drive to my university, I always felt like an outsider looking in (Covarrubias & Fryberg, 2015). I felt like an imposter in higher education, and unfortunately, this feeling still resonates with me today.

Nonetheless, I will never forget the emotions I experienced when I walked across the stage to receive my BA. I had made it: I felt like I had indeed defied my destiny. This has been the most emotional and accomplished day of my life to date. In that moment I became a different statistic as I became the first person in my family to attend and graduate from college. No one in my family—including me—could believe I had completed this daunting task. As I walked across that stage, I understood that it was safe to dream. This realization changed my life's outcome. Experiencing this shift allowed me to see that people constantly change in order to redefine and often reconcile disparate parts of themselves. I reconciled my past and present on that day, and for the first time, I could see a future in which I could be both a survivor and dreamer.

Once I entered graduate school, I slowly realized that people are complex in part because they have a past that continually impacts their current and future circumstances (Gutiérrez y Muhs et al., 2012; Stephens et al., 2012). My class identity is always with me. As a FGCS, this identity greatly disadvantaged my education process because I had no exposure to the questions I needed to ask. These parts of my identity are the most salient parts of who I am, although I understand how my intersecting identities impact how I live my personal and professional lives. Through my own naming process, I recognize that I am a White, working-class, heterosexual, partnered cis woman, who is also an Atheist and non-disabled person of size. I recently added staff psychologist to this list of claimed identities because I now work in a student counseling center at a higher education institution. There appears to be room for me within the academy.

In recent years, I have experienced some shifting in my identities, as I imagine all people do with the fluidity of their lives and experiences. Alcoff (2006) asserts that although some identities are more visible than others, identity variables may shift in their salience depending on the environment and life circumstances. Alcoff discusses how visible identities can impact people's sense of belonging, as others measure us based on the identities that they can see, rather than on the identities that may be most salient.

A salient shift in identity for me is related to class, which some may see as an invisible identity. In my thirties, I shifted in my social location such that I am now afforded opportunities from which I was once excluded. Despite my success, my FGCS identity is salient in all my academic spaces. Similar to other FGCS, I think about this part of my identity daily (Orbe, 2004). Being in a doctoral training program was an aspect of my recent life that I did not once believe would be possible. This shift was crucial for me, and has ultimately changed my life's outcome. Experiencing this shift personally allowed me to see that people constantly shift identities in order to redefine or reconcile some part of themselves.

Psychological and Educational Outcomes for FGCS

FGCS tend to lack the role models they need to succeed in college. Due to often needing to navigate college on their own, or with well-intentioned family members who are simply unable to provide necessary support, these students often experience profound consequences when they enter the academy (Covarrubias & Fryberg, 2015). Specifically, FGCS often struggle with low self-esteem and self-efficacy, as they have lacked reinforcement from others on their ability to achieve in college (Davis, 2010). Perhaps one of the most devastating outcomes for FGCS is that simply getting in the door to college does not mean that they will earn a degree (Stephens et al., 2012; Tate et al., 2015). Much like my experience, where I went to college briefly and had to leave due to financial reasons and role strain, many FGCS are unable to complete their degree within six years from graduating high school, thus leading to increased financial strain and a negative impact on mental wellness (Davis, 2010; Stephens et al., 2012; Tate et al., 2015).

Other stressors for FGCS identified by the literature include identity threat, psychological adjustment distress, difficulty maintaining or creating relationships, thus impacting their sense of social support, and feelings related to not adequately fitting in as a student (Stephens et al., 2012). These stressors impact student performance, which is likely to create a negative self-concept that may ultimately lead to students' decision to leave school to reconcile their discomfort or shame (Stephens et al., 2012; Tate et al., 2015).

If college is seen as the ticket to social mobility, and some students routinely and profoundly receive the message that they do not belong in higher education, what does that mean for their placement, and thus value, in society (Stephens et al., 2012)? The gap between FGCS and non-FGCS likely continues to widen even in college, wherein FGCS frequently fill roles outside their primary student role (Pascarella et al., 2004). These additional roles and responsibilities impact the cognitive and psychological functioning of FGCS, consequently resulting in less campus involvement, less time for studying or attending office hours, and perhaps lower academic performance (Pascarella et al., 2004). This is not to imply that FGCS cannot excel in college, because they certainly can; they simply need to put forth more effort and cross more barriers to do so.

Academic Programs and Inclusion

If I had to summarize my identity in one word, I would choose Advocate. Personally, this identity stems from what I have overcome in my life through advocating for myself, my beliefs, and my education. Growing up in a working-class family, I recognized the lack of formal education afforded to those of a less-privileged class status. My experiences led me to value education, and I grew to understand that by obtaining educational resources, I would be more capable of not only helping myself, but also would be able to aid others. Professionally, being an advocate means that I am a facilitator for change at the societal level. The intersection of my class identity, FGCS identity, and my recently obtained educational and professional privileges impact my desire to create safer spaces for students like me in academia, so first-generation students can not only feel accepted, but also welcomed to pursue their own dreams.

FGCS often find themselves needing more social support, tutoring, and care as they enter into college (Stephens et al., 2012). This was certainly the case for me, and I often found myself asking questions that I could tell others thought were foolish. The judgment I received from administrators and peers diminished my self-esteem, and was a new challenge for navigating this already difficult and unfamiliar environment (Pascarella et al., 2004; Stephens et al., 2012). If colleges and graduate-training programs, where even fewer college students identify as FGCS, could create mentorship programs where FGCS could share their experiences about navigating college, then perhaps more students could create a blueprint for their college experience. When the cultural norms one experiences differs from their macro-environment, they are unable to see how they fit within the greater context (Stephens et al., 2012). Quite literally, for FGCS it is the case that they cannot be what they cannot see.

There were few FGCS in my graduate-training program. I remember coming out as a FGCS in my first few weeks of graduate school, in my vocational psychology class. As I stood in front of my peers and shared my vocational and educational family tree, I could tell only one other student resonated with my upbringing. Thinking back, I wish my program had nurtured this part of my identity, because truthfully getting to graduate school as a FGCS is an enormous accomplishment. I spent many years hiding this part of my identity, rather than embracing it or celebrating this triumph part of myself. With few faculty members identifying as FGCS, it is likely that they, too, lack the blueprint for navigating academia. The first-generation identity is a diversity variable that warrants the same care and consideration of other diverse parts of a person. Without taking the time to understand the FGCS college experience and all the complexities of the identity, professors and peers are likely to misunderstand and enact microaggressions against FGCS, as I know from experience. If colleges and universities do not make adequate space for FGCS, they will continue to recapitulate elite environments that are safe for only the privileged (Stephens et al., 2012).

Psychologists and FGCS Support

In recent years, college counseling centers have experienced an increased demand for their services across all identity groups (Watkins, Hunt, & Eisenberg, 2012). Contrary to previous college cohorts, students come to college with previous mental health treatment; thus, psychologists must play a greater active role in securing the mental stability of the entire college population. A unique obstacle for FGCS and their families centers on mental health knowledge and stigma. Marginalized students may require the most support once they make it to college, yet they are the least likely to get their needs met through standard psychological practices geared towards treating non-FGCS (Watkins et al., 2012).

In my own experience as a staff psychologist, I have observed the complexity that the intersection of a FGCS identity and other marginalized identities present for students. Professionals struggle to understand the differences between factors of students' FGCS identity, and factors associated with other identities. Specifically, psychologists may under-estimate the role that a first-generation identity can play in students' lives, and therefore, may neglect to see students' identities in their entirety.

An additional factor includes the mental and emotional distress that FGCS may experience due to role strain, acculturation concerns, and depression and anxiety related to negative self-concept and fears about their future. Psychologists should be prepared to assist these students in both a clinical and skills-based capacity. Because mental health treatment can be misperceived as weakness, especially in working-class cultures, and FGCS often endure a real or perceived pressure to appear strong and capable, mental health providers must directly acknowledge the impact that FGCS identity has for students seeking support. Further, as a psychologist with a first-generation identity, I openly identify as a FGCS during outreach events, in counseling sessions, and in all my other professional settings. Visibility is everything. If just one person sees my success, then they may believe success can be their future, too.

In 2014, nearly 4.5 million FGCS were enrolled in higher education, and this number continues to climb as these students may see a baccalaureate degree as the way to change their financial landscape (Stebleton, Soria, & Huesman, 2014). Consistent with the literature, FGCS may feel a lack of belongingness at college, while simultaneously feeling disconnected from their home culture. FGCS need spaces that welcome diversity on college campuses as well as programming that follows both them and their families throughout their entire academic career. Perhaps a key component lacking from current programming is mentorship for FGCS and their families while the student is still in high school. The assumptions made about students' knowledge of how to navigate their college experience does not consider how FGCS lack the resources and exposure to educated mentors who can help them create a path for their future.

Psychologists play a pivotal role in creating space for FGCS on college campuses. It felt crucial for me to take up space at a university for my first job out of graduate school not because I wanted to prove something to myself, but because I want to advocate for FGCS. I network with other professionals who were FGCS, meet diversity leaders, and assert my desire to make college a second and comfortable home for FGCS. During my final year in graduate school, I created an outreach event for FGCS. Although few students attended, I intimately heard the stories of four women who have struggled to find their way at a STEM-focused university. They shared vulnerably and urged for more support on campus. Motivated by these experiences, I created a therapy group in the student counseling center for FGCS so they can find community. In future semesters, I intend to get outside of the counseling center and hold group meetings in an alternative space so that students who fear judgment about needing help can feel more at ease about using this resource. Something I keep in mind during my advocacy efforts for FGCS is to never give up or get complacent, even when attendance is low or the impact seems marginal. My job is to find these students and support them in a way that facilitates their connection to campus.

Additionally, psychologists can help other professionals on campus address FGCS' needs by establishing mentorship programs, designing print and online material that is easily accessible to this population, and encouraging faculty and staff to reach out to students. One of the greatest obstacles for FGCS is that they have a diminished sense of their own value, which impacts their ability to seek support from people on campus in authority positions. By creating spaces for FGCS on college campuses, professors, therapists, administrators, and other authority figures can physically go to the students, rather than expecting them to know how and when to seek support. People in authority positions on campuses need to literally create the blueprint for college for FGCS: They need to help them see their own value.

Closing Remarks: A Resiliency- and Empowerment-Based Approach to Advocacy

As I transition into my career's next stage to a professional role where I can impact students like me, I feel overwhelmed with joy for who I have become. I incorporate dreaming and resiliency into my empowerment-based clinical work, teaching, and perhaps most importantly, my everyday life. Through learning to dream, I discovered how to confront and surpass limits and live within all of my open space. My hope is to support clients and students through their own naming process while simultaneously encouraging them to dream. Only now, after years of metaphorically falling down, and dragging myself back up, and making mistake after mistake, that my perspective of myself and future has changed. Through my own dedication and willpower, I created a space for myself that no one else handed out to me. When it comes to the academy, I now fully see that I belong here, too.

References

Alcoff, L. M. (2006). *Visible identities: Race, gender, and the self* (Vol. 10). New York, NY: Oxford University Press.

Bound, J., & Turner, S. (2002). Going to war and going to college: Did World War II and the GI Bill increase educational attainment for returning veterans? *Journal of Labor Economics, 20*(4), 784–815. https://doi.org/10.1086/342012

Covarrubias, R., & Fryberg, S. A. (2015). Movin'on up (to college): First-generation college students' experiences with family achievement guilt. *Cultural Diversity and Ethnic Minority Psychology, 21*(3), 420–429. doi: 10.1037/a0037844

Davis, J. (2010). *The first-generation student experience: Implications for campus practice, and strategies for improving persistence and success.* Sterling, VA: Stylus Publishing.

Dennis, J. M., Phinney, J. S., & Chuateco, L. I. (2005). The role of motivation, parental support, and peer support in the academic success of ethnic minority first-generation college students. *Journal of College Student Development, 46*(3), 223–236. doi: 10.1353/csd.2005.0023

Gutiérrez y Muhs, G., Niemann, Y. F., González, C. G., & Harris, A. P. (Eds.). (2012). *Presumed incompetent: The intersections of race and class for women in academia.* Ogden, UT: Utah State University Press.

Lazerson, M. (1998). The disappointments of success: Higher education after World War II. *The Annals of the American Academy of Political and Social Science, 559*(1), 64–76.

Orbe, M. P. (2004). Negotiating multiple identities within multiple frames: An analysis of first-generation college students. *Communication Education, 53*(2), 131–149. https://doi.org/10.1080/03634520410001682401

Padgett, R. D., Johnson, M. P., & Pascarella, E. T. (2012). First-generation undergraduate students and the impacts of the first year of college: Additional evidence. *Journal of College Student Development, 53*(2), 243–266. doi: 10.1353/csd.2012.0032

Pascarella, E. T., Pierson, C. T., Wolniak, G. C., & Terenzini, P. T. (2004). First-generation college students: Additional evidence on college experiences and outcomes. *The Journal of Higher Education, 75*(3), 249–284. doi: 10.1353/jhe.2004.0016

Ryan, J., & Sackrey, C. (1996). *Strangers in paradise: Academics from the working class.* Lanham, MD: University Press of America.

Stebleton, M. J., Soria, K. M., & Huesman, R. L. (2014). First-generation students' sense of belonging, mental health, and use of counseling services at public research universities. *Journal of College Counseling, 17*(1), 6–20. doi: 10.1002/j.2161–1882.2014.00044.x

Stephens, N. M., Fryberg, S. A., Markus, H. R., Johnson, C. S., & Covarrubias, R. (2012). Unseen disadvantage: How American universities' focus on independence undermines the academic performance of first-generation college students. *Journal of Personality and Social Psychology, 102*(6), 1178–1197. doi: 10.1037/a0027143

Tate, K. A., Fouad, N. A., Marks, L. R., Young, G., Guzman, E., & Williams, E. G. (2015). Underrepresented first-generation, low-income college students' pursuit of a graduate education: Investigating the influence of self-efficacy, coping efficacy, and family influence. *Journal of Career Assessment, 23*(3), 427–441. doi: 10.1177/1069072714547498

Watkins, D. C., Hunt, J. B., & Eisenberg, D. (2012). Increased demand for mental health services on college campuses: Perspectives from administrators. *Qualitative Social Work, 11*(3), 319–337. doi: 10.1177/1473325011401468

Section Three: The Role of Intersecting Marginalized Identities in Institutional Socialization

11. Outside/Inside (Higher) Education: Colonizing Oppression, Intersectional Struggles, and Transformative Opportunities for Marginalized First-Generation College Students

XAMUEL BAÑALES

Introduction

The subject of first-generation college students (FGCS) is receiving more academic inquiry in recent years (Davis, 2010; Housel & Harvey, 2009; Jehangir, Stebleton, & Deenanath, 2015; McGlynn, 2011; Orbe, 2004; Ward, Siegel, & Davenport 2012). Increasingly, the topic is appearing in books, newspapers, magazines, media sites, or blogs, sometimes through the perspective of college students and academics who were first generation (Banks-Santilli, 2015; Greenwald, 2012; Hernández, 2017; Muñoz, 2017; Smith, 2015). Qualitative and quantitative studies on FGCS (Jehangir et al., 2015), and the range of research about them, collectively cover many issues. These include: definitions and theories to understand the term and group; the experiences, barriers, and challenges FGCS face; narratives of their personal empowerment and resilience; examinations of how higher education administrators, faculty, and staff can better understand and work with them; and recommendations for ways university strategies and practices can improve their academic success and graduation rates. Furthermore, initiatives in California like *I'm First!* and UC Davis' *First Generation Faculty* have emerged, among many reasons, to empower FGCS (I'm First! n.d.; First Generation Faculty, n.d.).

Two common, interrelated approaches in the literature and narratives about FGCS focus on constraints and merit. Restrictions may include parental income, psychological/emotional challenges, academic preparation, English language proficiency, ACT scores, and GPA. The limitation perspective is commonly based on a deficit view in which FGCS' obstacles determine or explain a lack of success in college (Banks-Santilli, 2015; Greenwald, 2012). At the same time, narratives about merit are premised on a myth of meritocracy, or the belief that everyone has an equal chance to succeed, and that individuals who are "smart" and determined deserve to be rewarded for their personal work ethic and achievements. Both the narratives of constraints and meritocracy are largely premised on and reinforce the larger, inaccurate myth of upward mobility of mainstream American/Western culture (Frank, 2016; McNamee & Miller Jr., 2014).

One way the deficit model is addressed in higher education is that university personnel make changes to their practices of working with FGCS. The adjustments can serve FGCS to better transition into the university—to "act on their behalf" (Greenwald, 2012). A college may enact a merit-based perspective when it showcases an overachieving FGCS, often of an underrepresented background, who "succeeds" despite limitations they experience in their academic journey (for one example, see Wanderer Films, 2016). One of the problems of FGCS narratives, especially those intersecting with a discourse of multiculturalism and diversity, is that they may serve as a guise that ultimately perpetuates Whiteness (Castagno, 2014). Moreover, these standpoints rarely critically examine social, structural, and institutional obstacles that FGCS face in a variety of spaces, including home, their communities, and society, and not only in college.

Fortunately, the literature about FGCS also includes more productive frameworks that take into account multiple identities and complex settings. To highlight one example, Jehangir et al.'s (2015) research report uses a developmental ecology model to examine intersecting contexts and identities of FGCS. The authors examine how FGCS interact with multiple dimensions and factors in their environments, such as socioeconomic background and class, race/ethnicity, and immigration status. Drawing from focus-group data at a predominantly White, Midwestern, research institution, the report analyzes the experiences of 39 study participants who were majority students of color (94%), female (62%), immigrants (48%), and received federal financial aid (85%). Although the study does not critically analyze important aspects of intersectional identity, such as sexuality, the report illuminates the heterogeneity of FGCS. Additionally, Jehangir et al. (2015) reveal several findings, such as how FGCS experience contradictions between "home" and "college" life and the varying expectations of these spaces; manage and become more adept at navigating and negotiating their contrasting worlds; and balance deep responsibilities to families and communities while asserting their independence that comes with career and personal choices.

Approaches that account for multiple contexts and complex identities are important and necessary because the category of FGCS is not synonymous to, but certainly may include, members of a variety of other underrepresented groups, such as those of racial/ethnic, disability, gender, or class backgrounds. Data shows that FGCS are more likely to be over the age of 24, female, low-income, of color (Black or Latinx), nonnative speakers of English, immigrant, single parents, and/or employed, and have a disability, and such aspects are likely to influence their experiences in the university (Jehangir et al., 2015). This is particularly important if one takes into account that college graduation rates vary widely along racial and ethnic lines, especially for Black and Latinx students who complete their credentials at lower rates (Tate, 2017).

Although scholarly and popular attention on FGCS has been generative, interconnected gaps emerge in the research and narratives. First, a critical assessment of higher education and Western society is overwhelmingly missing from the discourse on FGCS. In general, the literature on FGCS lacks a critical conversation about the highly problematic, exclusionary, and oppressive role that K–12 and higher education has played historically and in contemporary times, specifically for underrepresented communities. Those who focus on or write from the perspective as a FGCS often fail to problematize the Western university and modern society—the cultural norms and structures largely responsible for creating systemic inequities. Social and university structures make it difficult for marginalized students to complete their education, enter college, and succeed—regardless of if they are FGCS or not. Without critical attention on the systemic and oppressive forces that operate in society, one runs the risk of perpetuating a deficit or merit-based model and reinforcing the false myth of upward mobility in American culture, which largely places the fault or expectations on individuals. Second, although the topic of FGCS may include conversations on salient aspects of identity and background, such as race/ethnicity, nationality, or socioeconomic status, few critically engage the intersectionality of oppression across other forms of exclusionary structures of power, such as through gender and sexuality, especially as they relate to experiences before and after the university. More complex narratives of FGCS are necessary in order to further highlight this group's heterogeneity while also expanding awareness on the varying marginalizations that shape their experiences, and not only during college years. Finally, there aren't enough narratives of college students and academics of first-generation backgrounds that are committed to social change on multiple fronts. Learning more about the ways in which FGCS and academics work toward transforming their respective institutions and environments not only challenges deficit/merit-based models, but also addresses structural forces of marginalization and power.

Thus, this essay addresses such gaps by: (1) providing a general contextualization of public education in the United States, including the modern university, particularly in relation to colonization and racially underrepresented groups; (2) narrating intersectional struggles I have experienced and navigated before entering college, as a FGCS, and now as a faculty member, in relation to oppression and violence; and (3) calling attention to various forms of social change that have occurred at the university by FGCS, including many I have participated in and am currently enacting.

My general argument is that a critical assessment of FGCS' experiences through an intersectional lens cannot be divorced from society's oppressive institutional structures. Furthermore, I contend that if we want significant change in how intersectional identities of FGCS are understood, treated, or respected, they cannot be separated from the transformative changes that need to happen at the university and beyond. Placing attention on the relationship between marginalization and exclusionary structures of (higher) education in the U.S. provides an opportunity to shift the discussion on FGCS beyond deficit and merit to one of power, privilege, oppression, and transformation in society.

Colonizing Education, University, and Oppression

Although there have been many past individuals who were the first in their families to attend college and complete higher education degrees, the category of FGCS is a relatively recent one that emerged with post-World War II economic prosperity and global domination of the U.S. Prior to WWII, most people attending American universities were historically male and White, invariably children of parents who attended colleges who were most likely children of parents with higher education, and so on down the line (Davis, 2010). In the U.S. and other "First World" countries (or the "global North"), people of European origin have long dominated scholarship and higher education. Subjects such as history, literature, art, and society "were formerly always 'White Only' (and usually 'male only'), with other groups included only as problems, enemies, or outsiders" (Forbes, 2008, p. 59). Instead of learning about marginalized or underrepresented histories, students in public education are generally expected to know information that is considered standard, like the number of wives that Henry VII had, that Shake-speare was a famous playwright, or that Augustus Caesar was the emperor of the Roman Empire. As California school counselor Diana Martínez noted, "Many teachers who went through the system and received their credentials don't know [basic figures of Chicano History]" (Quoted in Santillano, 1994, p. 11). After the establishment of the GI Bill and state outreach programs like the Educational Opportunity Program, FGCS increased on American campuses in significant numbers. As a result, and after much protest, the university slowly became more diversified, including the curriculum, which I will address later in this essay.

Despite the increasing presence of FGCS at the university since the mid-twentieth century, many higher education institution officials are unfamiliar with this population's heterogeneity or have only recently become aware of them and their needs. Many college administrators, faculty, staff, and traditional students often do not understand why FGCS, especially those of underrepresented backgrounds, are most likely to drop out, take longer to graduate, get less out of a college education, or report feelings of low confidence and isolation when reflecting on their university experience (Davis, 2010). Literature on FGCS underscores several reasons that explain their "low success," such as having to work multiple jobs, attending to family needs, and/or being unfamiliar with college life and expectations. Unfortunately, many of these explanations reify a notion of merit or deficit. This individual-focused perspective is divorced from the systemic exclusionary ideologies and practices that are central to modern education and society. Thus, a general historical-social context of modern society and critique of the inequalities and oppression of systems of education, including the Western university, is needed in order to better understand the challenges and complexities of intersectional FGCS.

Underrepresented groups have a long history of epistemological violence and subjugation in educational systems and general American society (Takaki, 2008). This oppression has occurred since the country's settler-colonial days when education was mostly rural and organized around agricultural or religious practices. For example, early Protestant schools in the East, French Jesuits in the Midwest, and Spanish missionaries in the Southwest often aimed to convert Native Americans to Christianity and "save" them from what was perceived as savagery (Dunbar-Ortiz, 2014; Hale, 2002; Miranda, 2013). During the era of violent Westward expansion of the 1800s, supported by the doctrine of Manifest Destiny that justified American imperialism, Native Americans children and youth were required to attend undesirable boarding schools. At these schools, epistemological violence, cultural genocide, and sexual-mental-physical abuse frequently took place, whereby destroying tribal languages, customs, and beliefs (Archuleta, Child, & Lomawaima 2000; Hale 2002; Heape & Richie, 2008). U.S. history also includes legalizing slavery of African Americans in Virginia during the mid-1600s. Although several schools were established between 1774–1808 for Black people (at a time when over 90% of the population were slaves), gradually teaching them became prohibited and forbidden. After the Civil War, a series of racist, anti-Black policies and laws, particularly in the American South, such "black codes," Jim Crow Laws, and the ruling of Plessy v. Ferguson, state sponsored racial exclusion and segregation became enforced, including public education (Alexander 2012; Jackson, 2001). Other racialized groups, such as people of Mexican and Chinese backgrounds, have also been systemically oppressed in American public schools (Donato, 1997; Espinosa & Christopher, 1986; Kuo, 1998).

A way to understand this oppressive history of education and racially/ethnically marginalized groups in the U.S. is through the intimate connection between colonization and knowledge production. European colonization of the Americas created a violent state of war and a modern/colonial culture of power where racism, sexism, and heterosexism, among other hierarchies, were birthed and became central to society (Lugones, 2007; Maldonado-Torres, 2008; Quijano, 2000). Since the sixteenth century, colonization constructed a "hierarchy of superior and inferior knowledge and, thus, of superior and inferior people around the world" (Grosfoguel, 2007, p. 214). Additionally, Western hegemonic intellectual practices dominated and marginalized other cultures and knowledges by rewriting them through the lens of imperialism (Castro-Gómez, 2007; Mignolo, 2002, 2003). By the Enlightenment, the European paradigm of knowledge—a product of a subject-object relation—was made possible through the concept of rationality whereby epistemological violence became part of colonial/imperial expansion strategies.

The universal pretension of an epistemology founded during the sixteenth century in Eurocentric thought and experience, in the practice of imperialism and violence, continues to be implemented in the twenty-first century in higher education and elsewhere (Chatterjee & Maira, 2014). Despite the ruling of Brown v. Board of Education in 1954, which mandated the desegregation of educational institutions in the U.S., public schools have become significantly less integrated in contemporary times (Hurd, 2014). The university in the U.S., especially post-9/11, has become a charged space for debates about a variety of topics, including democracy, freedom, citizenship, patriotism, and nationalism. In addition, the growing privatization of the public university is progressively putting students into exorbitant amounts of debt and making it harder for people to access higher education (McClanahan, 2011).

More and more, academic freedom is undermined, nonconformist pedagogical and scholarly work is delegitimized, and a variety of oppressive logics, like those of warfare, nationalism, racism, sexism, heterosexism, and ableism, are centrally intertwined in the U.S. academy, like the rest of modern/colonial society (Chatterjee & Maira, 2014; Sandoval, Ratcliff, Buenavista, & Marín, 2016). The Western academy is an imperial university, whereby scholarship and intellectuals play a central role—wittingly or unwittingly—in legitimizing settler-colonialism and American exceptionalism, as well as rationalizing U.S. repression and expansionism domestically and across the globe (Chatterjee & Maira, 2014; Grosfoguel, Hernández, & Velásquez, 2016; Wallerstein, 1997).

Given this historical-social context of oppression and exclusion in systems of education, the struggles that many FGCS from underrepresented and intersectional backgrounds experience cannot solely be understood through the lens of deficit/merit or through ahistorical accounts of their identities and social environments. Furthermore, many marginalized people still carry the burden of feeling dehumanized, being bullied, and experiencing violence in educational institutions and elsewhere where heteropatriarchy and White supremacy are pervasive (Bowerman, Nelson, & May, 2016; Branson-Potts, 2017; Cianciotto & Cahill, 2012). They are often pushed out of their educational institutions before they complete high school because they lack a variety of things, such as stability, love, and the opportunity of choice. If people from marginalized backgrounds do attend college, they may face new challenges, like universities further contributing to their oppression. FGCS from underrepresented and intersectional backgrounds face vast and multifaceted obstacles. This is why we need to critically understand and highlight the social inequities requiring fundamental changes.

Marginalized Intersectional Struggles

My path into college was rather unusual, like it is for many FGCS of marginalized backgrounds who also lack appropriate mentors and resources. Neither of my parents had formal education, and my childhood experiences were largely shaped by growing up in an immigrant and poor working-class household. As a gardener, my father tended landscapes of wealthy millionaires who lived in our city's hills. My mother worked random jobs off and on while raising six children. Common to poor working-class immigrant people, my family moved around a few times, frequently sharing the house with external relatives, many of whom were undocumented. Moreover, in our majority Mexican neighborhood, we faced challenges that often accompany poverty: alcoholism, neglect, labor exploitation, racism, and lack of resources.

I attended a public school where most students were of Mexican origin, immigrant, and economically disadvantaged backgrounds. However, in middle school, my tests scores placed me in an academic track, which meant that I attended classes with mostly affluent youth from the hills. This experience was isolating and I increasingly felt inferior to my peers. Halfway through the ninth grade I dropped out/was pushed out (Harris, 2010), partly because I was already disengaged from my courses while also coming to terms with my Queer identity, which led to progressively feeling unsafe in school. I started working at 15 and, fortunately, thereafter found my way into the local community college. Working multiple jobs, I eventually transferred to the University of California at Berkeley (UC Berkeley) to complete my undergraduate degree and later doctorate.

I often wonder how I got through public education and the university, given that multi-marginalized people frequently experience violence. In the U.S. and elsewhere, violence is used to mark who is excluded from society, and it can easily emerge as a response to intersectional identities, especially for those who identify as queer and trans people of color (Harris-Perry, 2015; Human Rights Campaign and Trans People of Color Coalition, 2017; Mitchell, 2013). As I navigated K–12 education, I experienced violence in symbolic and physical forms. In elementary school, many identity markers made me a target of bullying and isolation, including speaking English "with an accent" or not following traditional gender norms (Bañales, 2015). Being placed in advanced education in middle school came at the expense of experiencing tacit and explicit modes of social, cultural, and economic exclusion. In the ninth grade, I experienced physical violence after school, which dramatically increased and confirmed how unsafe I felt in society. As Mitchell (2013) argues, violence delimits the boundaries of who belongs in society and who does not. I experienced what Anjaldúa (1987) calls "intimate terrorism," which accounts for hegemonic, colonizing violence that makes the world an unsafe place, and where the threat of violence exists every day.

In my journey through public education, I also experienced various forms of epistemological violence. This type of violence describes when a person is reduced to the status of an object, dehumanized through discourse or knowledge that forecloses non-Western ways of knowing (Spivak, 1988). In elementary school, I recall doing an in-class assignment where we had to write about what we wanted to be in the future. I wrote that I wanted to be an architect, get married, and have kids—similar to what many children in fourth grade wrote about. Classmates next to me read my assignment out loud, pointing and laughing at me, telling me that I could not have this future because, according to them, "I was a fag." Sobbing, I ran to the teacher for comfort. She took me outside to tell me that I was too sensitive and "needed to toughen up."

During my community college years, I remember stepping into an evening class after a long day of work. As soon as I walked into the classroom— before I even found a place to sit—the professor told me to stop. Raising his large body from behind the front table, he requested to see my schedule. "I need to check and make sure you are in the right class," he reported. Once I proved that I was indeed enrolled in the class, the professor warned: "You know, this is not an easy class; you should really think about taking this course." Baffled, I observed how he did not stop or warn anyone else entering the classroom.

In graduate school, one of my thesis advisors was erratic in communication style and behavior. Instead of providing appropriate academic guidance, the advice often dismissed my intellectual ideas and I was asked to redo my work. Even after I started from scratch, and despite that my other mentors had approved my new work, this advisor did not want to sign my thesis. Feeling vulnerable and insecure as the thesis deadline approached, this advisor eventually agreed to sign their approval. However, the advisor told me beforehand that they were signing not because they believed in my ideas, but rather because it was a procedural move.

Growing up marginalized in a colonizing society, where oppressed people are routinely reminded that they do not belong, and where violence is normalized, it is common to internalize self-doubt, fear, and insecurity. For example, in elementary school and into high school, I was pressured to follow traditional norms of masculinity and monitor how I behaved and spoke. This meant that I had to find creative strategies to avoid being harassed and bullied, such as walking home through longer routes or staying at school longer, while becoming very alert at my surroundings. After enrolling at my local community college, I experienced impostor syndrome, which describes feeling like a fraud or incompetent (Cokley et al., 2017; Roché & Kopelman, 2013;). Since I did not traditionally graduate from high school, I did not think I was prepared enough to complete the assignments or even college. When I transferred to the UC Berkeley as an undergraduate student, low-income students could live in affordable student cooperative housing. I chose the least expensive option, which unfortunately turned out to be a very negative experience. Limited with housing options, along with having economic stress and insecurity, I spoke to a counselor to begin the withdrawal. As a graduate student at the same university, I almost abandoned my studies halfway through the doctoral program. After years of being at the university with many privileged and mostly White generational academics and students who theorized about oppression and social justice, my lived experience felt invalidated, and I felt disconnected and with no sense of purpose. Even though I had funding for the upcoming academic year, I almost forfeited my fellowship and quit. In my journey through public education, I internalized that I was at fault, inadequate, deficit, and incomplete.

As a first-generation faculty (FGF), I still experience self-doubt and insecurity, partly due to the countless obstacles that marginalized professors' experience. Academics have examined diversity in higher educational courses and institutional contexts, with increased awareness of the politics of ability, class, race, ethnicity, nationality, gender, and sexuality on campus (Ahmed, 2012; Chesler & Young Jr., 2013; Fryberg & Martínez, 2014; Gutiérrez y Muhs, Niemann, González, & Harris, 2012; Pérez, 2012; Vance, 2007). This research highlights that White faculty, consciously or unconsciously, benefit from institutional racism and racial privilege. Chesler (2013) notes that White faculty generally "receive many benefits that includes the treatment of some kind of cultural stances and priorities as legitimate and others not, some faculty scholarly pursuits as normative and others not, and some ways of teaching and relating with students appropriate and rewarded and some not" (p. 2). In contrast, faculty of color, and especially those who are Queer/women, commonly deal with the burden of ontological politics in universities that are historically dominated by White heteronormative men. For instance, regardless of the competency in their teaching or the subject of courses, faculty of color experience many obstacles, including: receiving lower teaching evaluations from White students, having expertise challenged and feeling like one has to work harder to establish their credentials and maintain "authority" as an instructor and scholar, being stereotyped in relation to ethnic/identity background or cultural styles, having to prove competency and credibility, being accused of having biased curriculum or perspectives, or being the direct or indirect target of insults (Bañales & Roaf, 2016; Chesler & Young Jr., 2013; Gutiérrez y Muhs et al., 2012).

As a FGF teaching in a public university in California, I still experience similar challenges that I faced in K–12 and higher education. Like the rest of the country, California is becoming more ethnically/racially diverse. In many colleges, demographic diversity is often visible at the student-body level. However, in curriculum and faculty, the ethnic/racial composition repeatedly doesn't reflect the demographic changes, especially when one considers other intersecting forms of power and identity politics, including class, gender, and sexuality. For example, at the California State University at Stanislaus (Stanislaus State), where I currently teach, the student body is over-whelmingly Latinx FGCS, yet most faculty and administrators are White. It's very alarming to participate in faculty meetings at the college level where the lack of racial/intersectional diversity becomes accentuated, confirming that, the more one climbs the academic ladder, the less diverse/intersectional and more isolating the terrain. Even if there are faculty of diverse/intersectional backgrounds, this does not necessarily guarantee they are grounded in a crit-ical politic that does not privilege Western norms of standards. In fact, I've interacted with faculty of color who are rather normative and conservative, upholding colonizing ways of thinking. Although I generally connect with many intersectional FGCS, partly due to my life experiences and marginalized background, this does not exempt me from also replicating, wittingly or un-wittingly, forms of epistemic violence or problematical ways of being, too; the university is a hierarchical institution that seduces even the most conscious to follow oppressive practices. Fortunately, there are countless ways in which first-generation students and faculty have challenged institutional oppression and continue to transform their environments.

Transformative Opportunities

The university is a site of oppression, one that is intertwined with under-mining students and faculty of color and legitimizing or supporting settler colonialism, oppressive state policies, and warfare (Chatterjee & Maira, 2014; Gutiérrez y Muhs et al., 2012). However, it is also a contradictory space where transformative thinking and social change can occur (Oparah, 2014). Despite the limitations of higher education, being a college student or faculty of first-generation background may offer many productive opportunities, and there are not enough narratives that underscore the transformative change that these groups have established.

There is long history of activists, many of whom were from marginal-ized FGCS background. Many of these activists challenged the universi-ty's colonizing structures across multiple fronts, including racist, classist, and nationalistic lines. One significant example is the Third World Strike in the San Francisco Bay Area, California, which took place during a charged socio-political context that included urban violence, the Cold War, anti-Vietnam War protests, Civil Rights activism, and protest from radical Black, brown, red, yellow, feminist, and gay power movements (Ordona, 2000; Pulido, 2006). In 1968–69, a majority of students at San Francisco State University (and later at UC Berkeley) from African American, Chicano/Latino, Asian American, Native American backgrounds organized campus coalitions known as the Third World Liberation Front (TWLF). Many in the TWLF were FGCS who entered the university through the GI Bill or recently established state outreach programs. Once on campus, these students encountered a Eurocentric, hostile university that reflected society's exclusionary racial power dynamics. Along with informational picketing, blocking campus entrances, mass rallies, and teach-ins, the TWLF led the longest student strike in the country at the time. Hundreds of students were arrested and injured, and the National Guard became stationed at UC Berkeley (Asian Community Center Archive Group, 2009). The TWLF demanded the establishment of Third World Colleges comprised of departments of Asian American, African American, Chicano, and Native American Studies, and those in the struggle were influenced by global activism, revolutionary art and music, anti-colonial movements, and anti-racist scholarship (Biondi, 2012; Jackson, 2009; Okihiro, 2016).

FGCS and their allies are currently involved in many social change movements on campuses. One notable example is the activism from undocumented students who grapple with anti-immigrant sentiments in college and society, or lack adequate information, support, and resources to enter and thrive at the university (Negrón-Gonzales 2017; Zimmerman 2011;). Although many undocumented students are also FGCS, this group is heterogeneous. For instance, undocumented people come from many ethnic/racial backgrounds or may identify as Queer. Many had temporary relief and legal protection through Deferred Action for Childhood Arrivals (DACA) before it was terminated by the current president, though a significant number have families with mixed-legal status backgrounds, while some have relatives who have been deported. Despite the diversity of undocumented FGCS, many have participated in activism ranging from direct protest, establishing networks, participating in legislative and policy efforts, to using art, poetry, and digital media; for one example, see Dreamers Adrift (Hernández, Romero, Iñiguez, & Salgado, 2010).

The activism of undocumented students, family, and allies have produced important transformations such as changing the narrative of the immigrant rights movement (Nicholls, 2013) and creating new spaces. For instance, the Undocumented Student Program of the Dreamer Resource Center at UC Berkeley promotes pathways for engaged scholarship and supports the advancement of undocumented students in higher education (Undocumented Student Program, n.d.). Freedom University in Atlanta, Georgia, provides tuition-free education, college application and scholarship assistance, and activist training and leadership to undocumented students (Freedom University, n.d.). Last but not least, CSU Stan is in the process of instituting a Dreamers Center to support AB540 and undocumented students.

As a FGCS, I participated in social change in many ways. I do not come from a generational activist family, so I gradually figured out how to become civically involved with my community. When I was a junior college student, I volunteered at local community centers and was part of Movimiento Estudiantil Chican@ de Aztlán (MEChA), the Chicano/a student group that helped organize state-wide empowerment conferences and public cultural events. At UC Berkeley, I was involved with the award-winning student group Young Queers United for Empowerment (YQUE), which provides a safer, supportive, and active space for Queer Latinx students on campus. Because many felt that universities were hostile spaces for Queer students of color, YQUE helped organize the first Queer People of Color summits at UC Berkeley (2006–2008). Ten years later, the summit is now a Queer and Trans People of Color conference held at universities throughout California.

As a graduate student at UC Berkeley, I also participated in many activist efforts, including helping to organize the 40th anniversary of the Ethnic Studies Department, which was a conference that sought to create a version of a decolonized university (Harper & Hamilton, 2010). I was involved in co-ordinating a hunger strike on campus to pressure the chancellor to denounce Arizona's anti-immigrant law of SB1070 and work toward making the campus a safer space for undocumented students (Bañales, 2012; Public Affairs, 2010). Finally, I co-founded of the Association of Jotería Arts, Activism, and Scholarship (AJAAS) in 2011. AJAAS is a national collective of artist, activist, and scholars who actively collaborate on projects, including establishing biennial conferences throughout the country (Revilla, 2014).

Working toward social change did not end when I completed graduate school. The university where I currently teach is located in the Central Valley of California, which primarily covers the areas between Sacramento and Bakersfield, and has a rural landscape with disenfranchised urban cities. Demographically, the area has large populations of Whites and Latinx, as well as large concentrations of other groups, such as Hmong and Filipinx. Many counties in the Central Valley have some of the highest percentages of residents living below the poverty line and there is a large population of underrepresented groups in local colleges that are first generation and/or undocumented (Negrón-González, 2017). During my first year as an assistant professor, very little cultural or intersectional programming addressed or reflected the largely underrepresented student body or the region's local issues. Despite the job's overwhelming demands, in addition to using decolonial pedagogical methods in class (Bañales & Roaf, 2016), I collaborated with colleagues and students from largely FGCS backgrounds to organize a critical Ethnic Studies conference in the spring of 2017 (Santos & Olmos, 2017).

This event brought artists, scholars, and activists from a variety of racial/ethnic/gender/sexuality backgrounds to discuss the importance of the field as well address respective challenges of their communities or the region. Lastly, I recently created a social justice broadcast show on campus with students of first-generation or marginalized backgrounds and established the first annual Indigenous People's Day event on campus.

Such activism calls attention to how FGCS and faculty with intersecting marginalized identities can challenge epistemological violence and the Western university while working toward changing society. Many studies or narratives about FGCS often either position them as victims or as model success stories. In contrast, activism reminds us that focusing on individuals without attention to institutional and systemic oppression will not lead to transformative changes. A critical assessment of FGCS experience through an intersectional lens requires us to examine the relationship between marginalization, violence, and exclusionary structures of (higher) education as we work towards social change across power, privilege, and oppression, not only in the university, but also beyond.

Conclusion

Critical attention to the relationship between marginalization and exclusionary structures of (higher) education shifts the discussion on FGCS from deficit and merit to power, privilege, and oppression. One way we can avoid replicating such problematic models and perspectives is to historicize education, the university, and Western society, particularly as they relate to violence and colonizing systems of power. Furthermore, to understand FGCS' challenges and experiences through an intersectional lens, this essay underscores the need to make varied marginalizations of identities central to the inquiry before, during, after, and besides studying at the university. Last but not least, marginalized FGCS and allies have participated in many forms of social change, and critical assessment of these efforts can help us transform ourselves and decolonize the respective spaces that we inhabit in educational institutions and elsewhere.

References

Ahmed, S. (2012). *On being included: Racism and diversity in institutional life*. Durham, NC: Duke University Press.

Alexander, M. (2012). *The new Jim Crow: Mass incarceration in the age of colorblindness* (2nd ed.). New York: The New Press.

Anzaldúa, G. (1987). *Borderlands/La frontera: The new mestiza.* San Francisco, CA: Aunt Lute.

Archuleta, M. L., Child, B. J., & Lomawaima, K. T. (Eds.). (2000). *Away from home: American Indian boarding schools experiences, 1879–2000.* Phoenix, AZ: Heard Museum.

Asian Community Center Archive Group. (2009). *Stand up: An archive collection of the Bay Area Asian American movement 1968–1974.* Berkeley, CA: Eastwind Books.

Bañales, X. (2012). The future(s) of ethnic studies is in its past(s)... and in the surrounding possibilities. *Nineteen Sixty Nine: An Ethnic Studies Journal, 1*(1), 10–22.

Bañales, X. (2015). Spirit first, consequences, second: The politics of gender and culture in the playground. In J. Landsman, R. M. Salcedo, & P. C. Gorski (Eds.), *Voices for diversity and social justice: A literary education anthology* (pp. 117–122). Lanham, MD: Rowman & Littlefield.

Bañales, X., & Roaf, M. (2016). The battle to decolonize knowledge: Theories, experiences, and perspectives teaching ethnic studies in Arizona. In D. M. Sandoval, A. J. Ratcliff, T. L. Buenavista, & J. R. Marín (Eds.), *White washing American education: The new culture wars in ethnic studies* (Vol. 2) (pp. 69–94). Santa Barbara, CA: ABC-CLIO, LLC.

Banks-Santilli, L. (2015, June 3). Guilt is one of the biggest struggles first-generation students face. *The Washington Post.* Retrieved from https://www.washingtonpost.com/posteverything/wp/2015/06/03/guilt-is-one-of-the-biggest-struggles-first-generation-college-students-face/?utm_term=.83f7a51a6767

Biondi, M. (2012). *The Black revolution on campus.* Berkeley, CA: University of California Press.

Bowerman, M., Nelson, S., & May, A. (2016, August 25). Is 'college experience' synonymous with rape culture? *USA Today.* Retrieved from https://www.usatoday.com/story/news/nation-now/2016/08/25/college-experience-synonymous-rape-culture/89262712/

Branson-Potts, H. (2017, April 17). Cal State Stanislaus to investigate white supremacist student who punched woman in Berkeley melee. *The Los Angeles Times.* Retrieved from http://www.latimes.com/local/lanow/la-me-ln-nathan-damigo-stanislaus-state-20170417-story.html

Castagno, A. E. (2014). *Educated in whiteness: Good intentions and diversity in schools.* Minneapolis, MN: University of Minnesota.

Castro-Gómez, S. (2007). The missing chapter of empire: Postmodern reorganization of coloniality and post-Fordist capitalism. *Cultural Studies, 21*(2–3), 428–448.

Chatterjee, P., & Maira, S. (Eds.). (2014). *The imperial university: Academic repression and scholarly dissent.* Minneapolis, MN: University of Minnesota Press.

Chesler, M. A. (2013). The state of research with faculty identities in higher educational classrooms and institutional contexts. In M. A. Chesler & A. A. Young, Jr. (Eds.), *Faculty identities and the challenge of diversity: Reflections on teaching in higher education* (pp. 1–20). Boulder, CO: Paradigm Publishers.

Chesler, M. A., & Young, Jr., A. A. (Eds.). (2013). *Faculty identities and the challenge of diversity: Reflections on teaching in higher education*. Boulder, CO: Paradigm Publishers.

Cianciotto, J., & Cahill, S. (2012). *LGBT youth in America's schools*. Ann Arbor, MI: University of Michigan Press.

Cokley, K., Smith, L., Bernard, D., Hurst, A., Jackson, S., Stone, S., ... Roberts, D. (2017). Impostor feelings as a moderator and mediator of the relationship between perceived discrimination and mental health among racial/ethnic minority college students. *Journal of Counseling Psychology, 64*(2), 141–154.

Davis, J. (2010). *The first-generation student experience: Implications for campus practice and strategies for improving persistence and success*. Sterling, VA: Stylus Publishing.

Donato, R. (1997). *The other struggle for equal schools: Mexican Americans during the Civil Rights era*. Albany, NY: State University of New York.

Dunbar-Ortiz, R. (2014). *An indigenous people's history of the United States*. Boston, MA: Beacon Press.

Espinosa, P. (Producer), & Christopher, F. (Director) (1986). *The Lemon Grove incident* [Motion picture]. USA: Espinosa Productions.

First Generation Faculty. (n.d.). Retrieved from http://firstgen.ucdavis.edu/

Forbes, J. D. (2008). Ethnic or world studies: A historian's path of discovery. In T. P. Fong (Ed.), *Ethnic studies research: Approaches and perspectives* (pp. 59–92). Lanham, MD: AltaMira Press.

Frank, R. H. (2016). *Success and luck: Good fortune and the myth of meritocracy*. Princeton, NJ: Princeton University Press.

Freedom University. (n.d.). Retrieved from http://www.freedomuniversitygeorgia.com/

Fryberg, S. A., & Martínez, E. J. (Eds.). (2014). *The truly diverse faculty: New dialogues in American higher education*. New York: Palgrave Macmillan.

Greenwald, R. (2012, November 11). Think of first-generation students as pioneers, not problems. *The Chronicle of Higher Education*. Retrieved from https://www.chronicle.com/article/Think-of-First-Generation/135710

Grosfoguel, R. (2007). The epistemic decolonial turn: Beyond political-economy paradigms. *Cultural Studies, 21*(2–3), 211–223.

Grosfoguel, R., Hernández, R., & Velásquez E. R. (Eds.). (2016). *Decolonizing the Westernized university: Interventions in philosophy of education from within and without*. Lanham, MD: Lexington Books.

Gutiérrez y Muhs, G., Niemann, Y. F., González, C. G., & Harris, A. P. (Eds.). (2012). *Presumed incompetent: The intersections of race and class for women in academia*. Boulder, CO: University Press of Colorado.

Hale, L. (2002). *Native American education: A reference handbook*. Santa Barbara, CA: ABC-CLIO.

Harper, M. (Producer/Director), & Hamilton, J. (Editor). (2010, October 11). Decolonizing the university: Fulfilling the dream of the Third World College [Video file]. Retrieved from https://vimeo.com/15729523

Harris, W. (2010, March 31). Dropped out? No, pushed out. *Philadelphia Public School Notebook*. Retrieved from http://thenotebook.org/articles/2010/03/31/dropped-out-no-pushed-out

Harris-Perry, M. (2015, August 23). 17 trans women killed since start of 2015 [Video file]. *MSNBC*. Retrieved from http://www.msnbc.com/melissa-harris-perry/watch/17-trans-women-killed-since-start-of-2015-511515715961

Heape, S. R. (Producer), & Richie, C. (Director). (2008). *Our spirits don't speak English: Indian boarding schools* [Motion picture]. USA: Rich-Heape Films.

Hernández, D. (2017, July 2). A first-generation student's survival strategy: Work more, sleep less. *The Chronicle of Higher Education*. Retrieved from https://www.chronicle.com/article/A-First-Generation-Student-s/240476

Hernández, D., Romero, F., Iñiguez, J., & Salgado, J. (2010, October). *Dreamers adrift*. Retrieved from http://dreamersadrift.com

Housel, T. H., & Harvey, V. L. (Eds.). (2009). *The invisibility factor: Administrators and faculty reach out to first-generation college students*. Boca Raton, FL: BrownWalker Press.

Human Rights Campaign Foundation and Trans People of Color Coalition. (2017). *A time to act: Fatal violence against transgender people in America 2017, 1–47*. Retrieved from http://assets2.hrc.org/files/assets/resources/A_Time_To_Act_2017_REV3.pdf

Hurd, C. A. (2014). *Confronting suburban school resegregation in California*. Philadelphia, PA: University of Pennsylvania Press.

I'm First! (n.d.). Retrieved from http://www.imfirst.org

Jackson, C. F. (2009). *Chicana and Chicano art: ProtestArte*. Tucson, AZ: University of Arizona.

Jackson, C. L. (2001). *African American education: A reference handbook*. Santa Barbara, CA: ABC-CLIO.

Jehangir, R. R., Stebleton, M. J., & Deenanath, V. (2015). *An exploration of intersecting identities of first-generation, low-income students* (Research Report No. 5). Columbia, SC: University of South Carolina, National Resource Center for the First-Year Experience and Students in Transition.

Kuo, J. (1998). Excluded, segregated and forgotten: A historical view of the discrimination of Chinese Americans in public schools. *Asian American Law Journal, 5*(7), 181–212.

Lugones, M. (2007). Heterosexualism and the colonial/modern gender system. *Hypatia, 22*(1), 186–209.

Maldonado-Torres, N. (2008). *Against war: View from the underside of modernity*. Durham, NC: Duke University Press.

McClanahan, A. (2011). The living indebted: Student militancy and the financialization of debt. In M. Figlerowicz & S. Porzak (Eds.), *Qui parle: Critical humanities and social sciences, 20*(1), 57–77.

McGlynn, A. P. (2011). *Envisioning equity: Educating and graduating low-income, first-generation, and minority college students.* Madison, WI: Atwood Publishing.

McNamee, S. J., & Miller Jr., R. K. (2014). *The meritocracy myth* (3rd ed.). Lanham, MD: Rowman & Littlefield.

Mignolo, W. D. (2002). The geopolitics of knowledge and the colonial difference. *The South Atlantic Quarterly, 101*(1), 57–96.

Mignolo, W. D. (2003). Globalization and the geopolitics of knowledge: The role of the humanities in the corporate university. *Nepantla: Views from South, 4*(1), 97–119.

Miranda, D. A. (2013). *Bad Indians: A tribal memoir.* Berkeley, CA: Heyday.

Mitchell, K. (2013). Love in action: Noting similarities between lynching then and anti-LGBT violence now. *Callaloo, 36*(3), 668–717.

Muñoz, P. (2017, March 31). My guilt as a first-generation American student. *The Huffington Post.* Retrieved from https://www.huffingtonpost.com/entry/my-guilt-being-first-generation_us_58b85d88e4b051155b4f8ccb

Negrón-Gonzales, G. (2017). Constrained inclusion: Access and persistence among undocumented community college students in California's Central Valley. *Journal of Hispanic Higher Education, 16*(2), 105–122.

Nicholls, W. J. (2013). *The DREAMers: How the undocumented youth movement transformed the immigrants rights debate.* Stanford, CA: Stanford University Press.

Okihiro, G. Y. (2016). *Third World studies: Theorizing liberation.* Durham, NC: Duke University Press.

Oparah, J. C. (2014). Challenging complicity: The neoliberal university and the prison-industrial complex. In P. Chatterjee & S. Maira, S. (Eds.), *The imperial university: Academic repression and scholarly dissent* (pp. 99–121). Minneapolis, MN: University of Minnesota Press.

Orbe, M. P. (2004). Negotiating multiple identities within multiple frames: An analysis of first-generation college students. *Communication Education, 53*(2), 131–149.

Ordona, T. A. (2000). Coming out together: An ethnohistory of the Asian and Pacific Islander queer women's and transgendered people's movement of San Francisco (Unpublished doctoral dissertation). University of California, Santa Cruz, CA.

Pérez, W. (2012). *Americans by heart: Undocumented Latino students and the promise of higher education.* New York: Teachers College Press.

Public Affairs. (May 7, 2010). Chancellor Birgeneau denounces Arizona immigration bill. *Berkeley News.* Retrieved from http://news.berkeley.edu/2010/05/07/immigration/

Pulido, L. (2006). *Black, brown, yellow, & left: Radical activism in Los Angeles.* Berkeley, CA: University of California Press.

Quijano, A. (2000). Coloniality of power, eurocentrism, and Latin America. *Nepantla: Views from South, 1*(3), 533–580.

Revilla, A. T. (2014). The Association for Jotería Arts, Activism, and Scholarship: A movimiento for queer Chicana/os and Latina/os. *Aztlán: A Journal of Chicano Studies, 39*(1), 253–260.

Roché, J. M. (with Kopelman, A.). (2013). *The Empress has no clothes: Conquering self-doubt to embrace success.* San Francisco, CA: Berrett-Koehler Publishers.

Sandoval, D. M, Ratcliff, A. J., Buenavista T. L., & Marín, J. R. (Eds.). (2016). *"White" washing American education: The new culture wars in ethnic studies* (Vols. 1–2). Santa Barbara, CA: ABC-CLIO, LLC.

Santillano, D. (1994, March 4). Who was Cuauhtemoc...? *The Prospector,* p. 11.

Santos, F., & Olmos, V. (2017, April 3). First annual Ethnic Studies conference hosted at Stan State. *The Signal.* Retrieved from https://www.csusignal.com/campus_culture/article_d9192e00-17cf-11e7-a357-c7fa8e005667.html

Smith, A. A. (2015, November 10). Who's in First (Generation)? *Inside Higher Ed.* Retrieved from https://www.insidehighered.com/news/2015/11/10/who-are-first-generation-students-and-how-do-they-fare

Spivak, G. C. (1988). *Can the subaltern speak?* In C. Nelson & L. G. Grossberg (Eds.), *Marxism and the interpretation of culture* (pp. 271–313). Urbana, IL: University of Illinois.

Takaki, R. (2008). *A different mirror: A history of multicultural America* (2nd ed.). New York: Little, Brown, and Company.

Tate, E. (2017, April 26). Graduation rates and race. *Inside Higher Ed.* Retrieved from https://www.insidehighered.com/news/2017/04/26/college-completion-rates-vary-race-and-ethnicity-report-finds

Undocumented Student Program. (n.p.). Retrieved from https://undocu.berkeley.edu/haas-dreamers-resource-center/

Vance, M. L. (Ed.). (2007). *Disabled faculty and staff in a disabling society: Multiple identities in higher education.* Huntersville, NC: Association on Higher Education and Disability.

Wallerstein, I. (1997). The unintended consequences of Cold War area studies. In N. Chomsky, I. Katznelson, R. C. Lewontin, D. Montgomery, L. Nader, R. Ohmann, R. Siever, I. Wallerstein, & H. Zenn (Eds.), *The Cold War and the university: Toward an intellectual history of the postwar years* (pp. 195–231). New York, NY: New Press.

Wanderer Films [Username]. (2016, April 28). Stanislaus State University Equity & Diversity Video [Video file]. Retrieved from https://www.csustan.edu/diversity-matters

Ward, L., Siegel, M. J., & Davenport, Z. (2012). *Understanding and improving the experience from recruitment to commencement.* San Francisco, CA: John Wiley & Sons.

Zimmerman, A. M. (2011). A Dream detained: Undocumented Latino youth and the DREAM movement. *NACLA Report on the Americas, 44*(6), 14–17, 38.

12. Supporting the Lived Experiences of First-Generation College Students: Implications From the UNiLOA and DSDM Student Success Model

GLORIA AQUINO SOSA, PIETRO A. SASSO, AND TRACY PASCUA DEA

Introduction

This chapter presents a new model of student development and success, the *Dynamic Student Development Metatheodel* (DSDM), to examine the intersectionality of identities of first-generation college students (FCGS). We argue that the intersectionality of identities impacts how successfully FGCS traverse their college experiences. As higher education institutions become increasingly more diverse, they must conceptualize student populations using a multidimensional lens, rather than focusing on identities as independent from one another (NCES, 2013; The Pell Institute, 2015). Current college student identity models offer a one-dimensional approach as they view identities as separate entities. These existing models fail to address how college students develop identity. The existing models also do not consider the impact of converging identities on how students experience the college environment. We discuss the importance of having an intersectionality framework with a holistic view of college students' identity development. We place particular emphasis on student populations from underrepresented groups such as FGCS.

Intersectionality is a conceptual framework that considers people holistically, within the contexts of their environments, and with an emphasis on the gestalt, or whole, of each person. Conceived by feminist theorists (Crenshaw,

1989; hooks, 1981, 1984) and intertwined with the research on critical race theory (Delgado & Stefancic, 2001), intersectionality focuses on the experiences of historically marginalized populations in the context of dominant discourses that consider people through the most salient characteristic, setting aside the idea that *all* identities matter and impact an individual. This chapter will examine the concept as related to the DSDM student success model. The underpinnings of intersectionality highlight the multidimensional development of one's identities as shaped by one's interactions and experiences. Intersectionality describes the analysis of one's unique lived experiences established at the convergence of multiple social identities. The concept postulates that no one identity can be appreciated, litigated, or understood without examining its interactions with other identities (Crenshaw, 1989).

Intersectionality illuminates the concept that convergences exist within structures of power and inequity that create both privilege and oppression (Bowleg, 2008; Crenshaw, 1989; hooks, 1981, 1984; Shields, 2008; Thornton Dill, McLaughlin, & Nieves, 2007). Thus, inequities are never the result of single, explicit factors or the external characteristics of an individual. Rather, they are the outcome of junctures of distinct social locations, race and ethnicity, gender and gender expression, power relations, and experiences (Crenshaw, 1989; Hankivsky, 2014; hooks, 1981, 1984). Although there have been several models and theories explaining the development of college student identities, there is limited student affairs research addressing the complexities converged identities and how this impacts student success.

This chapter will provide a brief primer on social identity theories to introduce a new disruptive and conceptual meta-theory. This theory is the Dynamic Student Development Metatheodel (DSDM), which uses multiple (meta) theories (the) models (odel) grounded in an intersectionality lens to promote student success practices and stronger relationships between students, administrators, and faculty (Frederick, Sasso, & Barratt, 2015). Reynolds & Pope (1991) and Abes, Jones, and McEwen (2007) researched the expression of multiple identities; however, focusing on academic and psychosocial impact in college needs to be investigated and understood. Integration within the theoretical foundation of the DSDM allows for a holistic approach to student development and success not addressed in isolation by any singular theory. This chapter will apply the DSDM framework to FCGS students.

A key construct of the DSDM includes providing a more individualized focus on student development by attending to the affective domain. Individualized approaches are appropriate for college students in the context of their multiple identities when scaled to their developmental stage. The authors assert FGCS might be better served with specific and targeted interventions guided by the use of intentional student development theory. Thus, the DSDM provides a framework to support underserved populations, such as first-generation students, who have additional challenges as outlined within this chapter and throughout this text.

Background

FGCS and Intersectionality

According to the U.S. Department of Education (2010), FGCS constitute the fastest growing population of students entering college, comprising approximately 50% of enrolled students in both 2– and 4-year institutions (The Pell Institute, 2015). According to The Pell Institute (2015), as of 2012 there were 17,732,431 students enrolled in all college types, and thus nearly 9 million students who would fit some definition of FGCS. The definition of FGCS varies, and can be specific to an institution's designation or even a federal designation in the case of grant proposals; the authors recognize the definition can impact how proportions can be shaped for statistical purposes, institutional objectives, or otherwise. For the purposes of this chapter, the authors define FGCS as those whose parent/s or guardian/s have not attended or completed college in the United States (Nuñez & Cuccaro-Alamin, 1998).

Of those entering college who identify as first generation, a significant number are from historically underrepresented populations within higher education and marginalized populations such as low-income, Latino/Hispanic, and African American/Black. Other underrepresented populations such as American Indian/Alaskan Native and some Asian groups are also included as FGCS in many studies. The U.S. Department of Education National Center for Education Statistics (2010) held that students who identified as Asian constituted 32% of the first-generation population; 48.5% of Latino students had parents with no education beyond high school; and 45% of African American students were also in that category. In addition, American Indian students in the grouping comprised approximately 35%, and Caucasians represented 28% who self-identified as first generation. In addition to this designation, FGCS navigate multiple identities, further complicating their higher education journeys.

College Knowledge as Cultural Capital. Although defining the first-generation population seems to be cumbersome at best, there are a vast number of students who enter post-secondary education with little to no *college knowledge* (Vargas, 2004), leaving them with an increasingly monumental task to complete their undergraduate degrees. According to Vargas, *college knowledge* can be defined as information, often coming from family members, that provides insight into the challenges that make degree attainment difficult. College knowledge is a form of cultural capital—a Marxist concept expanded upon by Pierre Bourdieu (1986)—that refers to knowledge, skills, awarenesses, and other, often intangible concepts and understandings that relate to one's social standing and status. Having information that helps point out specifics about the college experience is an advantage that can, at the very least, provide students with academic and/or psychosocial confidence to move through the bureaucracy of a university or the conflicts that arise from living in a residence hall—and everything in between (Vargas, 2004).

While dissecting the varied processes associated with comprehending what one needs to know about entering college, students are, simultaneously, uncovering many layers of their identities (Chickering & Reisser, 1993; Erikson, 1963; Tinto, 1993). Students might also begin to recognize (though perhaps not know how to name) the lack of cultural capital they hold not only as FGCS, but also as a result of their intersecting identities. Conley (2005) highlighted that academic underpreparedness coupled with being an English Language Learner (ELL), for example, is a barrier FGCS students often face.

Saenz, Hurtado, Barrera, Wolf, and Yeung (2007) and Engle and Tinto (2008) confirmed that a lack of cultural capital negatively impacts student progress in college. Salkulku and Alexander (2011) provided an overview of the literature regarding imposter syndrome, defined as believing one is a fraud and has mistakenly been placed in a circumstance rather than having earned their place in that setting. Steele and Aronson (1995) and Steele (2010) researched stereotype threat, another phenomenon that highlights where FGCS may lack cultural capital, as they may perform academically and psychosocially to the stereotype of their group rather than to their capabilities. All of this research points to ways FGCS' manifestation of intersecting identities can negatively impact sense of belonging and connection to their colleges, not to mention to their peers. Lack of cultural capital can be detrimental to first-generation student success, and can make or break the student's capacity to continue in their pursuit of a higher education.

Together with a lack of cultural capital comes the difficulty of navigating developmental stages while discovering other identities (e.g., LGBTQ+) that traditionally-aged college students must traverse. The intersectionality of the varied selves being unearthed during the college years can create divergent and perhaps conflicting perceptions of self-discovery and identity synthesis (Chickering & Reisser, 1993; Erikson, 1963; Marcia, 1966); in FGCS, this confluence of selves can cause extreme turmoil at the crucial juncture of learning to interact with others while encountering these characteristics. In addition, while going through the process of self-discovery, students are impacted psychosocially as well as academically, and having connections to the college, to others who have had similar experiences, and to staff and faculty who understand these processes and can intervene can be an explicit and balancing force in the student's experience.

Student Success. Higher education administrators often use the term *student success* as though it is a clearly defined operational designation, and on that basis, administrators and governmental entities make decisions that affect the lives of faculty, staff, students, key stakeholders, and those outside the academy. *Student success,* however, is a broad and sweeping construct that can mean qualitatively different things. An institution's definition of student success essentially establishes a set of targets at which the organization can intentionally aim services, supports, interventions, and programs (SSIPs) that best address students' needs. In the High Potential Program at Saint Mary's College of California for example, SSIPs occur during the Summer Academic Institute for Leaders and Scholars (SAILS) the summer prior to the first year, throughout the first and second years through peer mentoring and counseling, and throughout all years through career and leadership development (Sosa & Pascua Dea, 2016). Student success, in its most useful iteration, can mean making it through the first year of college by accessing appropriately defined and relevant supports rather than arbitrary interventions that may miss essential needs of the target population.

Student Success and Intersectionality. Student success is impacted by every characteristic and experience of a student. Everything each person experiences impacts interactions, work, and one's psychosocial sense of self within any environment. Rendón (2006) articulated the importance of validating the lived experiences of students, and particularly those of FGCS, as they are often lumped in with students who have had a typical, so called *dominant culture* experience (Robinson-Wood, 2009). Students whose personal and academic achievements have occurred within a homogeneous environment demonstrate cultural capital within that context. Upon coming to college, FGCS are often no longer in a homogeneous environment, and may be considered no differently by administrators, faculty, and staff than their non-FGCS peers. The expectation that students will have few or no challenges in college can be detrimental to a first-generation student's initial launch into the college environment. The resilience and strengths exhibited by FGCS are often ignored, perhaps due to a willingness by college faculty and staff to treat everyone equally—or because there is an assumption FGCS have significant gaps in their academic preparedness. Though gaps might be present, and perhaps the concept of equal treatment seems positive, lumping students into one category, regardless of how they are then treated, actually negates and invalidates lived experiences that highlight the benefits of lauding intersectionalities to enhance student development (Rendón, 2006; Stephens, Hamedani, & Destin, 2014). The DSDM can help to address the varied aspects of student identity and contribute to a student's sense of belonging, which positively impacts students' academic and psychosocial success (Tinto, 1993).

New Model for Student Development

Dynamic Student Development Metatheodel

The intention of the DSDM, originally developed by Barratt and Frederick (2015), but further refined by Frederick et al. (2015), is to identify common themes or factors within sets of theories and models to better, and perhaps more appropriately, inform practice. A "metatheodel" joins multiple (meta) theories (the) and models (odel) focused on a broad construct; in this case, the construct of college student development.

The concept behind a metatheodel is to identify, define, and apply common elements to inform practice by establishing accurate operational definitions, planning and engaging appropriate supports, services, interventions, and programs (SSIPs), and actively assessing the outcomes of the application in practice. This is consistent with the notion of a *metatheodel*, a term created by the authors.

Growth, Learning, and Development (GLD). The dynamic student development metatheodel asserts that student GLD should be understood as an integrated phenomenon that best occurs within a set of assumptions, including that: (a) GLD is best supported within the confines of a trusting relationship; (b) GLD is an active as opposed to passive process; (c) the degree and level of GLD is improved as student internalization increases; and (d) upon entry to college, students possess a definable and acquired set of qualities, skills, and attributes that can be improved upon as a result of their collegiate experience. Understanding that GLD requires trust, active involvement, increasing student self-awareness, and highlighting student strengths demonstrates how a direct connection to a student necessitates observing and validating a first-generation student's intersections of identity. That connection is made by a *significant other* (SO).

Significant Other (SO). The role of the significant other (SO), a term first coined by Kegan (1982), evolves from being highly directive in the early portion of a student's academic years to that of a mentor/guide in the middle portion of the academic lifespan, and finally, to that of a "sounding board" and informal advisor in the latter portion of a student's college career. Each stage of the DSDM calls for the SO to manage different overarching goals in students' lives. An SO must have the knowledge, awareness, and skills to ascertain and encourage a student's exploration of self, and to engage in a mutual understanding of identity development. In fact, the SO can prove instrumental in celebrating the intersectionalities a student is discovering, and be a crucial partner in seeking out information for the student to learn even more about themselves.

Students have a profound need to connect with caring others, and SOs will also realize that they will be meeting the needs of their students while finding their own need for a sense of effectiveness, purpose, and connection with others will be satisfied. Early on, the role of the SO is to provide direct guidance and oversight of behaviors, to assist in the meaningful processing of the student's experiences, and to manage an ongoing conversation with the student focusing on meaning-making, identity formation, intentionality, and purpose. The role of the SO is to support students' internal processing in such a way that the students themselves will find their own answers.

Rogers (1969) held that "certain attitudinal qualities which exist in the personal relationship between the facilitator and the learner yield significant learning" (p. 106). The SO must assist the student in developing the skills of articulation to appropriately represent what the student is feeling, what they believe, or what they need. Recognition of the emergence of multiple identities is vital to the SO-student relationship, and validating the intersections of those identities can make a significant difference in how a student navigates their college experience. For example, a Catholic Latina student who identifies as part of the LGBT community may be wrestling with internal conflicts related to traditional beliefs of her religion and culture that would render her sexuality an aberration (Lakhani, 2015). The SO validates the student first through acceptance during their relationship, perhaps providing one of the first adult, unconditional relationships, then by supporting the student through her path to discovery and coming out, if desired. The SO can point the student in the direction of resources and provide a context for the student to understand more about her place in the family, the college, and the world.

Services, Supports, Interventions, and Programs (SSIPs). Each of the DSDM's stages calls for the development of SSIPs designed to assist in advancing student growth in specific functional areas, including critical thinking, self-awareness, communication, diversity, citizenship, membership and leadership, and relationships. SSIPs development should occur within a tripartite structure that includes the experiences students have within the spheres of: (a) academic emphasis, (b) co-curricular emphasis, and (c) environmental and process emphasis. These three areas exist as overlapping as opposed to independent areas of emphasis in the context of the institution and of the student. Changes to one will lead to changes in the others due to their unique relationship to one another, and rely on developing a sense of belonging. Beginning with Maslow's Hierarchy of Needs (1954) and continuing throughout most of the student development research, having a sense of belonging is vital to student success (Hurtado & Carter, 1997; Tinto, 1993; Walton & Cohen, 2011). SOs encourage co-curricular activities as a way to connect to the campus community, and further strengthen student capacity to engage and thrive. SSIPs that integrate and address students' holistic experience can actively combat daily microaggressions (Solórzano, Ceja, & Yosso, 2000), stereotype threat (Steele, 2010), and imposter syndrome (Sakulku & Alexander, 2011) that might be holding students back and keeping them from fully joining their academic and co-curricular communities.

Conceptualizing the DSDM in the Context of Intersectionality. Understanding the DSDM requires a new conceptualization of how traditional models and theories of college student GLD impact students. The DSDM attends to students' perceptions of their lived experiences while enrolled and it is the "sense they make" of their experience that drives their decisions to remain enrolled and the degree to which they will be actively involved in managing their own success. For this reason, among others, the DSDM is an ideal construct for understanding student success at the intersection of their identities.

Lived experiences occur within the three domains of cognition, behavior, and affect. While cognition and behavior are important and are the two domains on which higher education tends to focus, the affective domain exerts primary control over decision-making. The affective domain is so strong decisions are often made contrary to what would be cognitively supported. As FGCS begin to *feel* their place in the college environment, the varied and overlapping conceptualization of their identities can begin to formulate, perhaps creating angst at the least and manifesting in more serious iterations, such as depression and anxiety, in directing their college experience. For example, a student who identifies as Vietnamese and who is expected to come home each weekend to help the family elects to stay on campus to catch up on homework, but instead attends a party. The student is negating the pull toward family (affect) and instead convinces herself she will study (cognition), though instead attends the party (behavior). Reflection on just this one decision can cause the student much pause, and anxiety in three areas: family connection, attention to academics, and sense of belonging. The student's intersecting identities of student, Vietnamese daughter whose family has expectations, and person trying to connect to a new environment are in conflict.

Relationships are crucial to supporting the student's GLD, particularly within the turmoil that can surface when one begins to understand varying pieces of the self. The tenets of the DSDM and application of any models or theories of student GLD are grounded in relationships. As such, relationships constitute the very elixir by which FGCS can learn to traverse their perhaps newly emerging identities, including identity as a FGCS. The DSDM supports the intentional transition from first-year students' state of dependence, through independence, and finally, to the optimal state of interdependence with others and the environment. The DSDM is designed to "meet students where they are," as the vast majority of entering students come to college in a highly dependent state (Astin, 1999; Chickering & Reisser, 1993). This dependent state can result in low levels of performance and the belief that merely meeting minimal standards of GLD is necessary and sufficient to assure success in life. In an interesting twist to how FGCS connect to college, there is evidence that over-involvement by faculty or staff can retain the student's reliance on them, thus keeping the student in the dependent stage. This negates the importance of surfacing intersecting identities as well as intersecting behaviors and affects that could strengthen the student's movement towards independence and interdependence. As such, SOs, faculty, and staff who are over-involved with students to "support" them actually hinder the expression of the student's innate strengths and resiliency that blossoms when validated (Rendón, 2006; Sosa & Pascua Dea, 2016).

The DSDM presents in three stages with unique characteristics, goals, roles, and foci of the SSIPs. Due to the relative degree of dependency with which new students begin their college work, their ability to articulate or even understand their individual needs should not be assumed. The SO should initially maintain a higher degree of involvement and direction while balancing and creating space for students to affirm their developing identities. As stated, the SOs role evolves from being highly directive early on in the student's academic career to that of a mentor/guide, and finally, to a sounding board and informal advisor. Each stage of the DSDM calls for the SO to manage different overarching goals in students' lives, and recognizing how the student's academic and psychosocial development is complemented by attending to their multiple identities (Sue & Sue, 2016) adds to students' capacity for academic and psychosocial success. The following overview presents the essential elements to be addressed by the SO when working with students. While the elements listed are not exhaustive, attention to those listed will build a strong foundation on which additional elements can be focused, based on individual student needs.

Stage 1 includes full exploration of the student's dependency state and co-creation of concrete expectations of classroom attendance, completion of assigned homework, preparation for class participation and examinations, and engagement with the institutional community. Other expectations include self-exploration, identification of existing multiple identities, the creation of new self-management skills sets, and a heightened sense of self-agency. The broad goal of *Stage 1* is to assist in student identity development, the early establishment of positive habits, the creation and maintenance of a meaningful relationship with the SO, acclimation to the institutional environment, and finally, the development of an effective goal strategy.

Stage 2 is designed to assist student GLD through the state of independence. Self-agency, critical thinking, communication skills, appreciation for differences in others, community stewardship, working with others, and relationship management are learned through meaningful interactions with and modeling positive behaviors of the SO. In addition to modeling the SO, students become more conscious of their own qualities, skills, and attributes, their purpose for being, and their identity as college students in the context of learning and understanding the intersections of their identities. The SO encourages and expects students to become the primary decision-maker in their own lives, and to continue to establish self-assurance within the spaces of their gender expression, sexuality, racial and ethnic identities, and so on. The SO assumes the responsibility of a guide by offering suggestions, recommendations, and support for student independent decision-making. The intensity of support must remain flexible and applied appropriately to given situations and circumstances, and attention must be paid to the issues that arise when students are first recognizing who they are (Baxter-Magolda, 1998, 2014; Chickering & Reisser, 1993).

The DSDM's *Stage 3* outlines the level of interdependence. Interdependence cannot be achieved unless students fully understand who and what they are within the environment. They should have a clear understanding of their strengths and weaknesses and be focused on intentionality, all of which are supported and developed as a result of earlier work in *Stages 1* and *2*. Students having moved past being overly reliant on others or too focused on the self; interdependent students are capable of and want to help those around them, whether to meet individual or group goals or to engage in altruism with the intent of contributing to the betterment of both self and others. Rendón (2006), Schlossberg (1989), and Baxter-Magolda (1998, 2014) provided evidence that if students can align with their identity development and recognize that identity is dynamic, the environmental context will provide less of a challenge. Students can then focus on the strengths those identities reveal that had perhaps been considered deficits by institutional faculty and staff. Agency results in poise and conviction. Intersectionalities, when understood and applauded, complement those manifestations of self-assurance. A framework like the DSDM that functions as a strengths-based affirmation of sustainable self-efficacy is what all students need to succeed. Students whose intersections of identity might have been discounted or overlooked benefit significantly from having their full personhood considered and understood (Sosa & Pascua Dea, 2016).

First-Generation Student Success

Holistic Approach

No current theory of college student development incorporates existing elements of varying theories into a new model for student success. Few, if any, current student development theories or models exist that institutions can draw from to inform the holistic development of their students that positively affect both persistence through graduation and full-potential performance. Particularly, few if any, can be inclusive in recognizing intersectionality and the needs of FGCS. The DSDM as a metatheodel is built on multiple theories and model. These include: (1) Chickering's Identity Vectors (1969, 1993); (2) Astin's Model and Theory of Involvement (1999); (3) Tinto's Theory of Student Departure (1993); (4) Pascarella and Terenzini's General Model for Assessing Change (2005); (5) Bandura's Social Learning Theory (1977); (6) Baxter-Magolda's Theory of Self-Authorship (1998); (7) Schlossberg's Theory of Marginality and Mattering (1989); and (8) Kuh's Theory of Student Engagement (2001, 2008; Kuh, Kinzie, Schuh, Whitt, & Associates, 2005).

Integration within the theoretical foundation of the DSDM allows for a holistic approach to student development and success not addressed in isolation by any singular theory. While not an exhaustive list, some common factors within the theoretical foundation of the DSDM include strong, trusting relationships with others in the college environment; orientation to individuals' needs for growth and change through assessment and feedback; involvement and influence of the environment on students' sense of belonging and mattering; and support of students' attainment of self-actualization, which encompasses attention to identity development and the intersection and personal integration of those identities as they emerge (Baxter Magolda, 1998, 2014; Chickering & Reisser, 1993).

Belonging and Mattering

The theoretical foundation of the DSDM is not limited to one domain or position of any identified theory. The model is individualistic in forming to the needs of the student. This allows the model to be shaped around the student where they are in development, rather than a fixed model to which the student must be formed. In addition, the key is not for the institution to assess and interpret student experiences, but for students to do so themselves. However, this cannot be accomplished in absence of support and guidance of a significant other who validates and provides encouragement for personal and academic exploration and expression.

Current theoretical paradigms address students' cognitive and behavioral needs, but fail to consider students' affective needs, such as sense of belonging, affiliation, and connectivity, all integral to the student's quest to secure congruence with all parts of self. For FGCS, hiding parts of identity might have been a familial construct designed to ensure the student retains cultural congruence while moving into environments that negate the existence of multiple expressions of race, culture, and so on (Dey, Ott, Antonaros, Barnhardt, & Holsapple, 2010; Engle & Tinto, 2008; Saenz et al., 2007). The current paradigm also defines student success quantitatively while denying the complexities of persistence behavior that reflects students' engagement and identity development experiences in the college environment. The DSDM provides a bridge to practice that allows one to shape the complexities of theory into a model that is purely focused on student sense of membership and belonging in the academy, where processing along the affective domain is critical and required for congruent identity development.

As FGCS navigate discovery of their intersecting identities, freedom to explore and balance in developing relationships is crucial. According to Schlossberg (1989), people in transition often feel marginalized as they assimilate into a new environment or situation. This experience, when coupled with being part of an underrepresented group, can circumvent progress FGCS might have made in high school or if they participated in summer programs that involved staff and faculty who match the student's identities (Engle & Tinto, 2008; Saenz et al., 2007). Schlossberg (1989) highlighted the need to help students process their identity development while beholding individuality and diversity as central to their experiences. FGCS benefit from combining individuality and diversity with inclusion and collectivist ideals (Saenz et al., 2007). The role of the SO is to work with students to develop individualized plans as they assist in supporting students' transition from dependence to independence to interdependence, all while honoring and validating unique characteristics and intersectionalities of the student.

First-Generation Students and University Learning Outcomes Assessment

University Learning Outcomes Assessment

To further support the goals of the DSDM, the metatheodel was framed by the University Learning Outcomes Assessment (UniLOA), a national benchmark survey administered at Indiana State University from 2005–2016. Developed by Barratt and Mark in 2007, the UniLOA is a self-report, 70-item instrument with 13 demographic questions designed to measure student behaviors consistent with seven critical domains of *Growth, Learning, and Development* (GLD), including: (1) critical thinking, (2) self-awareness, (3) communication, (4) diversity, (5) citizenship, (6) membership & leadership, and (7) relationships. While they are important to student learning, cognitive and affective states are not measured by the UniLOA. Considering these critical domains in the context of intersectionality of multiple identities and psychosocial development of first-generation and/or low-income students can provide rich data regarding how identity resolution can positively impact student success and fidelity (identity commitment), as described in Erikson's stages of psychosocial development (1963, 1968).

Pascarella and Terenzini (1991) maintained that although classroom experiences have positive effects on gains, especially within disciplinary knowledge, those experiences alone have limited impact on learning from a holistic perspective. Rather, significant learning is the outcome of a combination of classroom-based academic work, more generalized types of campus and community involvement, and the successful management of meaningful relationships with others—experiences that are measured by the UniLOA. The UniLOA offers an opportunity to connect the three factors listed to first-generation and/or low-income student experiences, thus potentially uncovering the practices and interventions that can support rather than defeat student's navigation of their emerging multiple identities.

Outcomes of the UniLOA. Based on more than one-half million student responses, this section provides descriptive outcomes about how college students are behaving, which by inference can define their overall GLD. A profile will be presented below of UniLOA outcomes as related to the typical characteristics of FGCS.

(1) Socioeconomic status, as measured by qualification for receipt or non-receipt of a Pell Grant, seems to have very little impact on the frequency of behaviors along all seven domains of the UniLOA. This finding is striking in that persistence and graduation rates appear to follow SES

patterns; lower SES students fail to remain enrolled through degree completion than students from higher SES levels. This is consistent with FGCS who often fall into low SES categories (Engle & Tinto, 2008).

(2) Students with higher grade point averages and who reported they study more than 18 hours per week demonstrated higher UniLOA domain scores on all seven of the UniLOA's domains. In addition, scores tended to be highest in students reporting either they do not work at all or that they work less than 18 hours per week. Scores along all seven domains of the UniLOA decreased as more hours are spent watching television or engaging in online entertainment. This finding is especially challenging for first-generation students who often spend more than 20 hours per week working to cover their cost of attendance or to contribute to their family (Saenz et al., 2007). Moreover, transition to meeting college-level academic rigor is especially challenging for traditional-age FGCS. Having to work more hours per week limits study time, and having underdeveloped study skills and little encouragement to develop effective study habits reduces the possibilities of academic excellence.

(3) Students pursuing undergraduate degrees in pre-medicine, pre-dentistry, and social sciences score consistently higher along all domains. First-generation students are historically underrepresented in direct-entry majors (Harper, 2010).

(4) The highest UniLOA scores are produced by students reporting they hold two leadership positions. Student engagement is especially salient for first-generation students in building social capital, but often does not occur until the third and fourth years (Engle & Tinto, 2008).

(5) Students who engage in volunteer work score higher than those who do not. FGCS who spend time working and meeting family obligations often have little time outside of those commitments to participate in volunteer opportunities.

Conclusion

The purpose of this chapter was to integrate the DSDM (Frederick et al., 2015) framework to provide context to the lived experiences of FGCS and actively listen to their student voice as they work through identity development. Each person is an amalgamation of their intersecting identities, and how those are accepted, disregarded, or overlooked affects each individual (Crenshaw, 1989; Thornton Dill et al., 2007). The unique experiences of first-generation students are underscored as an example of how this fastest growing population of students (The Pell Institute, 2015) can benefit from program development that embodies a holistic approach to student achievement and multiple identity validation (Rendón, 2006).

This chapter also provided a statistical descriptive analysis of how college students are behaving, which by inference can define their overall GLD. A profile was presented of the "typical" FGCS, based on extracting first-generation student data from more than one-half million student responses to the Uni-LOA. Implications for practice were provided regarding how first-generation students can be better supported during their undergraduate experience at four-year institutions through the DSDM student success model's holistic approaches. Such implications for practice and interventions are designed to consider FGCS from a strengths-based (Saleebey, 1996) perspective that can increase students' self-confidence and cultural capital (Hiss & Franks, 2014; Sosa & Pascua Dea, 2016), rather than from a deficit-based perspective, all while validating their intersecting identities and recognizing how each faction of self can complement another (Rendón, 2006; Sosa & Pascua Dea, 2016). In addition, implications for understanding how students' multiple identities can influence their success is an important construct to be studied as students uncover these aspects of self during this dynamic developmental stage.

References

Abes, E. S., Jones, S. R., & McEwen, M. K. (2007). Reconceptualizing the model of multiple dimensions of identity: The role of meaning-making capacity in the construction of multiple identities. *Journal of College Student Development, 48*(1), 1–22.

Astin, A. (1999). Student involvement: A developmental theory for higher education. *Journal of College Student Development, 40*(5), 518–529.

Bandura, A. (1977). *Social learning theory.* Englewood Cliffs, NJ: Prentice Hall.

Barratt, W. R., & Frederick, M. A. (2015). *University learning outcomes assessment (Uni-LOA): National report of means.* Retrieved from http://www.uniloa.com/wp-content/uploads/2015/11/NationalNormsPublic.pdf

Baxter Magolda, M. B. (1998). Developing self-authorship in young adult life. *The Journal of College Student Development, 39*(2), 143–156.

Baxter Magolda, M. B. (2014), *Self-authorship. New directions for higher education,* 25–33. doi: 10.1002/he.20092

Bourdieu, P. (1986). The forms of capital. In J. Richardson (Ed.), *Handbook of theory and research for the sociology of education* (pp. 241–258). Westport, CT: Greenwood.

Bowleg, L. (2008). When Black + lesbian + woman does not equal Black lesbian woman: The methodological challenges of qualitative and quantitative intersectionality research. *Sex Roles, 59*(5–6), 312–325.

Chickering, A. W. (1969). *Education and identity.* San Francisco, CA: Jossey-Bass.

Chickering, A. W., & Reisser, L. (1993). *Education and identity* (2nd ed.). San Francisco, CA: Jossey-Bass.

Crenshaw, K. (1989). Demarginalizing the intersection of race and sex: A Black feminist critique of antidiscrimination doctrine, feminist theory and antiracist politics. *University of Chicago Legal Forum, (1)*8, 139–167. Available at: http://chicagounbound.uchicago.edu/uclf/vol1989/iss1/8

Conley, D. T. (2005). *College knowledge: What it really takes for students to succeed and what we can do to get them ready.* San Francisco, CA: Jossey-Bass.

Delgado, R., & Stefancic, J. (2001). *Critical race theory: An introduction.* New York, NY: New York University Press.

Dey, E. L., Ott, M. C., Antonaros, M., Barnhardt, C. L., & Holsapple, M. A. (2010). *Engaging diverse viewpoints: What is the campus climate for perspective-taking?* Washington, DC: Association of American Colleges and Universities.

Engle, J., & Tinto, V. (2008). *Moving beyond access: College success for low-income, first generation students.* Washington DC: The Pell Institute for the Study of Opportunity in Higher Education.

Erikson, E. H. (1963). *Childhood and society.* New York, NY: W.W. Norton.

Erikson, E. H. (1968). *Identity, youth, and crisis.* New York, NY: W.W. Norton.

Frederick, M., Sasso, P., & Barratt, W. (2015). Towards a relationship-centered approach in higher education: The Dynamic Student Development Metatheodel (DSDM). *The New York Journal of Student Affairs 15*(2), 1–26.

Hankivsky, O. (2014). *Intersectionality 101.* Retrieved from http://www.sfu.ca/iirp/documents/resources/101_Final.pdf

Harper, S. R. (2010). An anti-deficit achievement framework for research on students of color in STEM. In S. R. Harper & C. B. Newman (Eds.), *Students of color in STEM: Engineering a new research agenda. New Directions for Institutional Research* (pp. 63–74). San Francisco, CA: Jossey-Bass.

Hiss, W. C., & Franks, V. W. (2014). *Defining promise: Optional standardized testing policies in American college and university admissions.* Arlington, VA: National Association for College Admission Counseling. Retrieved from http://www.nacacnet.org/research/PublicationsResources/Marketplace/research/Pages/TestingCommissionReport.aspx

hooks, bell. (1981). *Ain't I a woman? Black women and feminism.* Boston, MA: South End Press.

hooks, bell. (1984). *Feminist theory: From margin to center.* Boston, MA: South End Press.

Hurtado, S., & Carter, D. F. (1997). Effects of college transition and perceptions of the campus racial climate on Latino college students' sense of belonging. *Sociology of Education, 70*(4), 324–345.

Kegan, R. (1982). *The evolving self: Problem and process in human adult development.* Cambridge, MA: Harvard University Press.

Kuh, G. D. (2001). Assessing what really matters to student learning: Inside the national survey of student engagement. *Change, 33*(3), 10–17.

Kuh, G. D. (2008). *High-impact educational practices: What they are, who has access to them, and why they matter.* Washington, DC: Association of American Colleges & Universities.

Kuh, G. D., Kinzie, J., Schuh, J. H., Whitt, E. J., & Associates. (2005). *Student success in college: Creating conditions that matter.* San Francisco, CA: Jossey-Bass.

Lakhani, N. (2015, August 12). LGBT in El Salvador: Beatings, intolerance, death. *Aljazeera.* Retrieved from http://www.aljazeera.com/indepth/features/2015/08/lgbt-el-salvador-beatings-intolerance-death-150805075132892.html

Marcia, J. E. (1966). Development and validation of ego identity status. *Journal of Personality and Social Psychology, 3*(5), 551–558.

Maslow, A. H. (1954). *Motivation and personality.* New York, NY: Harper.

National Center for Education Statistics. (2013). *National postsecondary student aid study.* Retrieved from http://nces.ed.gov/surveys/npsas/

Nuñez, A.-M., & Cuccaro-Alamin, S. (1998). First-generation students: Undergraduates whose parents never enrolled in postsecondary education (NCES 98–082). *U.S. Department of Education, National Center for Education Statistics.* Washington, DC: U.S. Government Printing Office.

Pascarella, E. T., & Terenzini, P. T. (1991). *How college affects students: Findings and insights from 20 years of research.* San Francisco, CA: Jossey–Bass.

Pascarella, E. T., & Terenzini, P. T. (2005). *How college affects students: A third decade of research* (Vol. 2). San Francisco, CA: Jossey-Bass.

Rendón, L. I. (2006). *Reconceptualizing success for underserved students in higher education.* Ames, IA: National Postsecondary Education Collaborative, Iowa State University.

Reynolds, A. L., & Pope, R. L. (1991). The complexities of diversity: Exploring multiple oppressions. *Journal of Counseling & Development, 70*(1), 174–180.

Robinson-Wood, T. L. (2009). *Convergence of race, ethnicity, and gender: Multiple identities in counseling* (3rd ed.). Boston, MA: Pearson.

Rogers, C. R. (1969). *Freedom to learn.* Columbus, OH: Charles E. Merrill.

Saenz, V. B., Hurtado, S., Barrera, D., Wolf, D, & Yeung, F. (2007). *First in my family: A profile of first generation college students at four-year institutions since 1971.* Los Angeles, CA: Higher Education Research Institute, UCLA.

Sakulku, J., & Alexander, J. (2011). The impostor phenomenon. *International Journal of Behavioral Science, 6*(1), 73–92.

Saleebey, D. (1996). The strengths perspective in social work practice: Extensions and cautions. *Social Work, 41*(3), 296–305. doi: 10.1093/sw/41.3.296

Schlossberg, N. K. (1989). Marginality and mattering: Key issues in building community. In D. Roberts (Ed.), *Designing campus activities to foster a sense of community* (New Directions for Student Services No. 48, pp. 5–15). San Francisco, CA: Jossey-Bass.

Shields, S. A. (2008). Gender: An intersectionality perspective. *Sex Roles, 59*(5–6), 301–311.

Solórzano, D., Ceja, M., & Yosso, T. (2000). Critical race theory, racial microaggressions, and campus racial climate: The experiences of African American college students. *Journal of Negro Education, 69*(1/2), 60–73.

Sosa, G. A., & Pascua Dea, T. J. (2016). *NextGenFirstGen© – Implementing a cultural shift and institutional change resulting in outcomes that matter.* Proceedings of the Consortium for Student Retention and Exchange. Norman, OK: CSRDE.

Steele, C. M., & Aronson, J. (1995). Stereotype threat & the intellectual test performance of African-Americans. *Journal of Personality and Social Psychology, 69*(5), 797–811.

Steele, C. M. (2010). Whistling vivaldi: And other clues to how stereotypes affect us. New York, NY: W. W. Norton.

Stephens, N. M., Hamedani, M. G., & Destin, M. (2014). Closing the social-class achievement gap: A difference-education intervention improves first generation students' academic performance and all students' college transition. *Psychological Science, 25*(4), 943–953. doi:10.1177/0956797613518349

Sue, D. W., & Sue, D. (2016). *Counseling the culturally diverse: Theory and practice.* Hoboken, NJ: Wiley & Sons.

The Pell Institute for the Study of Opportunity in Higher Education. (2015). *Indicators of higher education equity in the United States: 45-year trend report.* Retrieved from http://www.pellinstitute.org/downloads/publications/Indicators_of_Higher_Education_Equity_in_the_US_45_Year_Trend_Report.pdf

Thornton Dill, B., McLaughlin, A. E., & Nieves, A. D. (2007). Future directions of feminist research: Intersectionality. In S. N. Hesse-Biber (Ed.). *Handbook of feminist research: Theory and praxis* (pp. 629–637). Thousand Oaks, CA: Sage Publications.

Tinto, V. (1993). Leaving college: Rethinking the causes and cures of student attrition (2nd ed.). Chicago, IL: University of Chicago Press.

U.S. Department of Education, National Center for Education Statistics [NCES]. (2010). *Web tables: Profile of undergraduate students: 2007–2008.* Retrieved from http://nces.ed.gov/pubs2010/2010205.pdf

Vargas, J. H. (2004). *College knowledge: Addressing information barriers to college.* Boston, MA: The Education Resources Institute (TERI).

Walton, G. M., & Cohen, G. L. (2011). A brief social-belonging intervention improves academic and health outcomes of minority students. *Science, 331*(6023), 1447–1451. doi: 10.1126/science.1198364

13. Translating Knowledge Into Action: Making Intersecting Marginalized Identities Visible in the Classroom and Beyond

TERESA HEINZ HOUSEL

This book's chapters collectively affirm that first-generation college students (FGCS) are neither homogenous in their identities nor always visible to academic institutions and their staff. Identity and visibility, in fact, have a complicated relationship with marginalized identities. This book expands our understanding of intersecting marginalized identities through the chapters' examinations of visible and invisible identities across age, class, sexual orientation, gender, and many other identities. Identities further intersect in fragmented and overlapping ways across time and place. When we apply this knowledge of identities' juxtaposition to FGCS, we can see how intersecting marginalized identities are nuanced by first-generation status and become salient at different times across a person's educational experiences.

Storytelling's Role in Constructing Intersecting Identities

In this book's preface, Carolyn Calloway-Thomas notes that storytelling helps first-generation students manage the highly complicated process of, in many cases, leaving their home culture to enter the middle-class culture of higher education. Robillard (2003) points out that "narrative provides shape, order, coherence to events beyond our control" (p. 76) (see also Sennett, 1998; Fishman, 1981; Mahala & Swilky, 1996). Narratives give "'shape to the forward movement of time, suggesting reasons why things happen, showing their consequences'" (Sennett, 1998, p. 30, cited in Robillard, 2003, p. 76). Telling stories about themselves helps students process their present and past experiences to construct integrated and multiple identities based on new knowledge. As I co-edited my previous two books on first-generation students (Harvey & Housel, 2011; Housel & Harvey, 2009), I observed that a good portion of early writing about FGCS from academics tended to be narratives—autobiographies—rather than formal academic studies using qualitative or quantitative methodologies. For example, many early publications about first-generation faculty used narrative to illuminate oppressive discourses such as classism and sexism in academia. Particularly, Ryan and Sackrey's (1984) *Strangers in Paradise: Academics from the Working Class,* a ground-breaking work about working-class academics, used autobiography "as a way to reassert the importance of class in a society that denies class realities" (Mazurek, 2009, p. 152). Mazurek (2009) asserts that the collections of autobiographical essays by working-class academics underscore that "the personal is political" in the telling of stories against privilege and marginalization (p. 152; see also Green, 1999). To this end, Tokarczyk and Fay's (1993), *Working-Class Women in the Academy: Laborers in the Knowledge Factory,* and Barney Dews and Law's (1995) *This Fine Place So Far from Home: Voices of Academics from the Working Class* include autobiographical chapters in which the authors, many of whom are FGCS, working-class, and female academics working in the humanities and social sciences, reveal their experiences of marginalization based on class and other identities such as gender.

To complement the narrative-based collections about first-generation students, Vickie Harvey and I purposefully sought essays using qualitative and quantitative methodologies for our books because we wanted to demonstrate the breadth of rigorous research on this student population. However, since our two co-edited books' publication, I realize more than ever that storytelling is fundamental to FGCS research. Noting the "middle-class enterprise" nature of academia, Robillard (2003) argues against "distinguishing between narrative and the more privileged genres of analysis and argument" (p. 82). Robillard (2003) cites McMillan (1998) to advocate that story is "'central to all epistemological activity'" (McMillan, p. 133, cited in Robillard, p. 79), and that "social class consciousness is something that is developed through storytelling. Take away narrative and you take away any meaningful discussion of class" (Robillard, p. 79). When first-generation students enter academic culture, storytelling becomes a powerful tool for making sense of their identities in an unfamiliar environment. This present book's chapters represent a mix of research methodologies, but storytelling pervades the authors' interpretation of their intersecting identities, the respondents' descriptions of their educational journeys, and the statistical data that represent lived experiences. In sum, the stories reflect the complex and limitless intersections between marginalized identities.

I am closely attuned to how pain often penetrates these stories. FGCS frequently experience a strong sense of achievement for making it to higher education. However, this achievement can by tainted by accompanying grief, loss, and even guilt when a first-generation student leaves their family's culture, which is often working-class (Banks-Santilli, 2015). In my own case, I sensed that my single father was lonely after I moved to campus, but I usually avoided visits home because they made me feel anxious and culturally isolated within my own family. Although the student's family is usually proud of their child's success, "first-generation college students' desire for education and upward mobility may be viewed as a rejection of their past" (Banks-Santilli, 2015). My previous research asserts how this duality of identity manifests as family tension and the need for the child to straddle two cultures of campus and home (Housel, 2012; Harvey & Housel, 2011; Housel & Harvey, 2009). As I pointed out in both Chapter 7 and previously, my father encouraged me so much that I sometimes "forgot that my family was not on this journey with me" (Housel, 2012). I was starkly reminded of this fact when he sometimes accused me during visits home that I acted "too good" for the family; looking back now with an adult perspective, I realize that he must have experienced duality, too, as the daughter he thought he knew culturally slipped from his grasp. Like many other FGCS, I carefully managed my everyday cultural performances as I straddled campus and home cultures. This double consciousness forced me to masked my emerging new identity as a college student, though not always successfully, during visits home: "Many first-generation students speak of the fear of appearing too haughty if they reveal their college-learned knowledge through vocabulary, conversation topics, dress, or even how they carry themselves with newfound confidence" (Housel, 2012). To cope with the identity dissidence, I turned to storytelling as I wrote in my journal, and shared my story at various academic conferences and in articles and blogs over the years. This storytelling process, which helped me create meanings from my own history, gave me the necessary concrete sources from which I could abstract theories of identity, class, and gender in my research (see Robillard, 2003, p. 81).

Privilege influences what stories students predominantly encounter on campus, and what stories have preferred telling in class. Autobiographical writing by first-generation and/or working-class academics is frequently disregarded as not scholarly or rigorous enough. I argue that this devaluing has a deeper motivation other than just methodology. "As long as we continue to devalue the possibilities of narrative," states Robillard (2003), "we will continue to marginalize the possibilities for working-class students to develop an understanding of why things happen, their consequences, their material results in the [world]" (p. 76). Mazurek (2009) points out that narratives outside the established canon have essential functions. They critique prevailing cultural norms that are historically middle- and upper-class, White, and male in academia and other institutions; make visible the presence of classism, labor exploitation, and other oppressions in American culture; and build class solidarity (Mazurek, 2009, p. 152; Mazurek, 1995). Telling our stories as FGCS with intersecting marginalized identities makes what might be invisible visible. As McIntosh (1989) suggests, "Unless we study what we haven't noticed, we will never understand what we think we have noticed" (p. 11). Through storytelling and analyzing others' stories with research methodologies, this book's chapters cover intersecting marginalized identities that inform policy, pedagogy, and activism.

Reclaiming Intersecting Marginalized Identities in Advocacy for FGCS

Storytelling helps galvanize people into advocacy. Zandy (1994) points out in her introduction to *Liberating Memory: Our Work and Our Working-Class Consciousness* that "memory has purpose. It is a bridge between the subjective and the intersubjective—the private and unprivileged circumstances of individual lives—and the objective—the collective history of class oppression. It is a way of moving from personal pain to public and cultural work" (p. 4). Many of this book's contributors recount how their own experiences of marginalization led them to advocate for others. As I conclude this book, I emphasize the importance of applying knowledge to advocacy. Drawing from Mazurek's (2009) discussion of giving voice to working-class identity, I argue that advocacy for FGCS involves reclaiming intersecting identities as a "way of critiquing the dynamics of power within the academic world and beyond" (p. 152). Perspectives that focus just on FGCS' transition into academic culture implicitly put the responsibility to adapt and change on the first-generation student. However, this "assumption is always that it is 'the working-class individual who must adapt and change, in order to fit into, and participate in, the (unchanged) higher education institutional culture'" (Archer & Leathwood, 2003, p. 176). Institutions need FGCS as much as FGCS need them (Housel & Harvey, 2009; Harvey & Housel, 2011). FGCS increasingly attend colleges and universities, and thus more will progress onto graduate school and enter academic careers. However, academics from working-class and/or FGCS backgrounds are still a minority. Ryan and Sackrey (1984) cite a 1977 survey, which found that only

25% of academics self-identified as being from working-class backgrounds. A more recent 2001 study reported a similar percentage breakdown (see Muzzatti & Samarco 2006, p. 2). Institutions benefit when they consider FGCS and other identities in their diversity objectives.

Faculty, especially, may wonder what their role should be in increasing their students' sense of agency as they negotiate aspects of their identities. In addition to the implications for policy and daily practices discussed in this book's chapters, I offer additional possibilities for pedagogy and policy. First, faculty can assign readings that cover visible and less visible aspects of identity. Instructors can also add considerations of FGCS status and other marginalized identities to existing readings, assignments, and class discussions as they cover how privilege is enacted in everyday life and institutions. As Orbe (2004) points out, "This process can provide a productive point of reflection in terms of identifying course readings, assignments, and practices that may privilege certain group experiences over others" (p. 147). Assignments and class discussions could cover what identity messages that students send in their written, nonverbal, and verbal communication (Orbe, 2004, p. 147). When using these pedagogical strategies, educators must go beyond traditional considerations of identity such as race, ethnicity, and gender. In addition, broad considerations of identity should always examine identities' saliency across different contexts. This approach to identity is only possible if faculty and staff recognise the diversity within cultural group experiences; for example, not all FGCS have lower socio-economic backgrounds (see Orbe, 2004, p. 147).

Many of this book's contributors cite the importance of caring mentors such as family members, counselors, teachers/professors, and peer mentors. Institutions should use mentoring relationships in their programs for FGCS. For example, college ethnic- and race-focused student organizations have successfully developed social capital for FGCS through peer mentors who have demonstrated success in college. Faculty and staff advisors should not only support student organizations with established peer mentoring programs, but they must also use their expertise to establish peer mentor initiatives. When I was a faculty member at Hope College in Michigan, I worked with a colleague to develop training sessions for FGCS peer support groups. We focused on building social capital through a network of caring faculty, staff, and student peer mentors.

Research on FGCS repeatedly emphasizes the role of the student's family in mediating successful transition to college. Many scholars discuss the tensions in straddling home and campus cultures, managing financial stress, and confronting familial messages such as college not being 'real' work (Leyva, 2011), among many other challenges. Given these difficulties, I argue that institutions must consider the family relationship's role both before and during the student's college experience. Family support is linked to college retention (Chartrand, 1992). Yazedjian, Toews, and Navarro (2009) assert that institutions can offer orientations for parents of FGCS to help them understand about "new ways they can support their children throughout their time in college" (p. 476). For example, Mounts, Valentiner, Anderson, and Boswell (2006) suggests that parents can be encouraged to join their children at orientation and other campus events, send care packages, and maintain contact through phone calls and email. During my undergraduate education at Oberlin College, my parents were proud of my accomplishments, but they did not really know how to support me through practical, everyday behaviors. Thankfully, one of my mentors, Melody (discussed in this book's acknowledgments), knew the importance of these everyday actions in communicating support, and sent me care packages filled with snacks and items for decorating my dormitory room. These programs should also educate students and parents on how to convey such positive communication strategies to support the student and their familial relationships (Fass & Tubman, 2002).

First-generation student initiatives cannot be one-size-fits-all. Institutions need to reach out to their White first-generation students in different ways than their LGBT first-generation students or FGCS with disabilities, for example. To the first-generation students, faculty, staff, and administrators reading this chapter: Your strategies, insight, and yes, your stories are needed more than ever as more FGCS attend college in a society increasingly stratified between the haves and have-nots. I reiterate my call in Chapter 1 to invite readers to contribute their strategies for reaching FGCS at the classroom and institutional level to what I endeavour to be an online clearinghouse of resources at www. teresaheinzhousel.com/intersectionsofmarginality/. In addition, my New Zealand-based resource for first-generation students (referred to "first in the family" or "first in family" in Australia and New Zealand) is available for faculty, administrators, and staff working here: www.firstinthefamily.co.nz. I look forward to hearing from you and honoring your stories and intersecting identities, too.

References

Archer, L., & Leathwood, C. (2003). Identities, inequalities and higher education. In L. Archer, M. Hutchings, & A. Ross (with C. Leathwood, R. Gilchrist, & D. Phillips), *Higher education and class: Issues of inclusion and exclusion* (pp. 175–192). London: RoutledgeFalmer.

Banks-Santilli, L. (2015, June 3). Guilt is one of the biggest struggles first-generation college students face. *The Washington Post*. Retrieved from https://www.washingtonpost.

com/posteverything/wp/2015/06/03/guilt-is-one-of-the-biggest-struggles-first-generation-college-students-face/?utm_term=.83f7a51a6767

Barney Dews, C. L., & Law, C. L. (Eds.). (1995). *This fine place so far from home: Voices of academics from the working class*. Philadelphia: Temple University.

Fass, M. E., & Tubman, J. G. (2002). The influence of parental and peer attachment on college students' academic achievement. *Psychology in the Schools, 39*(5), 561–573. doi https://doi.org/10.1002/pits.10050

Fishman, J. (1981). Enclosures: The narrative within autobiography. *Journal of Advanced Composition, 2*(1–2), 23–30. doi: http://www.jstor.org/stable/20865483

Green, A. E. (1999). Writing the personal: Narrative, social class, and feminist pedagogy. In S. L. Linkon (Ed.), *Teaching working class* (pp. 15–27). Amherst, MA: The University of Massachusetts.

Harvey, V. L., & Housel, T. H. (Eds.). (2011). *Faculty and first-generation college students: Bridging the classroom gap together*. San Francisco: Jossey-Bass.

Housel, T. H. (2012, October 29). First-generation students need help in straddling their 2 cultures. *The Chronicle of Higher Education*. Retrieved from https://www.chronicle.com/article/Helping-First-Generation/135312

Housel, T. H., & Harvey, V. L. (Eds.). (2009). *The invisibility factor: Administrators and faculty reach out to first-generation college students*. Boca Raton, FL: Brown Walker Press.

Leyva, V. L. (2011). First-generation Latina graduate students: Balancing professional identity development with traditional family roles. In V. L. Harvey & T. H. Housel (Eds.), *Faculty and first-generation college students: Bridging the classroom gap together* (pp. 21–31). San Francisco: Jossey-Bass. doi: 10.1002/tl.454

Mahala, D., & Swilky, J. (1996). Telling stories, speaking personally: Reconsidering the place of lived experience in composition. *Journal of Advanced Composition, 16*(3), 363–388.

Mazurek, R. A. (1995). Class, composition, and reform in departments of English: A personal account. In C. L. Barney Dews & C. L. Law (Eds.), *This fine place so far from home: Voices of academics from the working class* (pp. 249–262). Philadelphia: Temple University Press.

Mazurek, R. A. (2009). Work and class in the box store university: Autobiographies of working-class academics. *College Literature, 36*(4), 147–178. doi: https://doi.org/10.1353/lit.0.0084

McIntosh, P. (1989). Feeling like a fraud: Part Two. *Wellesley College Center for Research on Women Working Paper Series, 37*, 1–14.

McMillan, J. (1998). Seeing different: A reflection on narrative and talk about social class. In A. Shepard, J. McMillan, & G. Tate (Eds.), *Coming to class: Pedagogy and the social class of teachers* (pp. 133–142). Portsmouth, NH: Boynton.

Mounts, N. S., Valentiner, D. P., Anderson, K. L., & Boswell, M. K. (2006). Shyness, sociability, and parental support for the college transition: Relation to adolescents' adjustment. *Journal of Youth and Adolescence, 35*(1), 71–80.

Muzzatti, S. L., & C. V. Samarco (Eds.). (2006). *Reflections from the wrong side of the tracks*. New York: Rowan & Littlefield.

Orbe, M. P. (2004) Negotiating multiple identities within multiple frames: An analysis of first-generation college students, *Communication Education, 53*(2), 131–149. doi: 10.1080/03634520410001682401

Robillard, A. E. (2003). It's time for class: Toward a more complex pedagogy of narrative. *College English, 66*(1), 74–92. doi: https://doi.org/10.2307/3594235

Ryan, J., & Sackrey, C. (1984). *Strangers in paradise: Academics from the working class*. Boston, MA: South End Press.

Sennett, R. (1998). *The corrosion of character*. New York: Norton.

Tokarczyk, M. M., & Fay, E. A. (Eds.). (1993). *Working-class women in the academy: Laborers in the knowledge factory*. Amherst, MA: University of Massachusetts.

Yazedjian, A., Toews, M. L., & Navarro, A. (2009). Exploring parental factors, adjustment, and academic achievement among White and Hispanic college students. *Journal of College Student Development, 50*(4), 458–467. doi: 10.1353/csd.0.0080

Zandy, J. (Ed.). (1994). Introduction. In J. Zandy (Ed.), *Liberating memory: Our work and our working-class consciousness* (pp. 1–15). New Brunswick, NJ: Rutgers University Press.

Contributors

Jenna Abetz (PhD, University of Nebraska-Lincoln) is an Assistant Professor in the Department of Communication at the College of Charleston. She investigates the construction and negotiation of identity, particularly during times of relational transition and contestation.

Xamuel Bañales is an Assistant Professor of Ethnic Studies at California State University, Stanislaus. Their research and teaching interests center on race/ethnicity, class, gender, and sexuality in relation to social movements, critical pedagogy, and decolonial theory and practice.

Carolyn Calloway-Thomas is Immediate Past President of the World Communication Association and Chair of African American and African Diaspora Studies at Indiana University. She is the author of *Empathy in the Global World: An Intercultural Perspective,* and co-author of *Intercultural Communication: A Text/Reader* and *Intercultural Communication: Roots and Routes.* Her co-authored *Handbook on Intercultural Communication between North Americans and Chinese* is forthcoming in 2018.

Kay-Anne P. Darlington is Assistant Professor of Communication at the University of Rio Grande.

Tracy Pascua Dea is the Assistant Vice Provost for Student Success at Saint Mary's College of California. She conducts research on student success with a focus on first-generation, low-income. and/or other underrepresented student populations, strengths-based institutional change, and the power of narrative for social change.

Leslie A. Frankel is an Assistant Professor in the Psychological, Health, and Learning Sciences Department at the University of Houston. Dr. Frankel's research focuses on parent-child relationships and how they impact early child development.

Danica A. Harris is a staff psychologist in the Student Counseling Center at the University of Texas, at Dallas, and an adjunct faculty member at Texas Woman's University. She presents on topics related to class issues, first-generation experiences, social justice in psychology, and sizeism. Her research focuses on trauma, and in particular trauma experienced by marginalized and oppressed groups.

Sascha Hein is an Assistant Professor in the Psychological, Health, and Learning Sciences Department at the University of Houston. His research interests include cognitive development in diverse cultures and delinquent behaviors in children and adolescents.

Teresa Heinz Housel is a Lecturer in the School of Communication, Journalism and Marketing at Massey University in Wellington, New Zealand. She was previously Associate Professor of Communication at Hope College in Michigan. She researches first-generation college students, housing and homelessness, and global media. Website: www.teresaheinzhousel.com.

Rebecca Mercado Jones is an Assistant Professor at Oakland University in Michigan. She tries to remember to whom she is accountable and tries her best to mentor students who come from similar humble beginnings.

Jonathan Mathias Lassiter is an Assistant Professor of Psychology at Muhlenberg College and Visiting Assistant Professor of Medicine at University of California, San Francisco. His research team investigates health at the intersections of race, spirituality, gender, and sexual orientation.

Andrea L. Meluch (PhD, Kent State University, 2016) is an Assistant Professor of Communication Studies at Indiana University South Bend. Meluch's research examines mental health issues in higher education.

Trott N. P. Montina is currently in his third year of study in Media & Communications, Africana Studies, and Doc-Storymaking at Muhlenberg College. His research interests include diversity in higher education and Black male mental health.

Paris Nelson (BS, University of Montevallo) is a recent first-generation college graduate. She is a passionate advocate for first-generation college students and enjoys exploring pathways to higher education.

Angela-MinhTu D. Nguyen is an Assistant Professor in the Department of Psychology at California State University, Fullerton. She conducts research on acculturation, bicultural identity, and the negotiation of multiple social identities.

Audra K. Nuru (PhD, University of Nebraska-Lincoln) is an Assistant Professor of Communication, and Chair of Family Studies, at the University of St. Thomas. She examines how individuals and families in underrepresented social groups negotiate multiple, and often contested, identities.

Jacob O. Okumu is Coordinator for Student Outreach and Developmental Services at Ohio University.

Paulette D. Garcia Peraza is a PhD Developmental Psychology student at the University of California, Santa Cruz. She conducts research on topics like intersectionality and cultural identity in ethnic minorities and first-generation college students.

Micaela Rodriguez recently earned her BS with Honors in Human Development and Family Studies from the University of Houston. Her future career goals center on improving the educational experiences of historically underrepresented student populations.

Pietro A. Sasso is an Assistant Professor in College Student Personnel Administration at Southern Illinois University, Edwardsville. His research focuses on social justice and diversity issues related to college student subcultures and populations. He is the co-editor and author of six texts, including *Today's College Students* (2014) and *Colleges at the Crossroads: Taking Sides on Contested Issues* (2018).

Gloria Aquino Sosa is the Chief Diversity Officer and an Associate Professor in the Counseling Department at Saint Mary's College of California. She is also a Licensed Professional Counselor (MI). She conducts research on entity renegotiation of first-generation and/or low-income students, strengths-based institutional change, and equity-based strategies to positively impact best practices in higher education.

Tiffany R. Wang (PhD, University of Nebraska-Lincoln) is an Assistant Professor in the Department of Communication at the University of Montevallo. She explores communication surrounding college transition in instructional and family contexts.

Index

A BOOK SERIES FOR EQUITY SCHOLARS & ACTIVISTS
Virginia Stead, H.B.A., B.Ed., M.Ed., Ed.D., *General Editor*

Globalization increasingly challenges higher education researchers, administrators, faculty members, and graduate students to address urgent and complex issues of equitable policy design and implementation. This book series provides an inclusive platform for discourse about—though not limited to—diversity, social justice, administrative accountability, faculty accreditation, student recruitment, admissions, curriculum, pedagogy, online teaching and learning, completion rates, program evaluation, cross-cultural relationship-building, and community leadership at all levels of society. Ten broad themes lay the foundation for this series but potential editors and authors are invited to develop proposals that will broaden and deepen its power to transform higher education:

(1) Theoretical books that examine higher education policy implementation,
(2) Activist books that explore equity, diversity, and indigenous initiatives,
(3) Community-focused books that explore partnerships in higher education,
(4) Technological books that examine online programs in higher education,
(5) Financial books that focus on the economic challenges of higher education,
(6) Comparative books that contrast national perspectives on a common theme,
(7) Sector-specific books that examine higher education in the professions,
(8) Educator books that explore higher education curriculum and pedagogy,
(9) Implementation books for front line higher education administrators, and
(10) Historical books that trace changes in higher education theory, policy, and praxis.

Expressions of interest for authored or edited books will be considered on a first come basis. A Book Proposal Guideline is available on request. For individual or group inquiries please contact:

Dr. Virginia Stead, General Editor | *virginia.stead@alum.utoronto.ca*

To order other books in this series, please contact our Customer Service Department at:

(800) 770-LANG (within the U.S.)
(212) 647-7706 (outside the U.S.)
(212) 647-7707 FAX

Or browse online by series at www.peterlang.com